Interest Groups, Advocacy and Democracy Series

Series Editor
Darren Halpin
Research School of Social Sciences
Australian National University
Canberra, Australia

The study of interest groups and their role in political life has undergone somewhat of a renaissance in recent years. Long standing scholarly themes such as interest groups influence mobilization, formation, and 'bias', are being addressed using new and novel data sets and methods. There are also new and exciting themes, such as the role of ICTs in enabling collective action and the growth of global advocacy networks, are being added. Contemporary debates about the role of commercial lobbyists and professionalized interest representation are also highly salient. Together, they draw an ever larger and broader constituency to the study of interest groups and advocacy. This series seeks to capture both new generation studies addressing long standing themes in new ways and innovate scholarship posing new and challenging questions that emerge in a rapidly changing world. The series encourages contributions from political science (but also abutting disciplines such as economics, law, history, international relations and sociology) that speak to these themes. It welcomes work undertaken at the level of sub-national, national and supra-national political systems, and particularly encourages comparative or longitudinal studies. The series is open to diverse methodologies and theoretical approaches. The book series will sit alongside and complement the Interest Groups & Advocacy journal.

More information about this series at
http://www.palgrave.com/gp/series/14850

James Dennis

Beyond Slacktivism

Political Participation on Social Media

palgrave
macmillan

James Dennis
Film, Media and Communication
University of Portsmouth
Portsmouth, Hampshire, UK

Interest Groups, Advocacy and Democracy Series
ISBN 978-3-030-00843-7 ISBN 978-3-030-00844-4 (eBook)
https://doi.org/10.1007/978-3-030-00844-4

Library of Congress Control Number: 2018956584

Cover image: "Lighting a match"
Cover credit: Matthew Elliott
Cover design by Laura de Grasse

This Palgrave Macmillan imprint is published by the registered company Springer Nature Switzerland AG
The registered company address is: Gewerbestrasse 11, 6330 Cham, Switzerland

For Mum. Thank you for always being there.

Acknowledgements

This book has benefited from the efforts of many people. I thank all those who dedicated their time to this study, including the staff and members of 38 Degrees and the participants who devoted three months of their life to the diary project. I am also incredibly grateful for the steadfast support from the editorial team at Palgrave Macmillan, in particular, Ambra Finotello and Katelyn Zingg. They made the seemingly insurmountable task of writing my first book manageable.

I am indebted to a number of academic friends and colleagues who have given their valuable time to offer feedback on various parts of this book as it has developed, in particular Nicholas Allen, Nick Anstead, Andrew Chadwick, Angela Crack, Martin Hampton, Dan Jackson, Wolfram Kaiser, Anastasia Kavada, Milan Kreuschitz-Markovič, Ben O'Loughlin, Zizi Papacharissi, Nora Siklodi, James Sloam, Amy P. Smith, Cristian Vaccari, Ariadne Vromen, Andrew Waterman, Ellen Watts, and Mundo Yang. A special note of thanks must go to Matthew Elliott, who took the excellent cover photo for the book and who kept me entertained throughout the writing process with a constant stream of memes and music suggestions.

My work has benefited tremendously from the vibrant research environment within the Department of Politics and International Relations at Royal Holloway and the School of Film, Media and Communication at the University of Portsmouth. I am particularly grateful to my subject area leads, Claire Perry and Mary Williams, for their encouragement throughout this process. Both institutions have also provided invaluable financial assistance to this project. The research phase for this book was funded by a Ph.D. studentship from the Economic and Social Research Council [Ref: 1094169]. The writing phase was supported by the Transnational Civil Society project at the University of Portsmouth.

A colleague recently told me that it is unprofessional to list your friends in the acknowledgements section of an academic monograph, but the patience required to tolerate hours-upon-hours of me complaining about Derby County or making obscure Pokémon references requires heartfelt thanks: Jack Alexander, Jack Bennett, Jenny Bennett, Matthew Benstead, Oliver Booth, William Brotherhood, Sean Coxhead, Kris Dennis, James Hare, Dida Markovič, Alex Matusiak, Caroline Rennie, Charlotte Richards, Olivia Rutazibwa, Naudia Salmon, William Whitehall, Naomi Whiteside, Luke Willis, Becca Woollgar, Geoff Woollgar, and Charli Wright. I am especially indebted to my family and my partner, Susana. Their love, support, and faith in me have been unwavering.

I acknowledge that some of the material presented in Chapter 4 appears in Andrew Chadwick and James Dennis (2017), "Social Media, Professional Media, and Mobilization in Contemporary Britain: Explaining the Strengths and Weaknesses of the Citizens' Movement, 38 Degrees," *Political Studies*, *65*(1), 42–60. I also thank the Reuters Institute for the Study of Journalism for giving permission to use data from the excellent Digital News Project for Chapter 7.

Finally, this book is dedicated to my Mum, Ali Bates. As a single parent of a working-class family, she sacrificed so much to ensure that my brother and I had every chance to succeed in our lives. I cannot thank her enough for everything that she has done for me.

Contents

List of Figures

List of Tables

CHAPTER 1

"It's Better to Light a Candle Than to Fantasise About a Sun"

Episode 1: #Kony2012

On 5 March 2012, Invisible Children, an American non-governmental organisation (NGO), released a 30-minute video entitled *Kony 2012*. The video was part of an ongoing campaign to raise awareness of the atrocities committed by Ugandan rebel Joseph Kony, leader of the Lord's Resistance Army (LRA), and increase pressure on the US federal government to ramp up their efforts to capture Kony. Featuring Hollywood-style editing and dramatic imagery, the video's primary focus was to highlight the role of Kony in the recruitment of children to fight in the LRA's militia. Released on YouTube and Vimeo simultaneously, the video took just six days to reach 100 million views, faster than the likes of Lady Gaga's video for *Bad Romance* and Susan Boyle's "iconic" performance on *Britain's Got Talent* (Wasserman 2012). The campaign witnessed an unprecedented level of sharing on the social networking sites Facebook and Twitter. The hashtag, #Kony2012, featured in a phenomenal 1200 tweets per minute at the campaign's peak (Lotan 2012), with over 12 million mentions of Kony on the service in total throughout March (Fox 2012). This was a result of the video's explicit encouragement of individuals to share the campaign within their online networks. In particular, those watching were asked to lobby a number of "elites" in order to raise awareness. These elites were not, as we may expect, exclusively politicians, but twenty so-called culturemakers,

J. Dennis, *Beyond Slacktivism*,
Interest Groups, Advocacy and Democracy Series,
https://doi.org/10.1007/978-3-030-00844-4_1

Fig. 1.1 A tweet from Rihanna in support of #Kony2012 (*Source* Rihanna [2012])

cultural icons with an extensive reach and influence across large networks online. This included the likes of Mark Zuckerberg, the founder and CEO of Facebook, and—as Fig. 1.1 illustrates—the pop star Rihanna.

Invisible Children raised over $5 million in just 48 hours. Overnight, the campaign put Joseph Kony, and Invisible Children co-founder Jason Russell, firmly at the forefront of popular discussion; the questionable impact of low-effort digital activism followed.

Debate ensued regarding the controversial narrative that some suggested was promoted through the video, that by simply clicking "share" or "retweet" you could make an observable difference in the world. This narrative spoke directly to an individual's sense of personal efficacy, "the feeling that individual political action does have, or can have, an impact on political processes" (Campbell et al. 1954: 187). A number of interconnected critiques quickly emerged in response to the video. Grant Oyston, a political science student at Acadia University, Canada, published a Tumblr post challenging the notion that by sharing a video or buying a wristband an individual could contribute to the political aim of justice against Kony (Oyston 2012). This argument gained increasing momentum as a number of bloggers began to delve into the financial accounts of Invisible Children; less than a third of its revenues from 2011 was spent on direct services in Uganda, while a significant proportion was used for promotional materials (Carvin 2012; Kersten 2012; Oyston 2012). Ultimately, the campaign was deemed unsuccessful. It failed to turn the extraordinary mass of online activity into offline mobilisation since the "Cover the Night" campaign—a call for activists to cover their neighbourhoods with images of the wanted warlord—amounted to little more than a few posters in major cities. The campaign failed to turn awareness into observable political change.

In terms of raising awareness and facilitating online discussion, #Kony2012 was a success, but for some commentators, this came at a high price. The campaign caused damage to public knowledge due to an emotionally provocative, but crucially misinformed, campaign message. The overly simplistic narrative used obfuscated the complex role of militias in Uganda, with potentially disturbing consequences. For example, Zuckerman (2012) argues that the video provided tacit support for Yoweri Museveni, a dictatorial leader renowned for his poor track record on civil rights. Furthermore, it propagated an ever-present ideal within advocacy that Africa is helpless and dependent on the West to act as its saviour (Drumbl 2012; Fisher 2012).

Rather than genuine commitment, the driving force of the widespread sharing of the video online was claimed to be political self-indulgence; self-interested political engagement intended to fulfil one's personal desire to have political impact or to boost one's feelings of personal efficacy. As Fig. 1.2 illustrates, a popular meme widely shared in response to the video, taking part was easy; just click a button and become an activist. This phenomenon is known as slacktivism, and this contentious concept forms the starting point of this book.

These questions surrounding the authenticity and impact of social media on political engagement form the basis of the slacktivist critique,

Fig. 1.2 A meme posted in response to #Kony2012

which has recently emerged in popular commentary about the Internet and politics. It refers to low-threshold forms of political engagement online, such as signing an e-petition, "liking" a Facebook page, or changing one's avatar on Twitter in support of a cause. These forms of digital micro-activism are perceived by many to have an insignificant effect on politics because they are characterised not by an ethic of solidarity or an individual's pre-existing political ideology and commitment, but merely the simulation of positive deeds or, worse still, inauthenticity (Morozov 2009, 2011; Gladwell 2010).

Set in the context of these recent debates about the rise of slacktivism, and due to the ubiquity of social media in everyday life, this research aims to explore empirically what effect the routine use of social networking sites has on political engagement and citizenship in Britain. This book examines slacktivism as a reflection of, and judgement on, this routine use of social media. This conceptual approach is adopted due to the popularity of the term to describe actions that a typical user may be expected to perform day-to-day. However, how accurate is the slacktivist critique in representing these everyday political experiences? I now move to the second episode from my ethnographic fieldwork that tells a remarkably different story. As Tufekci (2014) notes, "these symbolic, epistemic acts online—derided as "slacktivism"—may well be among the most important effects of the internet."

Episode 2: Don't Limit Our Access to GPs!

On 14 May 2013, the Conservative Policy Forum (CPF) issued a 12-page discussion paper to their national membership. The CPF is a policy discussion network formed of 250 local groups, which provides grass-roots members of the Conservative Party in the United Kingdom (UK) with a role in shaping party policy. This particular survey sought the opinions of party members on the ways in which local healthcare provision could be improved, with a focus on dentistry services and the care provided by local doctors' surgeries (Conservative Policy Forum 2013). The briefing paper included a list of statements on which respondents were asked to identify their level of agreement across a five-point scale. One such statement asked if "there should be no annual limit to the number of appointments patients can book to see their GP [General Practitioner]" (Conservative Policy Forum 2013: 11). This question was the trigger for a national mobilisation involving over 200,000 citizens.

The following Sunday, May 26, four newspapers covered the briefing paper: the *Daily Mail* (McCann 2013), the *Daily Mirror* (Beattie 2013), the *Independent* (Merrick 2013), and the *Daily Telegraph* (2013). These articles claimed that the Conservative Party was considering proposals to limit the number of GP appointments that a patient could make in a calendar year. The story prompted condemnation from the Royal College of General Practitioners, the professional body for GPs, and the leading opposition party, the Labour Party. Both argued that the proposal revoked a founding principal of the National Health Service (NHS), that access to treatment should be based on clinical need (Merrick 2013). As one may expect with a topic as politically charged as health care, the proposal was met with a mixture of outrage and disbelief.[1]

On Tuesday morning, May 28, 15 employees sat around a desk in a stylish office space in Farringdon, central London. This small group make up the leadership of 38 Degrees, a non-profit, political activist group based in the UK. The team, ranging from seasoned campaign professionals to bright-eyed volunteers, were deep in discussion. The conversation moved at a frenetic pace, darting between a rundown of what colleagues got up to over the bank holiday weekend and the important news stories that had emerged in their absence. After a few minutes, the hum of chatter fell away and the first meeting of the day began. This "huddle" is normal practice, as the staff sought to establish their workload for the week ahead. As is customary for the first working day of the week, the group discussed the results of a poll completed over the weekend. Each week, the leadership survey a random sample of the group's membership by way of tracking their priorities. The results showed that threats to the NHS were deemed to be the most pressing issue. Volunteers, who monitor communications on social media, noted that this issue also featured heavily in member correspondence over the previous week.

The team then moved on to determining which campaigns would take priority for the week ahead. For most pressure groups, this is a relatively straightforward process, as campaigns are planned weeks, or even months, in advance. For 38 Degrees, this is not the case. The staff monitors both the priorities of the membership and salient issues within professional news media to identify the point at which a campaign could have an impact. A campaign manager mentioned the reports from the Sunday papers, which suggested that the Conservative Party was considering limiting access to GP visits. The team agreed that based on the results of the weekly poll and feedback from social platforms, this might be something of interest to their membership.

A decision was made that members should be consulted over whether they should launch a campaign in response to the proposal. By midday, "Jonathan,"[2] a campaign manager, had posted a link to the *Daily Mail* article on the group's Facebook page (38 Degrees 2013a). As shown in Fig. 1.3, members were asked to indicate their approval by liking the post and were asked to offer suggestions about how, strategically, the organisation could respond.

Within a few hours, the post received 3289 likes, a clear signal of approval from those members who follow the group on Facebook.

Fig. 1.3 A screenshot of the leadership of 38 Degrees using Facebook to gather feedback from members (*Source* 38 Degrees [2013a])

A significant proportion of the 335 comments expressed outrage at the proposed restriction. Some reflected on how their own personal circumstances made regular contact with a GP a necessity. Others highlighted the potential risks to public health if sick people were discouraged from seeking medical attention. The post was also shared 788 times, raising awareness of the proposal amongst wider networks that may not have been exposed to the original media coverage.

An e-petition was launched on the back of this tacit approval, asking for confirmation from the Health Secretary, Jeremy Hunt, that the proposal would not be implemented. This is a typical first step for the organisation, as e-petitions are an efficient and widely used proxy for translating the disparate voice of its large membership into a tangible form of citizen action. The petition was shared through an email to the "full list" of 38 Degrees members, with members encouraged to amplify it on Facebook and Twitter. The email itself served two functions.[3] Firstly, as the excerpt from the email below illustrates, it was a call to arms, a way to rapidly mobilise members to take part in the campaign:

> This could be very serious. **The Conservatives are floating plans to cap the number of times we are allowed to visit our GP.** If we run out of visits – because we've got a sickly child or long-term health condition, for example – we could be forced to pay to go elsewhere.
>
> At the moment it's just a proposal. But if the Conservatives don't see a big public backlash, it could soon be a grim reality. **So let's raise an outcry as quickly as possible and push them to drop the idea immediately.**
>
> **Please sign the urgent petition now: tell health minister Jeremy Hunt to rule out limiting our access to NHS GPs.**

Secondly, the email also fulfilled an educative role. For each request, the leadership provide links to a range of sources from professional news coverage to detailed policy documents. This enhances the transparency of the group, providing an opportunity for members to consult source material prior to deciding whether or not to take part.

Particularly, striking here is the speed and responsiveness of these processes. In less than 24 hours, the group was able to identify a potential campaign that was in line with the priorities of their membership, measure the level of support for this specific issue, and launch a response.

The following day, May 29, saw the group's leadership take to Facebook once again, this time to drum up support for the campaign

(38 Degrees 2013b). One way in which the central team encourage engagement in an extended repertoire of actions is by using success as a motivational tool. In this example, the number of petition signatories, now over 145,000, was used to motivate members to share the petition. These personalised endorsements simultaneously expand the reach of an action and enhance the legitimacy of the group across the wider public.

On Thursday morning, as the campaign continued to gather momentum, Jeremy Hunt (2013) took to Twitter to offer a response. As shown in Fig. 1.4, Hunt refuted the story and questioned the organisation's intentions. By this point, the petition had reached over 200,000 signatures.

As news of Hunt's tweet filtered through the office, a meeting was called to discuss how to respond. The team were visibly perturbed by the allegation made regarding their neutrality, a trait that a number of members that I spoke to mentioned as a key reason for their involvement (Interview 15, August 2013; Interview 19, October 2013). "Amy," the campaigns director who was leading the meeting, pointed out that the campaign explicitly stated that this was a proposal and not policy. Jonathan noted that Hunt's response was a little ironic given that the CPF was seeking the opinions of its grass-roots members, asking "what can be more resolute than the voice of over 200,000 citizens?" The group agreed that this marked a significant victory and that this success should be shared with their membership.

As Jonathan prepared an email to update the membership on the turn of events, David Babbs, the Executive Director of 38 Degrees, consulted the group's Facebook page. The leadership had shared a screenshot of

Fig. 1.4 A response to the campaign on Twitter from the Secretary of State for Health, Jeremy Hunt MP (*Source* Hunt [2013])

Hunt's tweet immediately after it was posted (38 Degrees 2013c). The comments that followed were mixed, with some revelling in the organisation's success, while others were more sceptical of the accuracy of the petition. David fed a selection of these comments back to Jonathan as the email took shape. Here, Facebook provides a discursive space in which members can shape the leadership's actions. As David notes, "it's a very good way of bringing our members into the room" (Interview 7, June 2013). By late afternoon, an email had been dispatched to the full list of members, explaining the actions taken and the significance of their involvement throughout the campaign.

This example, which took place during a participant observation I conducted at 38 Degrees, provides a dramatic contrast to #Kony2012. It offers a very different perspective on the political utility of digital micro-activism, a term that I use to describe low-threshold interactions without normative judgement, with Facebook and Twitter being used to ascertain the will of the grass-roots membership, to mobilise a wider network of supporters, and as a space to interact with and lobby established elites. It illustrates the complex interdependency that exists between digital micro-activism and tried-and-tested activist repertoires. With this in mind, this book explores the extent to which slacktivism has value as a judgement on contemporary political action.

Beyond Slacktivism: Exploring the Individual Level

This study addresses the following research question: set in the recent debates around online slacktivism, what effect does routine social media use have on political engagement? A number of supplementary questions are used to guide this research and understand this relationship: what political information do citizens consume when using social networking sites, day-to-day? Do these social networking sites provide a space for discursive engagement, and if so, what is the nature of this discussion? And, crucially, do these low-effort interactions evolve into further participatory acts? If they do, what are the attitudinal motivations driving this involvement?

As Bimber et al. (2012: 1) note, much of the literature focuses on the organisational level when analysing the impact of digital media on political behaviour (e.g. see Bennett and Segerberg 2013; Karpf 2012). While these book-length studies have made significant contributions to our understanding of contemporary political communication, there is a gap in the literature for an in-depth study of the individual-level unit of analysis. As Howard (2011: 2) notes, when we adopt a network perspective on the media, individuals become meaningful objects of study as they have more control and autonomy over their identity. By adopting a "deep data" approach (Salmons 2012), through the collection of thick, descriptive data tailored around individual-level attitudes and behaviours, I analyse how and why digitally active citizens use Facebook and Twitter for political participation.[4]

Ultimately, this research seeks to establish the personalised context for the remarkable forms of digitally networked action that have taken place over the last decade; what happens before instances of collective, or connective, action (Bennett and Segerberg 2013)? I do this by exploring the relationship between routine social media use and political engagement in two different settings using an experimental, mixed-method research design. These represent the different spaces in which these tools can be used, outside of the isolated case studies offered by proponents of slacktivism. Firstly, in an activist context, through an ethnography of the political group 38 Degrees. Secondly, within day-to-day life, by combining evidence of participant behaviour online with reflective diaries.

Although big data studies and cross-national survey research provide vast amounts of detailed evidence on user behaviour, these findings can occasionally be superficial, focusing on specific actions or service functionality in isolation. As Neuman et al. (2011: 32–33) note, much of this research is based on indicators that are not designed with a "ubiquitous and universal" Internet in mind. Both approaches sometimes lack an understanding of the everyday experiences that drive behaviour online—the *why*. This book seeks to address that void by drawing on an alternative descriptive framework: the continuum of participation.

The Continuum of Participation

In order to critically evaluate the relationship between social media and political participation, it is necessary to form an understanding of the contexts in which these new modes of social and political self-expression take place. I dispute the notion that participation is a public-only phenomenon, as our private, everyday experiences shape our public actions. In order to empirically observe these personalised political attitudes and behaviours, an alternative theoretical approach—the continuum of participation—is proposed, designed to capture the nuance of mediated citizenship at varying scales.

Developing this descriptive framework was not my intention when embarking on this book. Rather this focus emerged from the conceptual limitations of the slacktivist critique, which evaluates the relationship between acts of digital micro-activism and the desired political outcome in isolation. As Rickett (2013) argues, "Facebook is not going to catch Joseph Kony and we won't tweet our way to peace in Syria." Such an approach implies that low-threshold interactions form a causal relationship with the desired political effect(s). This deterministic, causal relationship lacks an appreciation of the expansive, procedural foundations at the heart of political engagement (Arnstein 1969). Whether voting in an election or sending a tweet to an elected representative, active citizenship depends on access to informational resources, opportunities to take part in discursive spaces, and the capacity to organise. This focus on the macro-level as the arena in which power is contested and exercised omits the significance of the micro-level, and the attitudes and behaviours of individual citizens. Ultimately, the slacktivist critique is inherently disconnected from how citizens' experience politics, day-to-day. By exploring digital micro-activism across a continuum of participation, a process in which the interdependency between different acts sheds light on the normative value of democratic engagement, I provide context to the conditions under which the critique has relevance or can be challenged.

Based on the approach proposed by Carpentier (2011),[5] the continuum of participation consists of four stages. "Access" refers to cognitive engagement and how citizens pay attention to politics and public affairs. "Expression" encapsulates forms of political communication between citizens. The effects of expression can vary across the continuum depending on the motivations of the user, how receivers use this information, and the composition of the audience, such as one–many, real–imagined, online–offline, public semi-public. "Connection" represents the processes of political organisation, as citizens use social media to establish and join networks for a range of purposes. Finally, "action" signifies goal-orientated, public political acts, as social networking sites are used for digital activism, or form part of interconnected engagement repertoires. By conceptualising engagement as a process, rather than an outcome, connections can be observed between how citizens use social media to shape their political identity and the kind of political behaviour, if any, that occurs as a result.

There are two crucial conditions when using this theoretical device for empirical research. Firstly, behaviours under each category are inclusive of those undertaken in public, semi-public, and private settings. By emphasising the role of public political actions in isolation, we ignore the role of the receiver and the democratic goods that can be accrued through private forms of communication. Secondly, Chadwick's (2013) "hybrid media system" marks the parameters for media use, providing the context for media consumption and production at the individual level. In this hybrid logic, information is increasingly fragmented, and consumption is personalised. Within this book, media convergence is examined across this model to understand how citizens mix their use of social media with other forms of online and offline communication.

It is important to note that this framework is descriptive and does not advocate that a deterministic relationship exists; access to information and discursive opportunities do not guarantee that further civic or political actions will follow. Instead, this model is designed precisely to identify the conditions in which social media triggers attention and to trace how this relates to other expressive and participatory acts.

These effects are not always beneficial for democracy. Gladwell (2010) and Morozov (2009, 2011) shed some light on valid concerns within the context of this continuum. However, these get lost in the sensationalist, polarised debate between those that deem social media to be democratising by virtue of its networked design and the slacktivist critique. These so-called utopians and dystopians narrowly focus on social media in relation to monumental political change, such as the 2009 Iranian presidential election protests (Morozov 2011) or the use of Facebook and Twitter to overthrow the Communist Party in Moldova in 2009 (Shirky 2011), ignoring other incremental acts along the continuum. Rather than merely dismissing these acts as ineffectual or assuming that they are inauthentic, a process-based approach raises new questions regarding the conditions under which digitally mediated action becomes chaotic and unproductive or when it is beneficial for democracy.

The Organisational Management of Digital Micro-Activism

By drawing upon a three-month participant observation, ethnographic data from interviews with staff and members, as well as campaign emails, social media data, and online news articles, I illustrate how 38 Degrees seek to avoid slacktivism through their mobilisation strategy. In isolation, liking, commenting, and sharing on social media may seem trivial, but when examined at scale across a continuum of participation, these acts provide opportunities for meaningful involvement.

The leadership of 38 Degrees use social media to enable their members to guide the strategic direction of the group, from choosing what they should be fighting for to crowdsourcing their advice on how it should be done. This digital listening (see Karpf 2016) was a principal justification for involvement amongst those activists that I spoke to. Beyond these feedback loops, the central team in London deploys forms of digital micro-activism at strategically significant moments. The context of these actions is crucial to ascertaining their value as a form of democratic engagement. The leadership seek to maximise the impact of petitions, awareness-building on Facebook, and lobbying efforts on Twitter by drawing on their campaigning expertise to identify opportunities for impact.

When this political behaviour is examined outside of the isolation of a single act, it becomes clear that what has been dismissed as ineffectual narcissism may be a democratic shortcut, providing a bridge to sites of power for wider publics. This is what I describe as the organisational management of digital micro-activism; the leadership deploys these mundane tools in political contexts in which they are symbolically empowering *and* have material impact.

In this activist context, Facebook and Twitter also become important sites of activation. This study challenges the hypothesis that inauthentic reputation management or popularity underpins digital micro-activism on social media. Instead, 38 Degrees activists mobilise around campaigns that they are passionate about and that overlap with their political identity. This absence of ideology has been criticised in the past. As Dean (2005: 70) argues:

> By sending an e-mail, signing a petition, responding to an article on a blog, people can feel political. And that feeling feeds communicative capitalism insofar as it leaves behind the time-consuming, incremental and risky efforts of politics. MoveOn likes to emphasize that it abstains from ideology, from division … this sort of non-position strikes me as precisely that disavowal of the political I've been describing: it is a refusal to take a stand, to venture into the dangerous terrain of politicization.

This criticism overlooks the mobilisation strategy of groups like MoveOn (Karpf 2012), GetUp! (Vromen 2017), and 38 Degrees; digital micro-activism forms part of interconnected engagement repertoires that blend online and offline tactics. Some of the risky forms of high-cost activism are only made possible by the technological affordances of Facebook. In Chapter 4, I explore the "Save Our NHS" campaign, a series of local level efforts to galvanise resistance to the government's 2012 healthcare reforms. I illustrate how emotive self-expression within personalised networks on Facebook was integral to the rapid structural transformation that occurred mid-campaign, changing the focus of the campaign from a national, centrally managed e-petition, to the creation of over 150 semi-autonomous local groups.

The organisational management of digital micro-activism is not without limitations, however. When a campaign requires strong-tie relationships that are built around a collective identity, these democratic shortcuts are less useful. A common theme throughout this book is a rejection of the assumption that low-threshold online actions are *easy*. Although the leadership of 38 Degrees recognise that members are willing to express political opinions and share campaign material within their own networks on issues of personal relevance, there was a widespread reluctance to engage in conversation on the group's public Facebook page. This is not a refusal to take a stand or a non-position, as these same activists were often ready and willing to participate in high-threshold actions, but a specific cognitive load that some members face when faced with the prospect of public political expression on social media.

A Typology of Citizen Roles in Social Media Environments

In contrast to both my expectations and the hypotheses derived from the slacktivist critique, there is no evidence of a widespread self-expressive logic within this book. By adopting a mixed-method approach, that combines reflective diaries with evidence of user behaviour online, I analyse how digitally active citizens use Facebook and Twitter in their day-to-day lives. I reject the assumption that social networking sites cultivate public and semi-public expression by virtue of their design. Instead, many users take to semi-public and private spaces for political discussion. The findings illustrate how digital micro-activism represents a qualitatively different experience for some users than the assumed effortless proposed by the slacktivist critique. Many participants in this study were acutely aware of the social and reputational risks posed by public political expression to their real and imagined audience on social platforms.

Table 1.1 A typology of citizen roles in social media environments

Citizen role	*Description*	*Corresponding citizenship theory*
Civic instigator	Frequently share information, offer their opinion, and engage in forms of digital micro-activism by way of refining and honing their own political identity Most likely to engage in more substantive forms of political action	Actualizing citizen (Bennett 2008) Digitally-enabled citizen (Papacharissi 2010)
Contributor	Share political content but do so often without including any personal opinions Contributors seek to inform or entertain other users	
Active listener/ Passive listener	Active listeners frequently post content on non-political topics, but consciously avoid anything that they deem to be political Passive listeners use Facebook and Twitter to consume information but avoid public forms of expression entirely Use social media to consume political information. Take to private spaces to discuss politics, either online or face-to-face. Micro-activism deliberated over given the reputational dynamics of social media	Monitorial citizen (Schudson 1999) Standby citizen (Amnå and Ekman 2014)
Avoiders	Deliberately ignore posts on social media that have a political orientation	News resisters (Woodstock 2014)

A typology of citizen roles in social media environments is offered by way of identifying the different ways in which users engage with political material on Facebook and Twitter, as shown in Table 1.1. This challenges the claim that forms of micro-activism and online expression are lazy and easy forms of self gratification.

The typology of citizen roles in social media environments illustrates the complex attitudinal characteristics at the individual level. Bennett's (2008) "actualizing citizen" framework formed the basis of what I expected to find during my fieldwork. Although the majority of participants in the diary study did not reflect this, a small minority did. These citizens use Facebook and Twitter to shape news consumption around their individual preferences and frequently share political content, as the lines between content production and consumption become blurred. However, there was clear diversity within this group over the nature and motivations of this communication.

"Civic instigators" share personally expressive posts to challenge others. They refine their political identity based on this feedback.

As such, digital micro-activism forms part of an experiential learning cycle, as political talk and self-expression shape their political attitudes. "Contributors" also share political material to stimulate political learning amongst wider networks, but they do not share their opinions under normal circumstances. They are apprehensive about how their audience will perceive them. Instead, they see social media as a space to inform others and to learn, rather than to debate.

The majority of participants in this research refrained from public forms of political expression, either online or offline. Using the methodological orthodoxy of social media research, which emphasises publicly observable interactions, these "listeners" would not be accounted for. Such an interpretation, however, overlooks how information consumption on Facebook and Twitter is deeply ingrained within wider citizen practices in a hybrid media system. By operationalising the continuum of participation, it is possible to see how this consumption links to a variety of different forms of communication, which merge across different public, semi-public, and private settings. These are examples of Katz and Lazarsfeld's (1955) "multi-step flows of communication," with private modes of digital communication like Facebook Messenger and WhatsApp becoming sites for political talk. While these processes may not manifest in public-facing actions, there was evidence of cognitive engagement and discursive participation. These listeners are, in effect, on standby. They are politically interested and ready to mobilise around civic and political issues that resonate with their own private beliefs and personal identity (Amnå and Ekman 2014).

Outline of the Book

In this book, I aim to examine the theoretical and empirical relevance of the slacktivist critique by conducting rich, mixed-method research at the individual level. The book unfolds as follows.

Chapter 2 describes the utopian-dystopian dichotomy that has re-emerged within popular discourse on digital politics. Characterised by a prevalence of unsubstantiated generalisations, anecdotal case studies, and a lack of empirical testing, slacktivism forms part of this vague and imprecise dichotomy. The critique has become synonymous with a negative perception of the political value of social media. However, it is flawed by an overly narrow focus. The slacktivist critique cannot definitively represent everyday use, as it ignores the role that micro-activism plays in relation to other forms of political action, both online and offline. While each act, taken in isolation, may be deemed to be an "expression of benign idleness" (Rickett 2013), the critique ignores how micro-activism often complements other forms of participation and can lower the threshold for involvement for those traditionally marginalised by high-cost activism.

Chapter 3 develops the continuum of participation model, outlining the guiding theoretical and methodological assumptions for this book. I examine the characteristics of contemporary political participation, in which new emergent forms of group-based politics organised around personal identity challenge our understanding of collective action. By combining Bennett's (2008) concept of the "actualizing citizen," Papacharissi's (2010) concept of the "private sphere," and Chadwick's (2012) hypothesis that social networking sites create new conditions for individuals' political learning, I offer an alternative prognosis to challenge the hypotheses derived from the slacktivist critique.

Chapter 4 focuses on the use of Facebook and Twitter in an activist context through an ethnographic study of 38 Degrees. By exploring the group's use of social media across a process-based definition of participation, this study challenges the attitudinal and behavioural claims of the slacktivist critique. In what I describe as the organisational management of digital micro-activism, the leadership uses Facebook and Twitter to inform members, to involve them in the organisation's decision-making, and to activate wider publics for further online and offline action. This has significant implications when we consider the slacktivist critique. Integral to the critique is the claim that low-threshold digital interactions have no material impact; they do not form a link to institutional decision-making or the policymaking process. By designing campaign actions that are granular and by using technologies that are widely diffused amongst their membership, the leadership provides a bridge between digital micro-activism and sites of power.

The following two chapters examine how 29 digitally active citizens use social media within their day-to-day lives. Chapter 5 explores news consumption on Facebook and Twitter. As citizens have increasing control over the information contained on their social media news feeds, fears exist that a lack of agreement about what constitutes public issues may threaten societal bonds that are essential to a democracy. Despite this, this chapter argues that individual media habits are considerably more complex and less damaging than first feared. By comparing the content of the diaries with the lead stories of four British newspapers, I show that personal identity increasingly drives more individualised forms of news consumption. The implications of this personalisation for democratic engagement do not reflect the ominous forecasts of the slacktivist critique; in this study, there was no evidence of selective exposure leading to harmful audience fragmentation. The comparison between the diaries and newspaper coverage illustrates that this personalisation was balanced by moments of collective exposure, as citizens focused their attention on public issues.

By observing the different ways in which the diarists use social media for self-expression, political talk, and democratic engagement, Chapter 6 outlines a typology of citizen roles in social media environments that challenges both the attitudinal and behavioural logics that sustain the slacktivist critique. The media diaries show that, for some citizens, these acts are not easy as they are keenly aware of their audience online. The majority of participants in this research were listeners, using Facebook and Twitter to consume political information but refraining from public forms of expression. Instead, they take to private spaces to discuss politics, either online or face-to-face. These participants keep themselves informed about politics by bringing up political issues in everyday life. When listeners do undertake acts of digital micro-activism, they are not easy, low-threshold behaviours, but painstakingly deliberated over. For those that do post political updates regularly, this is a way of raising awareness for causes they deem to be significant. Self-expression on social media is not immediately disregarded, as predicted by the slacktivist critique, but forms part of their political socialisation and political identity formulation.

The final chapter brings together the results from the two empirical studies to analyse the relationship between routine social media use and political participation in Britain. I return to the quote that opens this book: "It's better to light a candle than to fantasise about a sun." Those scholars involved in the utopian-dystopian divide at the heart of this topic narrowly focus on social media in relation to monumental political change. They treat social media as a sun, a panacea for democracy across the globe. By conceptualising participation as a process and exploring the relationships formed between social media use and other modes of public and private communication, this study illustrates how Facebook and Twitter create new opportunities for cognitive engagement, discursive participation, and political mobilisation. Digital micro-activism and online self-expression are not lazy and easy forms of self-gratification, but symbolic acts that provide evidence of active citizenship.

Notes

1. For instance, see this discussion thread on the entertainment forum, Digital Spy: https://forums.digitalspy.com/discussion/1830281/now-the-tories-want-to-limit-gp-visits.
2. Pseudonyms are used throughout this book to protect the anonymity of participants. These are denoted by the first mention of a participant being included in quotation marks. Gender should not be implied from the pseudonyms.
3. action@38degrees.org.uk, 2013. NHS: A serious threat. [email]. Sent May 28, 2013. Retrieved May 28, 2013.
4. These services have been selected due to their popularity with both citizens (Kemp 2017) and political groups in Britain (Obar et al. 2012). As of January 2017, survey data suggests that 73% of Internet users in the UK use Facebook, while 41% regularly use Twitter (Kemp 2017: 193). Other online services will be examined as a by-product of their overlap with Facebook and Twitter.
5. Carpentier (2011: 69) argues that access to political content and involvement in socio-communicative relationships cannot be equated to participation because of their less explicit emphasis on power dynamics and decision-making. In Chapter 2, I argue that this is conceptually problematic, as power is diffuse across the model: access and interaction are inextricably linked to participation.

References

38 Degrees. (2013a, May 28). The Conservatives Seem to Be Considering Plans to Limit the Number of Times We'd Be Allowed to Visit a GP… *Facebook Update*. Retrieved July 10, 2014, from https://www.facebook.com/peoplepowerchange/posts/10152866604640788.

38 Degrees. (2013b, May 29). Already 145,000 of Us Have Signed the Petition to Jeremy Hunt Telling Him Not to Limit How Many Times We Can Visit Our GP!… *Facebook Update*. Retrieved July 10, 2014, from https://www.facebook.com/peoplepowerchange/posts/10152869643835788.

38 Degrees. (2013c, May 30). Fantastic News! Our People-Powered Petition of 182,000 People Has Obviously Had the Right Effect! *Facebook Update*. Retrieved July 12, 2014, from https://www.facebook.com/peoplepowerchange/photos/a.457255765787.382103.200006375787/10152872307590788.

Amnå, E., & Ekman, J. (2014). Standby Citizens: Diverse Faces of Political Passivity. *European Political Science Review*, *6*(2), 261–281.

Arnstein, S. R. (1969). A Ladder of Citizen Participation. *Journal of the American Institute of Planners, 35*(4), 216–224.

Beattie, J. (2013, May 27). Secret Tory Plan to Limit Your Number of GP Appointments. *Daily Mirror.* Retrieved May 31, 2013, from http://www.mirror.co.uk/news/uk-news/secret-tory-plan-cap-gp-1914881.

Bennett, W. L. (2008). Changing Citizenship in the Digital Age. In W. L. Bennett (Ed.), *Civic Life Online: Learning How Digital Media Can Engage Youth* (pp. 1–24). Cambridge: MIT Press.

Bennett, W. L., & Segerberg, A. (2013). *The Logic of Connective Action: Digital Media and the Personalization of Contentious Politics.* Cambridge: Cambridge University Press.

Bimber, B., Flanagin, A. J., & Stohl, C. (2012). *Collective Action in Organizations: Interaction and Engagement in an Era of Technological Change.* Cambridge: Cambridge University Press.

Campbell, A., Gurin, G., & Miller, W. E. (1954). *The Voter Decides.* Evanston, IL: Row, Peterson and Co.

Carpentier, N. (2011). *Media and Participation: A Site of Ideological-Democratic Struggle.* Bristol: Intellect.

Carvin, S. (2012, March 7). *Invisible Children—Pretty Dang Visible.* Retrieved March 12, 2012, from http://duckofminerva.blogspot.com/2012/03/invisible-children-pretty-dang-visible.html.

Chadwick, A. (2012). Recent Shifts in the Relationship Between the Internet and Democratic Engagement in Britain and the United States: Granularity, Informational Exuberance, and Political Learning. In E. Anduiza, M. Jensen, & L. Jorba (Eds.), *Digital Media and Political Engagement Worldwide: A Comparative Study* (pp. 39–55). Cambridge: Cambridge University Press.

Chadwick, A. (2013). *The Hybrid Media System: Politics and Power.* Oxford: Oxford University Press.

Conservative Policy Forum. (2013, May 14). *Local Health Discussion Brief.* Retrieved July 2, from http://www.conservativepolicyforum.com/sites/www.conservativepolicyforum.com/files/local_health_discussion_brief.doc.

Daily Telegraph. (2013, May 26). Conservatives Consider Limit on GP Visits. *Daily Telegraph.* Retrieved July 9, 2014, from http://www.telegraph.co.uk/health/healthnews/10081220/Conservatives-consider-limit-on-GP-visits.html.

Dean, J. (2005). Communicative Capitalism: Circulation and the Foreclosure of Politics. *Cultural Politics, 1*(1), 51–74.

Drumbl, M. A. (2012). Child Soldiers and Clicktivism: Justice, Myths, and Prevention. *Journal of Human Rights Practice, 4*(3), 481–485.

Fisher, M. (2012, March 8). The Soft Bigotry of Kony 2012. *The Atlantic*. Retrieved December 31, 2012, from http://www.theatlantic.com/international/print/2012/03/the-soft-bigotry-of-kony-2012/254194/.

Fox, Z. (2012, April 24). The Decline of Kony 2012: Where Did the Online Buzz Go? *Mashable*. Retrieved December 31, 2012, from http://mashable.com/2012/04/24/kony-2012-decline/.

Gladwell, M. (2010, October 4). Small Change: Why the Revolution Will Not Be Tweeted. *The New Yorker*. Retrieved November 3, 2010, from https://www.newyorker.com/magazine/2010/10/04/small-change-malcolm-gladwell.

Howard, P. N. (2011). *Castells and the Media*. Cambridge: Polity Press.

Hunt, J. [Jeremy_Hunt]. (2013, May 30). In Case Being Misled by 'Neutral' 38 Degrees E-Petition, It Is Not and Was Never Going to Be Conservative Policy to Limit GP Appointments. *Tweet*. Retrieved July 10, 2014, from https://twitter.com/Jeremy_Hunt/status/340046406926598144.

Karpf, D. (2012). *The MoveOn Effect: The Unexpected Transformation of American Political Advocacy*. Oxford: Oxford University Press.

Karpf, D. (2016). *Analytic Activism: Digital Listening and the New Political Strategy*. Oxford: Oxford University Press.

Katz, E., & Lazarsfeld, P. F. (1955). *Personal Influence: The Part Played by People in the Flow of Mass Communications*. New York: The Free Press.

Kemp, S. (2017, January 24). Digital in 2017: Global Overview. *We Are Social*. Retrieved January 30, 2017, from https://wearesocial.com/special-reports/digital-in-2017-global-overview.

Kersten, M. (2012, March 7). Taking 'Kony 2012' Down a Notch. *Justice in Conflict*. Retrieved March 7, 2012, from http://justiceinconflict.org/2012/03/07/taking-kony-2012-down-a-notch/.

Lotan, G. (2012, March 14). [Data Viz] Kony2012: See How Invisible Networks Helped a Campaign Capture the World's Attention. *SocialFlow*. Retrieved December 31, 2012, from http://blog.socialflow.com/post/7120244932/data-viz-kony2012-see-how-invisible-networks-helped-a-campaign-capture-the-worlds-attention.

McCann, J. (2013, May 26). Fury as Tories Look to Limit the Number of Times You Can See Your GP Each Year. *The Daily Mail*. Retrieved July 9, 2014, from http://www.dailymail.co.uk/news/article-2331068/Fury-Tories-look-limit-number-times-GP-year.html.

Merrick, J. (2013, May 26). Cap on Number of GP Visits Being Considered by Tories. *The Independent*. Retrieved May 31, 2013, from http://www.independent.co.uk/life-style/health-and-families/health-news/cap-on-number-of-gp-visits-being-considered-by-tories-8632396.html.

Morozov, E. (2009, May 19). The Brave New World of Slacktivism. *Foreign Policy*. Retrieved April 18, 2011, from http://neteffect.foreignpolicy.com/posts/2009/05/19/the_brave_new_world_of_slacktivism.

Morozov, E. (2011). *The Net Delusion: How Not to Liberate the World*. London: Penguin.

Neuman, W. R., Bimber, B., & Hindman, M. (2011). The Internet and Four Dimensions of Citizenship. In R. Y. Shapiro & L. R. Jacobs (Eds.), *The Oxford Handbook of American Public Opinion and the Media* (pp. 22–42). Oxford: Oxford University Press.

Obar, J. A., Zube, P., & Lampe, C. (2012). Advocacy 2.0: An Analysis of How Advocacy Groups in the United States Perceive and Use Social Media as Tools for Facilitating Civic Engagement and Collective Action. *Journal for Information Policy, 2*, 1–25.

Oyston, G. (2012, March 8). *We Got Trouble*. Retrieved March 8, 2012, from http://visiblechildren.tumblr.com/post/18890947431/we-got-trouble.

Papacharissi, Z. (2010). *A Private Sphere: Democracy in a Digital Age*. Cambridge: Polity.

Rickett, O. (2013, November 22). Want to Change the World? It Won't Happen Via Your Mouse Button. *The Guardian*. Retrieved March 20, 2014, from http://www.theguardian.com/commentisfree/2013/nov/22/change-the-world-charity-facebook-e-petition.

Rihanna [rihanna]. (2012, March 6). Please Go to http://Www.Invisiblechildren.Com Even If Its 10 Minutes… Trust Me, You Need to Know About This! #1Love. *Tweet*. Retrieved December 31, 2012, from http://twitter.com/rihanna/status/177302109937614848.

Salmons, J. (2012, November 16). *Deep Data: Digging into Social Media with Qualitative Methods*. Retrieved January 20, 2013, from http://nsmnss.blogspot.co.uk/2012/11/deep-data-digging-into-social-media_16.html.

Schudson, M. (1999). *The Good Citizen: A History of American Public Life*. Cambridge, MA: Harvard University Press.

Shirky, C. (2011, January/February). The Political Power of Social Media: Technology, the Public Sphere and Political Change. *Foreign Affairs*. Retrieved March 15, 2011, from http://www.foreignaffairs.com/articles/67038/clay-shirky/the-political-power-of-social-media.

Tufekci, Z. [zeynep]. (2014, February 2). These Symbolic, Epistemic Acts Online—Derided as "Slacktivism"—May Well Be Among the Most Important Effects of the Internet. *Tweet*. Retrieved February 3, 2014, from https://twitter.com/zeynep/status/430093891300524032.

Vromen, A. (2017). *Digital Citizenship and Political Engagement: The Challenge from Online Campaigning and Advocacy Organisations*. Basingstoke: Palgrave Macmillan.

Wasserman, T. (2012, March 12). 'Kony 2012' Tops 100 Million Views, Becomes the Most Viral Video in History [Study]. *Mashable*. Retrieved December 31, 2012, from http://mashable.com/2012/03/12/kony-most-viral/.

Woodstock, L. (2014). The News-Democracy Narrative and the Unexpected Benefits of Limited News Consumption: The Case of News Resisters. *Journalism, 15*(7), 834–849.

Zuckerman, E. (2012, August 3). *Unpacking Kony 2012*. Retrieved March 11, 2012, from http://www.ethanzuckerman.com/blog/2012/03/08/unpacking-kony-2012.

CHAPTER 2

#stopslacktivism: Why Clicks, Likes, and Shares Matter

Current popular debate on social media and politics reveals a number of fundamental deficiencies amongst both proponents and critics of online activism. These include, for example, analysing social media in isolation from other media, the use of anecdotal generalisations based on context-dependent case studies, and hard technological determinism. As a result, there has been a return to the utopian-dystopian dichotomy that bedevilled the social science of the Internet during the 1990s. Slacktivism forms part of this vague and imprecise dichotomy. This chapter will outline the flaws present within the slacktivist critique and propose a new research agenda in order to systematically analyse the relationship between routine social media use and political engagement.

Click Here to Save the World: The Roots of Slacktivism

> It has never been so easy to change the world; a horrible world, full of bigotry and social injustice and bankers and Starbucks and oblivious politicians. All you have to do is sit down at your computer screen, take a deep breath and tap a key. Abracadabra: suddenly, the politicians are a little less oblivious. And you, with your sense of common decency and rectitude, are empowered. That's all it took, a second, maybe a fraction of a second if your computer has a good connection. You might not even feel the need to take a deep breath.
>
> (Liddle 2013)

J. Dennis, *Beyond Slacktivism*,
Interest Groups, Advocacy and Democracy Series,
https://doi.org/10.1007/978-3-030-00844-4_2

As Liddle's quote alludes to, popular debate on the political value of social media is often framed as part of a deterministic dichotomy; either social media will usher in a new era of mass participation and political equality, or it will enable a dystopian, Orwellian future (see O'Loughlin 2011; Wright 2012 for an overview). This debate may invoke a sense of déjà vu, as similar divides have accompanied new communication technologies throughout history (Carpentier 2011; Chadwick 2006: 18; Negroponte 1995). This divide between the so-called utopians (Carswell 2012; Jarvis 2009, 2011) and dystopians (Bauerlin 2009; Gladwell 2010; Keen 2008) is illustrated through the work, and conflicts, of Clay Shirky (2008, 2010, 2011) and Evgeny Morozov (2011, 2013). According to Shirky (2011), as networked communities expand and become normalised within everyday communications, it is irrefutable that social technologies will be used for all future coordination of rapid and mass political mobilisation. Morozov's stance is markedly different. He refutes the ideals of the so-called cyber-optimists, instead arguing that social networking sites are simply entertainment platforms that distract citizens. These passive political acts compromise legitimate forms of offline activism (Morozov 2009, 2011, 2013).

This dichotomy is fraught with inaccuracies that fail to comprehensively explore the relationship between the use of social media and political participation. The literature too often relies on anecdotal case studies to formulate generalisations on the dynamics of political behaviour (Wright 2012: 248). For instance, Gladwell (2010) and Morozov (2011: 190) refer to just a handful of Facebook groups in constructing their critique of slacktivism. While their criticism of groups such as "Saving the Children of Africa" (Morozov 2011: 190) and the "Save Darfur Coalition" (Gladwell 2010) are not without foundation, they are in no way indicative of the democratic value of Facebook as a platform. A great deal of rigorous academic research now exists on the potential of social media for citizens' participation in political life (Boulianne 2015). This includes compelling findings on how social media use impacts a wide range of activities deemed important for political citizenship, such as news consumption (Fletcher and Nielsen 2017a, b; Kümpel et al. 2015; Valeriani and Vaccari 2016), discursive engagement (Bode 2017; Chadwick et al. 2017; Gil de Zúñiga et al. 2014; Vaccari et al. 2015a), and community formation (Bennett and Segerberg 2013; Chadwick 2013; Karpf 2012). However, the slacktivist critique still persists in popular commentary.[1] The problem at the heart of these debates is that both sides attempt to generate definitive conclusions about the nature of technological effects where none can be made. Furthermore, by resorting to hyperbole rather than rigorous empirical analysis, the debate has established a pervasive "either-or" frame in which academic work is often pigeonholed.

Given the polarised literature from which slacktivism originates, the term's precise definition is somewhat unclear. For example, slacktivism and clicktivism are often used interchangeably in popular discourse, despite clicktivism referring to a specific form of low-effort, online participation (Halupka 2014), and slacktivism being used as a more general critique of participation that requires minimal effort (Karpf 2010). Evidently, the term has undergone a radical transformation since its inception, as it was originally coined by Clark to describe small, personal scale activities undertaken to benefit a community (Christensen 2011). Therefore, it is important to clearly define the term.

The interpretation of slacktivism used in this book comes from the *Oxford English Dictionary* definition, referring to "actions performed via the Internet in support of a political or social cause (e.g. signing an online petition), characterised as requiring little time, effort, or commitment, or as providing more personal satisfaction than public impact."[2] I use slacktivism, rather than clicktivism, as it is the more commonly used term within the field of political communication (Christensen 2012: 3). In this study, I predominantly focus on digital forms of micro-activism on Facebook and Twitter. Actions include "liking" a Facebook post, commenting on another user's content or "retweeting" a post on Twitter.

Christensen (2011, 2012) identifies two themes that link the term's use in academic (Karpf 2010; Morozov 2011; Rotman et al. 2011; Shulman 2009), journalistic (Gladwell 2010; Morozov 2011; Rickett 2013), and activist (Khazan 2013; White 2010, 2011) circles. Firstly, low-effort forms of online engagement are less effective than traditional, offline methods of participation. As Morozov (2011: 190) argues, these actions make "online activists feel useful and important while having preciously little political impact." Secondly, the futility of these actions is of paramount concern due to the substitution thesis, in which low-effort, online methods of engagement replace tried and tested activist repertoires.

This criticism of political behaviour is not new. Whether on the effectiveness of mass email action (Shulman 2009) or "chequebook activism," in which political involvement amounts to little more than occasional financial donations (Hensby et al. 2011; Jordan and Maloney 2007; Putnam 2000), others have denounced activism that reduces the demands of a participant to ensure high levels of engagement. Those advocating the slacktivist critique argue that metrics, such as tracking the click-through rate on campaign material or the number of shares on a post, are an indication of successful engagement on social networking sites, rather than the substance, depth, or impact of a political action (White 2010, 2011). By reducing the demands of a participant to ensure high levels of participation, a mirage of active citizenship is cultivated, one that mistakes quantity for quality (Gladwell 2010; Morozov 2011).

The slacktivist critique also questions the legitimacy of the attitudes that underpin this political behaviour (see Halupka 2018). Slacktivism is perceived to have an insignificant effect on politics because it is characterised not by an ethic of solidarity or an individual's pre-existing political ideology and commitment, but merely the simulation of positive deeds or, worse still, inauthenticity (Gladwell 2010; Morozov 2011: 186). These low-threshold acts offer a quick and easy fix to satisfy one's desire for political involvement (Halupka 2014: 124–125), and a means of cultivating one's image amongst networked peers (Morozov 2011: 186). In essence, the slacktivist critique mirrors Olson's (1971) free-rider problem, as citizens avoid effort-intensive activism in favour of the civic and reputational benefits of easy, micro-activism online.

These attitudinal claims can be linked to existing research on political mobilisation. The critique emphasises the importance of personal efficacy, "the feeling that individual political action does have, or can have, an impact on political processes" (Campbell et al. 1954: 187). Existing research has widely documented how modern citizenship is characterised by self-actualisation (see Chapter 3). As a result of this pursuit of autonomy and influence, Gladwell (2010) and Morozov (2011) argue that citizens are drawn to political campaigns on social media as they often lack a hierarchical structure. In this way, each participant feels like they are making a difference. While citizens may seek this kind of influence, Morozov (2011: 197) suggests that an excess of communication undermines collective action. Furthermore, these horizontal networks are identified as unsuitable for political activism because of the relationships within them. As Gladwell (2010) notes, "the ties that bind people to the group are loose." While weak ties can be useful for activists seeking to mobilise large groups (Granovetter 1973), strong relationships based on mutual trust are required for high-risk activism (Morozov 2011: 196).

The selection of those campaigns that result in large-scale mobilisation online also comes under scrutiny. Given that affective expression is structurally embedded within the design of platforms like Facebook (e.g. the "Like" button) (Wahl-Jorgenson 2018), emotional contagion is a factor commonly linked to slacktivism. The significance of emotion to the slacktivist critique can be illustrated by #Kony2012, the video-based campaign examined in Chapter 1. Featuring Hollywood-style editing and dramatic imagery, the video's main focus was to highlight the role of Joseph Kony, leader of the Lord's Resistance Army (LRA), in the recruitment of children to fight in the LRA's militia. The campaign was widely criticised for its overly simplistic, "good versus evil" narrative, one that obfuscates and misrepresents the complex issue of child soldiers (Drumbl 2012; Gregory 2012). Described as "emotional exploitation" (Madianou 2013: 257), the affective pull of this video is key to understanding why so many people took part. In their audience-focused study, Engelhardt and Jansz (2014) describe how the campaign built up a sense of moral responsibility to participate. Taking part was deemed a social necessity; the simplistic narrative compelled those conscious of their virtual identity to become involved. How could you not take a stance against a man accused of recruiting thousands of children for military combat? While Jasper (1997) recognises the mobilising role of emotion in all forms of political action, this pressure is exacerbated and potentially distorted as a result of the social dynamics of online networks. In what Sunstein (2007: 84) describes as "cybercascades," online audiences are susceptible to the sway of popular opinion as they seek to secure the approval and validation of others. In this way, quick emotional triggers may take precedence over thoughtful and rational critique. Given that other research challenges this hypothesis, showing that emotive communication on social media can mobilise networks around under-represented viewpoints (Papacharissi 2014: 130–131), there is an evident need to explore the motivations of those taking part in digital micro-activism.

I argue that the slacktivist critique is indicative of the polarised dichotomy from which it originates. The critique is based on a series of causal assumptions that fail to comprehensively account for the potential use of these new technologies within everyday life. By focusing on these low-threshold behaviours in isolation, many of the benefits outlined by existing studies are overlooked. Revisions are therefore required to extract the relevant concerns and create a new, systematic research agenda for understanding the environment in which these new forms of social and political expression take place.

Refuting the Assertions of Slacktivism

> These myths of technologically enabled utopias or dystopias then predispose our reaction to technological innovations in ways that operate outside the realm of pragmatism.
>
> (Papacharissi 2010: 8)

Slacktivism has become synonymous with a negative perception of the political value of social media. However, as Papacharissi (2010) observes, the critique is flawed by an overly narrow focus, analysing micro-activism in isolation from other modes of engagement, and from other forms of media. As such, the critique lacks an appreciation for the complexity of normalised use, relying on anomalous case studies to support vague, grand theories of Internet usage where none can be made. In order to critically evaluate the relationship between social media and political engagement, one must first develop a comprehensive understanding of the environment in which this usage takes place. This book will examine the relationships formed between social media and other forms of online and offline communication, exploring the role of Facebook and Twitter as part of broader engagement repertoires. It is in the interactions that form between different modes of engagement and across mediated and non-mediated spaces that we will discover substantive findings on the relationship between social media and political participation.

The intention of this chapter is not to discard the hypotheses of the slacktivist critique, especially without any empirical evidence. Instead, I propose a number of theoretical problems. In order to provide a more accurate reflection of day-to-day use, the theoretical scope must be broadened. An alternate research agenda is proposed based on five key revisions.

Understanding Political Participation as a Process

> Politics is not defined by the *locus* of its operation but by its nature as a *process*.
>
> (Hay 2002: 3, emphasis in original)

Firstly, the slacktivist critique evaluates the relationship between acts of digital micro-activism and the desired political outcome in isolation. This deterministic, causal relationship lacks an appreciation of the expansive, procedural foundations at the heart of political engagement (Arnstein 1969; Carpentier 2011; Fung 2006; Vegh 2003) and, as Hay (2002: 3) argues, politics more generally. This emphasis on observable political behaviour actions ignores the role that social networking sites play in relation to information exchange, discursive engagement, and political mobilisation.

A key theme amongst proponents of the slacktivist critique is that campaigns conducted on social networking sites are ineffective in producing political change. However, as Fig. 2.1—a meme shared in the aftermath of the #Kony2012 campaign—shows, this critique implies that low-threshold interactions form a causal relationship with the desired political effect(s). In doing so, the critique ignores the complex array of factors that result in a political outcome. Moreover, conventional forms of participation seldom bring such immediate results, be they party membership, voting, or even a large-scale protest. Take, for instance, the 2003 protests which saw around two million people take to the streets of London to object to the imminent Iraq War (Kettell 2006: 96). This shortcoming is exacerbated when these acts of micro-activism are compared to revolutionary change (Gladwell 2010; Morozov 2009, 2011; White 2010, 2011). Instinctively, low-effort forms of online engagement will not feasibly produce systemic political change on their own. By focusing on this deterministic relationship, the slacktivist critique ignores the process of engagement that enables an individual to participate.

Fig. 2.1 A meme created in response to #Kony2012

Moreover, forms of symbolic participation, like self-expression on social media, commonly complement other direct and representative forms of participation (Bode et al. 2014; Chadwick and Dennis 2017; Kristofferson et al. 2014; Vaccari et al. 2015b; Yang and DeHart 2016).

These forms of symbolic involvement are overlooked because the slacktivist critique focuses on the macro-level as the arena in which power is contested and exercised. This emphasis on observable political actions omits the significance of the micro-level and the attitudes and behaviours of individual citizens. As Wright (2012: 249) notes, it may be the case that more democratically important political and social changes occur amongst the interactions of ordinary citizens. Although a number of studies describe the individualisation of political identity and the rise of post-materialist political action (Dalton 2008; Giddens 1991; Inglehart 1990; Norris 2011; Theocharis and van Deth 2016), few studies of online engagement account for attitudinal measures (Boulianne 2009). I argue that our definition of political participation should be broadened, taking into account this process of enablement.

There are a number of frameworks that develop this idea for the study of digital political communication. Vegh (2003: 72) notes that online activism generally falls into three distinct categories across a "ladder of engagement," each of which can either be Internet-enhanced, supporting offline efforts, or Internet-based: (1) awareness and advocacy, (2) organisation and mobilisation, and (3) action/reaction. The slacktivist critique isolates the action stage. As such, the potential of online technologies to share informational goods, as a means for symbolic participation, and as an organisational tool, is discounted. Similarly, Carpentier (2011) offers a process-based approach entitled the "access, interaction and participation model," arguing that access to political content and socio-communicative relationships represent prerequisite conditions for participation.

However, while access and interaction remain important conditions for participation, Carpentier (2011) argues that they cannot be equated to participation. In doing so, he disagrees with Jenkins (2006; Jenkins and Carpentier 2013) who describes information consumption and political discussion as participatory acts. As Carpentier (2011: 69) notes, "they are distinct from participation because of their less explicit emphasis on power dynamics and decision making." As such, this model reinforces the concept of slacktivism by isolating acts that explicitly display the contestation of power between actors. I argue that this is conceptually problematic for a number of reasons.

Firstly, power is diffused across the model as access and interaction are inextricably linked to participation. An awareness and understanding of a political issue, formed through media consumption or interpersonal discussion, may well define how a citizen acts. The consumption of information empowers a citizen, as it provides them with the informational goods on which to act (Delli Carpini et al. 2004). Power is also evident in the way that information is communicated between a producer and a receiver, a process defined as "framing," "selecting and highlighting some facets of events or issues and making connections amongst them as to promote a particular interpretation, evaluation or solution" (Entman 2004: 5). Traditionally, this meant that elite actors exercised power by using media frames to shape how those consuming the information made sense of an event or issue (Castells 2009: 115; Graber 2004: 548). Networked communications pose new questions regarding these established logics, as individual citizens can bypass traditional frames, challenge them, and even create new ones (Chadwick 2011; Gallagher et al. 2018; O'Loughlin et al. 2017). As such, the desire and means to participate depend upon how political information is framed.

Similarly, interaction, by definition, is always relational and power dynamics are displayed in the exchanges between actors (Jenkins and Carpentier 2013). This is especially true on social media, given the discrepancies in visibility and influence between users (Couldry 2012: 122; Graham and Wright 2014). On the other hand, interpersonal discussion can help citizens contextualise and understand political information (Eveland and Hively 2009; Hardy and Scheufele 2006; Scheufele 2001; Valenzuela et al. 2011). As McLeod et al. (1999: 329) note, "communication plays a critical role in either motivating participation or making it possible." Therefore, political conversations, either face-to-face or online, shape the conditions for participation.

However, although I argue that access, interaction, and participation are interconnected, they do not necessarily form a causal model. Public actions are not guaranteed to follow, as information consumption and interactions may remain confined to private spaces. Bakardjieva (2009: 96) describes this as "subactivism," "small-scale, often individual decisions and actions that have either a political or ethical frame of reference (or both) and remain submerged in everyday life." Actions include reading a newspaper, conversations with friends, either face-to-face (Eliasoph 1998) or with networked peers (Graham and Wright 2014), playing video games (Skoric and Kwan 2011), and watching television (Coleman 2007; Jones 2005). Power is contested in these seemingly insignificant activities. The information that an individual consumes and the interactions that they have, even if mundane or informal, can have an effect on the formation of their political identity (Bakardjieva 2009; Couldry et al. 2010). Furthermore, these micropolitical behaviours can wield substantial political power when considered collectively, either as a challenge to elites (Chadwick 2012: 54; Margetts et al. 2015), or in reinforcing the authority of a political community (Bucy and Gregson 2001: 357; Svensson 2011: 649).

This public–private distinction that Carpentier draws on also becomes more complex given the porousness of visibility online. Since clicks are measurable and can be easily visualised, they become an easy proxy for engagement within the slacktivist critique. However, this neglects the complexity of how we use social media, as the boundaries between mass and interpersonal communication become blurred (Baym 2010; Papacharissi 2010). Online self-expression can be published to public, semi-public, or private spaces depending on the service functionality. For example, a post to another user's "wall" on Facebook, or a tweet directed at another user, can be interpersonal in that this communication is intended for another individual, but, under normal use, these can also be viewed by a wider audience. Others may then use this information for a range of purposes, including what Anstead and O'Loughlin (2015) describe as "semantic polling" techniques, which involve pulling vast data sets from Twitter to try and understand public opinion (see Karpf 2016: 37–41). Thereby, user-generated content can even have political effects without the expressed intent of the user.

Owing to these limitations, the access, interaction, participation model (Carpentier 2011) is too restrictive, neglecting the important power dynamics that citizens encounter in everyday life. The socio-communicative relationships that Carpentier distinguishes from participation are also sites of power, as individuals or groups try to persuade and shape the preferences of others through forms of communication (Lukes 2005). However, the model does offer a way of overcoming the active-passive dichotomy in political participation research (Amnå and Ekman 2014; Bucy and Gregson 2001; Fox 2014; Theocharis 2012). Carpentier links these seemingly passive behaviours, which are often ignored, to forms of political action. Based on the process-based approaches proposed by Vegh (2003) and Carpentier (2011), I offer an alternative model, the continuum of participation, illustrated in Fig. 2.2.

The continuum of participation reflects the idea that engagement is a process, rather than an outcome. The descriptive model consists of four stages. Access refers to cognitive engagement and the ways by which citizens pay attention to politics and public affairs. Expression encapsulates forms of political communication between citizens. The effects of expression can vary across the continuum depending on the motivations of the user, how receivers use this information, and the composition of the audience, such as one–many; real–imagined; online–offline; and public–private. Connection represents the processes of political organisation, as citizens use social media to establish and join networks for a range of purposes. These consist of both strong and weak tie relationships, depending on the issue and the campaign. Finally, action signifies goal-orientated, public political acts, as social networking sites are used for digital activism, or form part of interconnected engagement repertoires. By using this approach and exploring the relationships between the different stages, a new set of questions emerge regarding the value of social media as a tool for political learning, for the honing of personal identity, for discursive participation, and for public forms of self-expression. This model is developed in Chapter 3.

The marriage equality campaign lead by the Human Rights Campaign, an LGBTQ equal rights organisation based in the USA, demonstrates that a new theoretical approach is needed as the boundaries between self-expression and instrumental action become blurred. In March 2013, the group shared a red version of its logo to coincide with the Supreme Court hearing two, potentially groundbreaking, cases on marriage equality. The organisation encouraged its supporters to change their profile picture on a number of social networking sites to show their support (Knibbs 2013). Advocates, in the form of

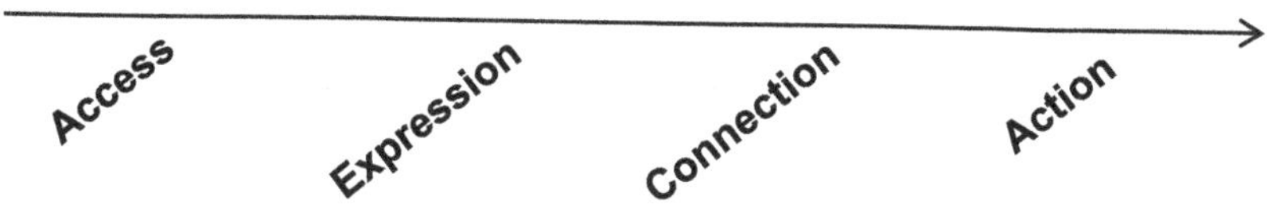

Fig. 2.2 The continuum of participation model

individual supporters, other political groups, and commercial brands, went one step further and remixed the logo, fusing it with a variety of political and cultural icons, including the US Constitution; the popular video games character "Super Mario"; the film franchise *Star Wars*; and the Internet meme "Grumpy Cat," as shown in Fig. 2.3 (Garcia 2013). If evaluated as a direct tactic to sway the opinion of those Justices adjudicating the case, as the slacktivist critique would propose, the campaign was most likely a failure. However, this overly simplistic approach lacks an awareness of the wider benefits of the campaign, which can be seen when mapped on the continuum of participation. Supporters personalised pre-existing content to fit the narrative and, in doing so, were simultaneously raising awareness and providing a platform for further action.

This book describes how different forms of engagement enmesh across the continuum of participation and the role that social networking sites play within these repertoires. Do social media form part of a meaningful participatory model, or do services like Facebook and Twitter prove unsuccessful when trying to turn awareness into action?

Fig. 2.3 Examples of campaign images from the Equal Rights Campaign, March 2013 (*Source* Adapted from Garcia [2013])

Accounting for Media Convergence

> If we understand political participation as solely within party, campaign, or movement organizations and if we look at its varieties (e.g., conventional and unconventional) as somewhat alternative to each other, then we lose sight of the many ways in which old and new political organizations and their supporters are integrating different modes of political engagement in everyday activities.
>
> (Vaccari 2013: 222)

The slacktivist critique focuses on social media in isolation. By claiming that tried and tested offline methods are more effective than digital micro-activism, the slacktivist critique falls foul of "digital dualism," the belief that online and offline are distinct and separate realities (Jurgenson 2011). As such, the critique fails to account for the empirical reality of contemporary activism, as fluid online and offline tactics intersect throughout the continuum of participation. Low-effort, high-volume micro-activism makes up just a single tactic in the strategic repertoire of actions used by both citizens and organisations (Karpf 2010: 28). Drawing on Vaccari's (2013: 222) observations above, the interconnectivity of social media, coupled with the mass adoption of services such as Facebook and Twitter, provides political parties, pressure groups, and social movements with a body of activists and organisational tools for collective action. As such, micro-activism often compliments other online and offline tactics (Bode 2017; Boulianne 2015; Christensen 2012; Vaccari et al. 2015b).

Furthermore, the condemnation of an entire communication medium as low-effort lacks an awareness of similar, relatively easy, offline political tasks such as political consumerism, postcard campaigns, or even voting (Christensen 2011; Karpf 2010). Moreover, users can also undertake high-effort acts on social networking sites, by creating political groups or devoting hours to civic discussion. It is therefore not a question of engagement on social networking sites being defined by low-effort slacktivism, but a renewal of these engagement forms within a new communicative space.

In highlighting the weaknesses of digital micro-activism and claiming that offline activism is more effective, the medium itself supersedes user behaviour as the focus of analysis. However, technology does not possess some innate quality to influence human behaviour. Therefore, the slacktivist critique represents a form of technological determinism, as the characteristics of the technology shape political behaviour, rather than the intentions of the user. If we are to understand the democratic potential of digital micro-activism, we must account for media convergence across three areas.

Firstly, social networking sites are often used to support other forms of online and offline engagement as part of interconnected engagement repertoires, where repertoires refer to the participatory tactics and structural form adopted by a political group. Traditionally, different organisational structures adopt different repertoires depending on their position and goals within a political system (Chadwick 2007: 285). However, Chadwick (2007: 286) argues that different organisational forms are becoming increasingly hybridised as they adopt "digital network repertoires," where online and offline techniques are being amalgamated, with new kinds of actions accompanying classic ones at the local, national, and transnational level. This blurring of engagement tactics is evident in a survey of 53 pressure groups in the USA, where Obar et al. (2012: 10) found that groups adapted their use of social media to suit specific organisational goals at particular points in a campaign.

Theocharis (2012) has also demonstrated this organisational flexibility in a study of the 2010 university occupations against the UK government's planned cuts to higher education. He notes two distinct contexts in which Twitter can be used. Firstly, the "mobilising stage," where Twitter was used to provide information to wider audiences, set an agenda for the movement through communication with other activists, and for the logistical planning of future protest events. Secondly, the leadership used Twitter during the demonstrations to disseminate crucial information to activists on the ground in real time, in what Theocharis characterises as "dynamic" or "demonstrational" use. Subsequently, the use of Twitter was not simply an easy, symbolic online action, but a fusion of online and offline engagement tactics that were fluid throughout the mobilisation process.

Therefore, social media enable a great deal of flexibility at the organisational level, as groups can vary their action repertoires depending on the issue or campaign (Bennett and Segerberg 2013; Bimber et al. 2012; Chadwick 2013). The speed and reach of networked communication platforms enable groups to switch and change their engagement tactics during a campaign. As such, social media do not replace the established norms of collective action, as claimed in the substitution thesis, but they empower political parties, pressure groups, and social movements to diversify their engagement tactics. Furthermore, these technological affordances have enabled the growth of entirely new political organisations (Chadwick and Dennis 2017; Hall 2017; Karpf 2016; Vromen 2017). As Karpf (2012: 156) argues, "a new generation of netroots organisations has emerged… Their advocacy work extends well beyond 'clicktivism,' engaging supporters in large-scale, sustained collective action. Their work routines and campaign strategies are built around the Internet." It is therefore crucial to evaluate the role of Facebook and Twitter within these wider engagement repertoires.

Secondly, by focusing on social media in isolation, the slacktivist critique constructs an arbitrary barrier between online and offline that ignores the impact of media convergence on information consumption and interpersonal discussion (Chadwick 2013; Graham et al. 2015; Jenkins 2006). The slacktivist critique detaches moments of discussion and expression, focusing on just one service or one event. This is problematic, as our everyday political experiences are fundamentally diffuse. We don't simply discuss politics in one place or using one technology, but civic discussion takes place across a whole range of overlapping mediated and non-mediated spaces (Wright 2012: 254). Moreover, this one-dimensional approach neglects how our behaviours on social networking sites influence our offline relationships and networks (Baym 2010; Ellison et al. 2007; Valenzuela et al. 2011). As such, a new approach is required that accounts for the convergence of media.

Chadwick (2013: 3) argues that Britain and the USA now have "hybrid media systems," which are built upon the interactions within and between different forms of media. He uses hybridity and flux to conceptualise a holistic approach to the study of media. Rather than differentiating between "new" and "old" media logics—where logics are defined as "technologies, genres, norms, behaviors, and organizational forms"—he argues that power in empirical studies of political communication can only be understood in the relationships and tensions that form between them. The increasingly fluid power dynamics between content producers and consumers, both professional and amateur, is leading to significant changes for political citizenship in Britain:

> This goes beyond the simple fact that citizens are now able to express themselves online in public forums. In the hybrid media system, it is older media's systemic integration and expectation of citizen expression occurring in newer media environments that often makes the difference.

> Internet-driven norms of networking, flexibility, spontaneity and ad hoc organizing have started to diffuse into our politics and media and these norms are generating new expectations about what counts as effective and worthwhile political action.
>
> (Chadwick 2013: 210)

These expectations are not present in accounts of slacktivism, where traditional modes of political activity are deemed sacrosanct. Therefore, the hybrid media system is an important theoretical step in bypassing the aforementioned utopian-dystopian dichotomy. It expands the parameters of media use rather than isolating a specific social networking site or detaching participation as an offline-only practice.

This is not to say that the hybrid media system approach necessarily equates to a more inclusive form of democracy. While Chadwick (2013: 58–59) does propose that hybridity presents opportunities in which citizens can exert power, traditional elites can, and do, adapt to these new environments (see Chadwick et al. 2016; Anstead and Chadwick 2018). In what Kreiss (2012) defines as "structured interactivity," political parties restrict the agency of social media users by directing citizen participation to those tasks that the leadership need completing. Likewise, broadcast media are still a central cog in the mechanics of media production. For instance, most user-generated content is dependent on the informational resources provided by mass media, including newspaper, radio broadcasting, and television. However, as media systems become more hybridised, the control an actor has over these information flows weakens and more opportunities exist for citizens to disrupt and influence the framing of an agenda, issue, or event.

This augmentation of digital and broadcast media can be illustrated by the convergence of television and social media. Putnam (2000) argues that television weakens citizen engagement as isolated viewers passively consume television. However, interactive digital platforms change the viewing experience, creating what Anstead and O'Loughlin (2011: 441) describe as the "viewertariat," users who comment, share, or remix content on social platforms as they watch television. Jenkins (2006) argues that these new behaviours mark a cultural shift in which consumption is no longer passive but active, breaking down the distinctions between producer and consumer. This trend is increasingly apparent across television, with audience participation a key feature of reality shows (Coleman 2007), sports programming (Aslan et al. 2015), and live coverage of political events (Chadwick et al. 2017; Gil de Zúñiga et al. 2014; Vaccari et al. 2015a).

This activity is what Karpf (2012: 166–168) describes as "activated public opinion," disorganised forms of online political speech that do not mesh with our traditional understanding of political participation or communication. Social networking sites offer a venue for citizens to speak out, share opinions, and spread news. What is so unique about this digital self-expression is the diverse range of effects seemingly identical acts can produce. A tweet can be an isolated instance of opinion expression. However, when undertaken collectively, the same action can be part of powerful, co-ordinated political action.

For example, in September 2012, the American weekly magazine *Newsweek* used a controversial headline, "MUSLIM RAGE," to describe a number of anti-US protests in the wake of a YouTube trailer for the low-budget film, *Innocence of Muslims.* Twitter users across the globe took offence to this sensationalist headline and the generalisations made from a protest in which only a few hundred participated (Nasr 2012). A hashtag, #muslimrage, was created to contest and reframe the narrative, drawing on a mixture of humour and personal anecdotes (see Amry 2012). This new narrative, generated by disorganised, large-scale self-expression, fed into broadcast media coverage, as the reaction was reported in the *Guardian* (Hotz 2012), the Huffington Post (Mirkinson 2012), and the *New York Times* (Kirkpatrick 2012). This example illustrates the complex power dynamics within the hybrid media system, as new and old media logics intertwine. Self-expression online often depends on the informational resources and reach of professional media, but simultaneously wields the potential to challenge established information hierarchies (see Meraz and Papacharissi 2013). In isolation, this self-expression may seem trivial or insignificant, but using the theoretical lens of the hybrid media system we can see the disruptive effects of so-called slacktivism.

This example of remix culture, where existing content is adapted or built upon to convey a different meaning, highlights a third area of convergence: the diffusion of the political into social, especially entertainment-orientated, spaces (Lessig 2008; Jenkins 2006). The slacktivist critique tends to be dismissive of social media, arguing that it generally serves to entertain and distract a user with gossip, lolcats, and dank memes, rather than provide civic or political informational goods (Morozov 2009, 2011: 81–82). However, the boundaries between what is deemed to be political and non-political are not static and vary from person to person.

Political decisions are often made based on everyday experiences. As Delli Carpini and Williams (2000: 161, emphasis in original) argue, "individuals are *simultaneously* citizens, consumers, audiences, family members, workers, and so forth." Our personal life and private experiences shape the conditions of our participation (Bennett 2012; Dahlgren 2009: 27–33; Giddens 1991; Papacharissi 2010, 2014; Wright 2012). As such, those conversations on social media that seem trivial may have unseen political consequences. Latent political actors exist in the form of those users who become accustomed to the self-expressive norms of social networking sites, sharing aspects of their daily life. Therefore, it is necessary to adopt a porous definition of the political in order to understand engagement at the individual level.

We can see evidence of this porousness in "infotainment," television programmes that blend entertainment and political information (Bastien 2009; Baym 2005; Coleman 2007; Jones 2005). Television shows, like *The Daily Show* in the USA (Baym 2005) and *Have I Got News for You* in Britain (Jones 2005), use humour to lower the entry costs to news and political debate. Likewise, the blurring of civic issues and popular culture online has led to the birth of new cultural artefacts. These include, for example, "memes": an image, typically humorous in nature, that is copied, adapted, and built upon and then spread online (Davison 2012; Shifman 2013). Jurgenson (2012) argues that memes represent an active attempt to assert individual autonomy. An individual chooses what to share and repositions a mass, cultural artefact as a statement about oneself; "the meme is personal is political" (Jurgenson 2012). This is an example of what Jenkins (2006: 16) describes as "convergence culture," a process by which the audience moves beyond passive consumption and has the tools to archive, annotate, appropriate, and recirculate media content. On social media, users have more autonomy over their own identity, forming connections with others around niche cultural phenomena. Politics becomes part of this cultural fragmentation, with creative citizens combining popular culture with meaningful political messages. This is evident on the "The Simpsons Against the Conservatives" Facebook page, where users combine political commentary with memorable moments from the animated TV show, *The Simpsons*. Figure 2.4 shows a meme created in the aftermath of the 2017 UK general election.

As such, the civic culture in Britain is far removed from the one described by Almond and Verba (1963). Dahlgren (2005, 2009) argues that we now have multiple civic cultures in which different cultural and social groups can express civic commonality in different ways. These civic cultures serve as the pre-conditions for participation, the everyday experiences that guide our sense-making processes and stimulate political participation (Dahlgren 2005: 157–158). In exploring these new civic cultures, we must engage with a diverse range of seemingly non-political, often informal, spaces, in which political issues emerge organically (Couldry 2012; Dahlgren 2009; Deuze 2012; Wright 2012).

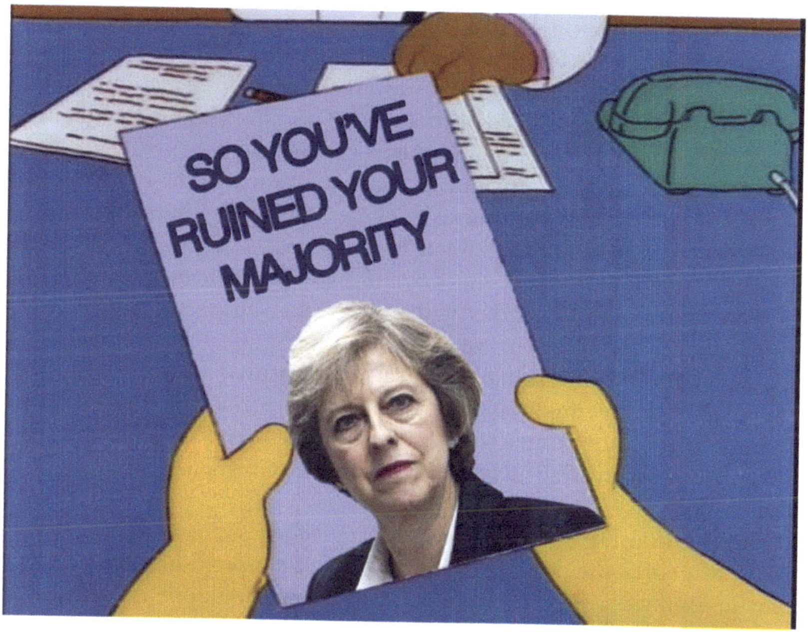

Fig. 2.4 A meme posted on "The Simpsons Against the Conservatives" Facebook page following the 2017 UK general election (*Source* The Simpsons Against the Conservatives [2017])

The transition from a broadcast era to a hybrid media system opens up a number of questions. Rather than focusing on examples of slacktivism in isolation, this study will examine the three dimensions of convergence outlined. Firstly, in an activist context, how are Facebook and Twitter used alongside other modes of political action? Secondly, in day-to-day life, how do citizens combine forms of traditional media with social media? Is the audience now active? Finally, using a diary methodology, I will examine in what spaces—online and offline—citizens consume political information, discuss issues, and engage in digital micro-activism.

A Matter of Scale: Time, Granularity, and the Digital Divide

A central component of the slacktivist critique is effort. Slacktivism is often described as a "lazy person's activism," as activists abandon effort-intensive, real space political action in favour of easier methods online. As Morozov (2011: 190) argues, "thanks to its granularity, digital activism provides too many ways out." Although this granularity—defined as "the extent to which the creation of informational public goods may be disaggregated into tasks of varying degree" (Chadwick 2012: 40)—may amplify the number of participants involved, those advocating the slacktivist critique argue that this masks the effortless and largely ineffective actions undertaken (Gladwell 2010; White 2010).

However, how is effort defined in this context? If we return to the definition of slacktivism in the *Oxford English Dictionary*, it is apparent that effort is synonymous with time. This suggests that the depth of someone's commitment to a cause, or the quality of democratic engagement at the individual level, can be measured by time. However, it is dangerous to simply assume that the more time a citizen devotes to politics, the more impactful their actions will be. Furthermore, it is unrealistic to claim that active citizenship requires such high levels of commitment.

This relationship ignores the importance of scale in two respects. Firstly, it ignores the power of volume. A single e-petition signatory may seem insignificant, but collectively, thousands or millions of signatories can have significant gravitas (Bochel 2013). Secondly, scale is an important characteristic of the continuum of participation. If we consider the time pressure that citizens experience on a daily basis, then the granularity of digital engagement represents an important means of maintaining awareness, keeping a toe in the water so to speak, sometimes sparking further involvement at opportune moments. Therefore, it is important to examine the context in which these apparent quick fixes take place.

Time is a resource that has unique properties. Everyone, regardless of their place within society, has just twenty-four hours in a single day, making it a resource that is inherently scarce (Goodin et al. 2008: 3). As such, it is rational to assume that the amount of time that we allocate to politics indicates the strength of our involvement. But such an assumption disregards the complexity of political behaviour at the individual level, ignoring how our perception of time affects our actions. In their study on citizenship in Britain, Pattie et al. (2004: 175) argue that citizens increasingly seek to make an observable impact with, often, the lowest time demands. This is a result of rising timepressure, the all too common feeling that we just don't have enough hours in the day to fulfil all of our ambitions (Goodin et al. 2008: 69).

In order to understand well-being in contemporary society, Goodin et al. (2008) argue that we need to move away from financial measurements and focus on time. They compare the amount of "discretionary time" that a person has control over across six countries. More commonly referred to as "spare time," they argue that the two terms are conceptually different. Discretionary time is the amount of time that an individual has autonomous control over after deducting what is strictly needed for *necessary* activities, identified as bodily, financial, and household requirements (Goodin et al. 2008: 35). However, people do more to fulfil these three necessities than is needed. Spare time is defined as "the amount of time you have left over after all the time you actually devote to paid labour, unpaid household labour and personal care" (Goodin et al. 2008: 36). Typically, the amount of spare time available to a citizen is much less than the level of discretionary time.

Two factors account for this perceived restriction of temporal autonomy. Firstly, flux and instability characterise modern work, as citizens shift between different careers, temporary work, and spells of unemployment, a consequence of which is both an increase of autonomy but also stress (Bennett 2012: 25). This anxiety permeates into our domestic duties, especially with the rise of single-parent families. Secondly, being busy has become a social symbol, as people work harder for the microeconomic benefits and status derived from career progression. This is not to say that past generations did not possess a strong work ethic, but that these changes must be understood as part of broader cultural developments. Inglehart (1990) describes this as a by-product of the value change from materialism to post-materialism, as citizens seek more freedom over their time to pursue the things that they enjoy or, more broadly, value.

The sum effect of these changes is the existence of a "time-pressure illusion," the gap between one's perception of their spare time and the actual level of discretionary time available to them (Goodin et al. 2008). The anxiety and strain itself is evidently not an illusion, but the sense of pressure stems from the impression that work beyond a level of necessity is required. Evidently, this sense of time pressure varies at the individual level, as restrictions to one's temporal autonomy depend on their lifestyle choices. However, unlike many other resources, the acute feeling of time pressure is somewhat universal. Those citizens on a low income must spend more time to fulfil their basic necessities, while those on a high income exist within a culture of success that benefits those who work hardest. These economic and sociopolitical changes mean that, as time becomes increasingly scarce, individuals prioritise involvement with issues of their choosing (Dahlgren 2009; Dalton 2008; Norris 2011; Pattie et al. 2004). What is derided as low-effort slacktivism may actually be a time-efficient way of maintaining an interest in politics.

Given the time-pressure illusion that citizens experience day-to-day, the diverse array of engagement opportunities online poses new challenges for how we conceptualise active citizenship. It is true that those acts labelled as slacktivism often require small amounts of effort, or time, from the individual, but they are often designed with this very much in mind. By making political actions more granular, the barrier of entry to political participation is lowered. Such an interpretation challenges the model of citizenship inferred from the slacktivist critique. This critique suggests that the ideal citizen is one who devotes the most time to their activism. However, such a definition is problematic; this dedicated, informed activist type does not, and cannot, exist in most advanced democracies (Coleman and Blumler 2009; Couldry et al. 2010; Dalton 2008; Dahlgren 2009; Graber 2004; Papacharissi 2010; Schudson 1999; Stoker 2006).

As Graber (2004: 561–562) notes, it is not feasible to stay fully informed about all political developments, all of the time. In *The Good Citizen*, Schudson (1999) argues that the "monitorial citizen" model characterises the conditions of modern citizenship, as citizens need only survey the news enough to identify those political issues that have personal relevance. Despite this, much of the debate on citizenship in popular discourse is framed around whether citizens are engaged or apathetic (Fox 2014; Hooghe and Dejaeghere 2007). This dichotomous approach obfuscates the value of scale, and what Amnå and Ekman (2014: 263) describe as the "standby citizen," "those who stay alert, keep themselves informed about politics by bringing up political issues in everyday contexts, and are willing to participate if needed." This citizen type, an extension of Schudson's monitorial citizen, is normatively separate to those disengaged or disillusioned citizens who are similarly perceived to be apathetic. These citizens monitor those issues that have personal significance, and are prepared to take action, should circumstances warrant them to. Therefore, participatory shortcuts can be beneficial to active citizenship.

This book examines what value Facebook and Twitter have, if any, in providing participatory shortcuts across the continuum of participation. Past studies have shown that those who benefit from the political use of the Internet, in general, tend to be skewed heavily in favour of those well-educated, computer savvy, and socially confident citizens (Brundidge and Rice 2009; Mossberger et al. 2003). Mossberger et al. (2003: 9) argue that the "digital divide" refers to more than simply an issue of access; a fully immersive experience online depends on a number of skill sets. One must possess a variety of technical competencies and information literacy skills to use these resources to their full potential. However, as of writing, little empirical research has been undertaken that examines whether social media can help bridge these social and technical divides in Britain.

Intuitively, by their very design, social networking sites can offer information shortcuts to those who may have become marginalised or excluded from political life. Through interpersonal communication and asymmetric sharing on social media, users are exposed to political information they may not have intended to consume (Chadwick 2012; Fletcher and Nielsen 2017b; Valeriani and Vaccari 2016). For example, "Trending Topics" on Twitter often includes news updates, political events, and, crucially, different information from a user's own personal feed. Similarly, empirical research has shown how citizens on Facebook and Twitter can encounter political ideas that differ from their own (Bakshy et al. 2015; Barberá et al. 2015).

Outside of these informational benefits, Jenkins (Jenkins and Carpentier 2013) and Zuckerman (2008) have argued that regular access to social networking sites for personal enjoyment creates the latent capabilities for political action. Zuckerman's (2008) "cute cat theory of digital activism" states that through the extended use of digital media tools for entertainment and social relations, citizens develop the organisational and technical capacities to use these tools for political ends, under the right circumstances. However, outside of technical proficiencies, this theory assumes that all users are equally comfortable with political self-expression online. Closer examination indicates that many citizens are uneasy about digital forms of interaction, as opposed to face-to-face communication. Tufekci (2012: 43) labels this characteristic as "cyber-asociality," "the inability or unwillingness of some people to relate to others via social media as they do when physically-present." These feelings are in flux over time, depending on technological developments, personal circumstances, and the nature of the particular networked contact(s). As Rainie and Wellman (2012: 9) note, citizens must build upon their existing social skills in order to make the most of this expansive networked environment. Undoubtedly, this social divide can impact a citizen's ability to use the Internet in ways beneficial for democracy. Just because the threshold of access to social media is lower does not necessarily mean that the opportunities gained through their use are evenly distributed across society. As such, the social divide must be factored into any conclusions drawn on the impact of Facebook and Twitter across the continuum of participation.

Morozov (2011: 194) contends that social networking sites lead to information overload, as lazy, but image conscious, users share their political perspectives and obstruct collective action efforts in the process: "not everyone can be Che Guevara." But users aren't trying to be full-time activists. The reality is that a majority of citizens balance civic and political interests with the trials of daily existence. Therefore, scale is essential when we consider the relationship between routine social media use and political engagement. Citizens are not conveniently divided between those who are active and those who are passive; engagement is not akin to an on/off switch. At various times, we are more or less involved, depending on our personal circumstances. With this in mind, the granularity built into social media must be explored across the continuum of participation, rather than in isolation as in the slacktivist critique.

The Feel-Good Factor: Authenticity and the Digital Self

> "Slacktivism" is an apt term to describe feel-good online activism that has zero political or social impact. It gives those who participate in "slacktivist" campaigns an illusion of having a meaningful impact on the world without demanding anything more than joining a Facebook group.
>
> (Morozov 2009)

As Morozov (2009) argues, the underlying motivational logic behind acts of slacktivism is self-gratification. This can be interpreted in two ways. Firstly, the aspiration to feel good by doing good. Critics denounce the effortlessness of slacktivism, providing cognitive rewards for the participant while minimising their contribution. However, this judgement is only valid when applied to the context of the action itself. If we isolate a Facebook post or a tweet, and then compare the depth of one's participation with what are often ambitious aims, it may seem that a participant's involvement is self-serving. However, what happens *after* and *alongside* these acts of slacktivism? Research has shown that those users engaging in digital micro-activism do so alongside a wide range of other civic and political activities (Bode et al. 2014; Boulianne 2015; Chadwick and Dennis 2017; Christensen 2012; Kristofferson et al. 2014; Vaccari et al. 2015b; Yang and DeHart 2016). What may seem to be a low-effort, self-indulgent act in isolation could in fact lead to further involvement, a process in which the interdependency between different acts sheds light on the normative value of democratic engagement.

Secondly, the slacktivist critique argues that actors are more concerned by social presentation than the cause itself, as users seek to cultivate a particular image. In both cases, one's actions are deemed to lack authenticity, as narcissism trumps genuine intent. Flawed or problematic campaigns become viral at the expense of other, more deserving or urgent, causes due to this perceived self-indulgence (Gladwell 2010; Morozov 2009, 2011). As Morozov (2011: 194) notes, "while many students are wasting their energy on 'saving' Darfur by joining Facebook groups, their own universities are run without the scrutiny they deserve from the student body." Well-documented examples include: the hundreds of thousands of Twitter users who made their avatars green in solidarity with the Iranian election protests in 2009; those Facebook users who changed their profile picture to include the French flag following the terror attacks in Paris in November 2015 (O'Loughlin et al. 2017); and the aforementioned #Kony2012 campaign. In each of these cases, the psychological or social benefits to the participant are seen to far outweigh any observable, "real world" impacts (Morozov 2011: 186).

However, this take on authenticity is imprecise as it conflates two interpretations of the term; authenticity refers to both the sincerity of political behaviour and whether the campaign is accurate and based on fact. This confusion is understandable as the *Oxford English Dictionary* definition of authenticity refers quite clearly to both interpretations.[3] However, it is important to distinguish between the two definitions when analysing political behaviour, as they are not one and the same. Someone may sincerely act on an issue that may be constructed on a suspect narrative. I know when I shared the #Kony2012 campaign video to my Facebook network on the morning of 5 March 2012, I had nothing but honest intentions. In order to understand the complex personal motivations that occur prior to acts of digital micro-activism, it is important to differentiate authenticity from information accuracy. This will also highlight if, and under what conditions, the relationship between the two concepts becomes empirically significant.

In this book, I define information accuracy as the factual precision of the information on which political behaviour is based. A measure of this kind can be highly subjective and difficult to operationalise methodologically. For example, a post on a social networking site may be more factually accurate than some news articles. However, as illustrated by #Kony2012, it is important to analyse what type of information sparks viral attention and digital micro-activism, examining both the format in which it is presented (e.g. a video, an image, or text) and the way that the content is framed. Authenticity is understood as "the quality of truthful correspondence between inner feelings and their outward expression." Drawing on qualitative techniques, I examine the extent to which behaviour is genuine as opposed to the result of external social pressures (Yacobi 2012).[4] These questions regarding authenticity have become of particular significance given the emphasis on individual autonomy as an explanatory factor for political engagement (see Chapter 3).

Concern over the accuracy of information stems from the ease of use of social media, coupled with the speed of information dissemination online. The desire to produce content that reaches as many users as possible produces "a race to the bottom," as actors seek to compress and simplify campaigns to suit the granular medium (White 2010). Although a political network can be activated quickly and passionately around a specific, single issue goal using these platforms, this may come at the cost of context and depth in understanding. These fears are heightened amongst younger citizens given the ongoing debates surrounding media literacy skills (Kahne et al. 2012; Livingstone 2011; Toff and Nielsen 2018).

This unease is exacerbated by the growing prominence of a new group of influencers online and the uncertain role that they play in shaping the preferences of other users. Described as "tastemakers" (Allocca 2011), "superparticipants" (Graham and Wright 2014), and "culture-makers" (Lotan 2012), these are users who wield significant social influence, usually due to their reach over large networks. For some users, celebrities in particular, this means additional influence within unfamiliar territories. As such, mobilising key influencers has become a key feature of campaign strategy for many pressure groups.

However, these critiques are based on an analysis of each action, case, or information source in isolation. If we explore the reaction to these digitally mediated behaviours over time, it is evident that some citizens do not just passively consume content online regardless of the provider (Hargittai et al. 2012). Sharing information publicly online opens up channels of contestation, providing opportunities for users to challenge and correct misinformation. For example, research conducted following the 2011 riots in England suggests that social media enabled users to verify information and dispel rumours, such as the speculation that a lion had escaped from a zoo in London (Procter et al. 2013). Similarly, a number of studies on #BlackLivesMatter, the protest movement formed following the acquittal of George Zimmerman in the killing of teenager Trayvon Martin, have shown how hashtags can be used to amplify marginalised voices, spread messages outside of the restrictions of main stream media, and foster debate (Freelon et al. 2016; Gallagher et al. 2018). Conversation helps citizens process, understand, and question information, ultimately moderating participatory behaviour (Baek et al. 2012; Delli Carpini et al. 2004; Fletcher and Nielsen 2017a; Hardy and Scheufele 2006), although these benefits are dependent on the extent to which disinformation is embedded within a media system (Bennett and Livingston 2018).

Furthermore, the role of these new influencers should be contextualised within the broader literature on media effects (Bennett 1990; Entman 2004). As Deuze (2012: xi) notes, "media benchmark our experience of the world, and how we make sense of our role in it."

Mass media and face-to-face communication have an equally important role in shaping our political attitudes, a role that is similarly prone to abuse. The processes that citizens use to form opinions are, and have always been, based on emotion and vulnerable to manipulation. The likelihood of achieving organised, rational, consensus-driven deliberative communication is highly unlikely (Bennett and Pfetsch 2018; Chadwick 2012). As such, it is vital to remain realistic and understand that throughout history audiences have been susceptible to trends or the sway of popular opinion; this is not a phenomenon that is exclusive to social media.

Following #Kony2012, Zuckerman (2012) posed two important questions. Can any political campaign truly be of mass interest without oversimplifying? And how do we balance the need for mass engagement, as a way of legitimising representative democracy, against the dangers of oversimplification? The slacktivist critique disregards the unique attitudinal factors that lead a person to a point of engagement. A more expansive approach is required to interpret how citizens consume, process, and act upon the information that they consume online.

The slacktivist critique also proposes that the audience exert social pressure that may cause a citizen to act inauthentically, as citizens ignore their own personal opinion and go along with the crowd in order to secure approval and validation from others. This audience is both real and imagined, as users also envisage the wider audience who may view their post in a public or semi-public space and their potential reaction (Marwick and boyd 2011; Papacharissi 2012). As a result, some users may refrain from political expression through fear of damaging one's reputation. In a survey conducted by the Pew Research Center's Internet and American Life Project, 73% of social networking site users admitted encountering political content that they disagreed with, but only 23% responded with comments of their own (Rainie and Smith 2012). This pressure originates from the very design of social media, as users struggle to manage their digital identity in public and semi-public networks (Baym 2010).

The user profile, a mandatory feature of most social networking sites, is designed to encourage transparency over anonymity. Users are asked to hand over personal information, offering a virtual representation of the self to their network, in an attempt to form a direct link between online and offline identity. As such, the boundaries between what Couldry (2003) describes as the "media world" and the "ordinary world" are in a constant state of flux. This calls into question the ways in which we construct our identities and manage our relationships with others, as users have multiple personas that they must manage across and within different services, with both real and imagined audiences in mind (Baym 2010; Deuze 2012; Marwick and boyd 2011; Papacharissi 2010, 2012; van Dijck 2013). The public and private converge on social media as private behaviours are broadcast publicly. As we navigate this treacherous and fluid terrain of public, semi-public, and private spaces, our personal identity must be reflexive.

Based on the interpretation of authenticity provided in this book, I argue that a citizen can authentically cultivate multiple representations of the self; self-awareness and individual choice are deemed to be the central tenets of authentic living. In *The Presentation of Self in Everyday Life* (1990), Erving Goffman states that human beings rely on appearance and perception to guide how they judge others when they interact (Goffman et al. 1997: 21). The observer relies on the subject's representation of the self in order to make a judgement. As to avoid misrepresentation, we try to manage the impression we give to others. We choose to adapt our persona depending on our audience, our own needs, and the technological affordances a platform provides (Deuze 2012: 247). As such, the social self that we display on Facebook is normally very different, for example, to the professional image that we relay on LinkedIn (van Dijck 2013: 204). What the slacktivist critique may deem to be narcissistic or inauthentic practice may be more accurately conceptualised as a consequence of our pursuit of individual autonomy.

By presenting authenticity as a binary condition, we lack understanding of the complexity of personal motivation. As Baym (2010: 108) argues, "impression management may involve outright deception, total honesty, or, most often, a strategic balance of sharing, withholding, and distorting information." It is not my intention to disregard the threat to democracy that reputational cascades pose, but to reframe the debate outside of the reductive labels that are applied within the slacktivist critique. Instead, we must explore both the informational sources that trigger micro-activism and also the complex, personal contexts that precede it.

The Importance of Technological Specificity and Service Design

A problem that is pervasive across those accounts advocating the slacktivist critique is the reference to social media as a homogenous entity. When making claims on the impact of social media on democracy, it is imperative that we clearly stipulate to which social networking sites they apply. Definitions frequently fail to note the fundamental differences between services. This is problematic given that site-specific design can influence the type and availability of information, while also shaping discursive opportunities and the possibilities for expressive engagement (Baym 2010; boyd and Ellison 2007; van Dijck 2013). For example, some sites, like Facebook, strongly support pre-existing offline relationships, while others, such as Twitter, facilitate connections between new contacts over shared interests. Moreover, this potential must be clarified as social networking sites are, first and foremost, commercial entities; they do not seek to amplify the agency of citizens (Andrejevic 2009).

Kaplan and Haenlein (2010: 61) define social media as "a group of Internet-based applications that build on the ideological and technological foundations of Web 2.0, and that allow the creation and exchange of User Generated Content." User-generated content refers to the various forms of informational goods that are created and produced by end-users.A more precise definition is offered by boyd and Ellison (2007), who describe social networking sites as "web-based services that allow individuals to (1) construct a public or semi-public profile within a bounded system, (2) articulate a list of other users with whom they share a connection, and (3) view and traverse their list of connections and those made by others within the system." In this study, social media and social networking sites are used interchangeably; both terms refer to this definition.

Two distinctions are significant when comparing the democratic potential of different social networking sites. Firstly, one must differentiate between synchronous and asynchronous communication, as the difference in temporal context can affect user behaviour (Baym 2010: 7–8; Valenzuela et al. 2011). For instance, the immediacy of synchronous communication can make the information provided seem more personable (Ryan 2007: 238–239), posing questions on whether this affects the likelihood of digital micro-activism. Secondly, different platforms produce different information flows between users. Symmetric sharing is common on Facebook, where each user confirms a connection and then content is shared privately or semi-publically. The default sharing mechanism on Twitter is asymmetric, where a user shares content publically and anyone can subscribe to their updates. Although this description is somewhat reductive, as it does not account for the variety of information flows that exist within each of these social platforms, a consideration of specific service functionality is essential.

This call for clarity may seem contradictory given the emphasis on media convergence throughout this chapter; how do we account for this and, at the same time, recognise technological specificity? I argue that it is possible to do both. Unlike the slacktivist critique, this book will not generate conclusions about the impact of each service in isolation; this would be problematic, as Facebook and Twitter do not exist in a vacuum. By using qualitative techniques, this study will analyse the role that Facebook and Twitter play within a hybrid media system, examining the functions of each service in-depth.

Conclusion

This chapter has illustrated the problematic nature of the slacktivist critique as a reflection of the relationship between routine social media use and political engagement. An alternate research agenda was proposed based on five key revisions. Firstly, the critique evaluates the relationship between acts of so-called slacktivism and the desired political outcome in isolation. It implies that easy online actions, like sharing a tweet, form a causal relationship with the desired political effect. However, in doing so this ignores the complex array of factors that result in any political outcome. Focusing on the relationship in this way lacks an appreciation of the procedural foundations at the heart of political engagement. By thinking of participation as a process, a new set of questions emerge regarding the value of social media as a tool for deepening knowledge, for political discussion, and for public forms of symbolic self-expression.

Secondly, empirical research on social networking sites must account for the three dimensions of media convergence outlined. Digital micro-activism often makes up just a single tactic in the vast strategic repertoire of political activism. By focusing on one social networking site or one event, we ignore the relationships formed between symbolic digital micro-activism and other forms of online and offline engagement. Furthermore, by focusing on social media in isolation the slacktivist critique treats online and offline as distinct and separate realities. Rather than differentiating between new and old media, Facebook and Twitter must be understood within the expansive, hybrid media system that such tools operate within (Chadwick 2013). This must be inclusive of what Wright (2012) describes as “third spaces,” non-political discussion forums—online and offline—where political talk emerges within everyday conversations.

Thirdly, slacktivism is often deemed to be lazy activism, as activists abandon effort-intensive, on-the-ground political action in favour of easier methods online. This suggests that the depth of someone's commitment to a cause, or the quality of democratic engagement at the individual level, can be measured by time. However, it is dangerous to assume that the more time a citizen devotes to politics the more impactful their actions will be, and it is unrealistic to claim that active citizenship requires such high levels of commitment. If we consider the time pressure that individuals experience on a daily basis, then the granularity of digital engagement affords an important means of maintaining awareness, sometimes sparking further involvement at opportune moments. Therefore, it is important to examine the context in which these "quick fixes" take place.

Fourthly, digital micro-activism is often labelled as inauthentic. However, this definition of authenticity is inaccurate, as it refers to both the sincerity of political behaviour and whether the campaign is accurate and based on fact. It is necessary to distinguish between attitudinal motivations and information accuracy when analysing political behaviour online, as someone may sincerely act on an issue that is constructed on a suspect narrative. Furthermore, I argue that self-presentation online can be authentic. As users navigate the fluid terrain of public, semi-public, and private spaces online, our personal identity must remain reflexive. Personal motivations must be explored as users cross within and between these spaces.

Finally, I argue for more clarity in our definition of social media, as service design can shape how these tools impact democratic engagement.

Slacktivism is indicative of the dichotomous literature from which it originates. The critique refers to just a tiny proportion of actions that are in no way indicative of how the use of social media may benefit, or harm, a user's understanding of and engagement with politics. Scale and context are crucial to understanding political behaviour. In this book, I adopt what Chadwick (2013: 5) describes as, "hybrid thinking," "nudging us away from 'either/or' patterns of thought and toward 'not only, but also' patterns of thought." By focusing on an action, we analyse the technological functionality rather than how citizens use the tool. In order to critically evaluate these new forms of social and political self-expression, we must analyse them within the media environment in which they take place. This must be inclusive of both the multifaceted engagement strategies that political actors employ when using social media and the expansive media system that such tools operate in. It is within these interactions that we will discover more substantive findings about the relationship between the routine use of social media and political engagement. The next chapter will explain the theoretical basis for this process-based approach before outlining a deductive framework, which offers an alternative prognosis to the slacktivist critique.

Notes

1. See, for example, the commentary pieces published in reaction to the hashtags #NeverAgain and #EnoughIsEnough (Gallucci 2018; Willingham 2018), used by Never Again MSD, an American student-led gun control organisation formed following the mass shooting at Marjory Stoneman Douglas High School in February 2018.
2. Slacktivism [Def. 1]. (2018). In *Oxford English Dictionary*, Retrieved April 23, 2018, from http://www.oed.com/view/Entry/51394141.
3. "The fact or quality of being true or in accordance with fact; veracity; correctness. Also accurate reflection of real life, verisimilitude." Authenticity [Def. 1]. (2018). In *Oxford English Dictionary*, Retrieved April 23, 2018, from http://www.oed.com/view/Entry/13325.
4. This definition intentionally avoids the debates surrounding what it means to live authentically, as it is necessary to operationalise a somewhat limited definition in order to empirically analyse individual-level motivations.

References

Allocca, K. (2011, February 1). Why Videos Go Viral. *TED*. Retrieved May 1, 2012, from http://www.ted.com/talks/kevin_allocca_why_videos_go_viral.html.

Almond, G., & Verba, S. (1963). *The Civic Culture: Political Attitudes and Democracy in Five Nations*. Princeton, NJ: Princeton University Press.

Amnå, E., & Ekman, J. (2014). Standby Citizens: Diverse Faces of Political Passivity. *European Political Science Review*, *6*(2), 261–281.

Amry, H. [LibyaLiberty]. (2012, September 17). I'm Having Such a Good Hair Day. No One Even Knows. #Muslimrage. *Tweet*. Retrieved April 24, 2018, from https://twitter.com/LibyaLiberty/status/247737358320037888.

Andrejevic, M. (2009). Critical Media Studies 2.0: An Interactive Upgrade. *Interactions: Studies in Communication & Culture*, *1*(1), 35–51.

Anstead, N., & Chadwick, A. (2018). A Primary Definer Online: The Construction and Propagation of a Think Tank's Authority on Social Media. *Media, Culture and Society*, *40*(2), 246–266.

Anstead, N., & O'Loughlin, B. (2011). The Emerging Viewertariat and BBC Question Time: Television Debate and Real-Time Commenting Online. *International Journal of Press/Politics, 16*(4), 440–462.

Anstead, N., & O'Loughlin, B. (2015). Social Media Analysis and Public Opinion: The 2010 UK General Election. *Journal of Computer-Mediated Communication, 20*(2), 204–220.

Arnstein, S. R. (1969). A Ladder of Citizen Participation. *Journal of the American Institute of Planners, 35*(4), 216–224.

Aslan, B., Dennis, J., & O'Loughlin, B. (2015). Balding Goes Trolling? Amplification, Engagement and Controversy at the 2012 Olympics. *Participations: Journal of Audience & Reception Studies, 12*(1), 577–607.

Baek, Y. M., Wojcieszak, M., & Delli Carpini, M. X. (2012). Online Versus Face-to-Face Deliberation: Who? Why? What? With What Effects? *New Media & Society, 14*(3), 363–383.

Bakardjieva, M. (2009). Subactivism: Lifeworld and Politics in the Age of the Internet. *The Information Society: An International Journal, 25*(2), 91–104.

Bakshy, E., Messing, S., & Adamic, L. (2015). Exposure to Ideologically Diverse News and Opinion on Facebook. *Science, 348*, 1130–1132.

Barberá, P., Jost, J. T., Nagler, J., Tucker, J. A., & Bonneau, R. (2015). Tweeting from Left to Right: Is Online Political Communication More Than an Echo Chamber? *Psychological Science: A Journal of the Association for Psychological Science, 26*(10), 1531–1542.

Bastien, F. (2009). Beyond Sex and Saxophones: Interviewing Practices and Political Substance on Televised Talk Shows. *The Canadian Political Science Review, 3*(2), 70–88.

Bauerlin, M. (2009). *The Dumbest Generation: How the Digital Age Stupefies Young Americans and Jeopardizes Our Future or Don't Trust Anyone Under 30*. New York: Tarcher.

Baym, G. (2005). The Daily Show: Discursive Integration and the Reinvention of Political Journalism. *Political Communication, 22*(3), 259–276.

Baym, N. K. (2010). *Personal Connections in the Digital Age*. Cambridge: Polity.

Bennett, W. L. (1990). Toward a Theory of Press-State Relations in the United States. *Journal of Communication, 40*(2), 103–125.

Bennett, W. L. (2012). The Personalization of Politics: Political Identity, Social Media, and Changing Patterns of Participation. *The ANNALS of the American Academy of Political and Social Science, 644*(20), 20–39.

Bennett, W. L., & Livingston, S. (2018). The Disinformation Order: Disruptive Communication and the Decline of Democratic Institutions. *European Journal of Communication, 33*(2), 122–139.

Bennett, W. L., & Pfetsch, B. (2018). Rethinking Political Communication in a Time of Disrupted Public Spheres. *Journal of Communication, 68*(2), 243–253.

Bennett, W. L., & Segerberg, A. (2013). *The Logic of Connective Action: Digital Media and the Personalization of Contentious Politics.* Cambridge: Cambridge University Press.

Bimber, B., Flanagin, A. J., & Stohl, C. (2012). *Collective Action in Organizations: Interaction and Engagement in an Era of Technological Change.* Cambridge: Cambridge University Press.

Bochel, C. (2013). Petitions Systems: Contributing to Representative Democracy? *Parliamentary Affairs, 66*(4), 798–815.

Bode, L. (2017). Gateway Political Behaviors: The Frequency and Consequences of Low-Cost Political Engagement on Social Media. *Social Media + Society, 3*(4). Retrieved from https://doi.org/10.1177/2056305117743349.

Bode, L., Vraga, E. K., Borah, P., & Shah, D. V. (2014). A New Space for Political Behavior: Political Social Networking and Its Democratic Consequences. *Journal of Computer-Mediated Communication, 19*(3), 414–429.

Boulianne, S. (2009). Does Internet Use Affect Engagement? A Meta-Analysis of Research. *Political Communication, 26*(2), 193–211.

Boulianne, S. (2015). Social Media Use and Participation: A Meta-Analysis of Current Research. *Information, Communication & Society, 18*(5), 524–538.

boyd, d., & Ellison, N. B. (2007). Social Network Sites: Definition, History, and Scholarship. *Journal of Computer-Mediated Communication, 13*(1), Article 11.

Brundidge, J., & Rice, R. E. (2009). Political Engagement Online: Do the Information Rich Get Richer and the Like-Minded Get More Similar? In A. Chadwick & P. N. Howard (Eds.), *Routledge Handbook of Internet Politics* (pp. 144–157). Abingdon: Routledge.

Bucy, E. P., & Gregson, K. S. (2001). Media Participation: A Legitimizing Mechanism of Mass Democracy. *New Media & Society, 3*(3), 357–380.

Campbell, A., Gurin, G., & Miller, W. E. (1954). *The Voter Decides.* Evanston, IL: Row, Peterson and Co.

Carpentier, N. (2011). *Media and Participation: A Site of Ideological-Democratic Struggle.* Bristol: Intellect.

Carswell, D. (2012). *The End of Politics and the Birth of iDemocracy.* Hull: Biteback Publishing.

Castells, M. (2009). *Communication Power.* Oxford: Oxford University Press.

Chadwick, A. (2006). *Internet Politics: States, Citizens and New Communication Technologies.* Oxford: Oxford University Press.

Chadwick, A. (2007). Digital Network Repertoires and Organizational Hybridity. *Political Communication, 24*(3), 283–301.

Chadwick, A. (2011). The Political Information Cycle in a Hybrid News System: The British Prime Minister and the Bullygate Affair. *The International Journal of Press/Politics, 16*(1), 3–29.

Chadwick, A. (2012). Recent Shifts in the Relationship Between the Internet and Democratic Engagement in Britain and the United States: Granularity, Informational Exuberance, and Political Learning. In E. Anduiza, M. Jensen, & L. Jorba (Eds.), *Digital Media and Political Engagement Worldwide: A Comparative Study* (pp. 39–55). Cambridge: Cambridge University Press.

Chadwick, A. (2013). *The Hybrid Media System: Politics and Power*. Oxford: Oxford University Press.

Chadwick, A., & Dennis, J. (2017). Social Media, Professional Media and Mobilisation in Contemporary Britain: Explaining the Strengths and Weaknesses of the Citizens' Movement 38 Degrees. *Political Studies, 65*(1), 42–60.

Chadwick, A., Dennis, J., & Smith, A. P. (2016). Politics in the Age of Hybrid Media: Power, Systems, and Media Logics. In A. Bruns, E. Skogerbø, C. Christensen, A. O. Larsson, & G. Enli (Eds.), *Routledge Companion to Social Media and Politics* (pp. 7–22). London: Routledge.

Chadwick, A., O'Loughlin, B., & Vaccari, C. (2017). Why People Dual Screen Political Debates and Why It Matters for Democratic Engagement. *Journal of Broadcasting & Electronic Media, 61*(2), 220–239.

Christensen, H. S. (2011). Political Activities on the Internet: Slacktivism or Political Participation by Other Means? *First Monday, 16*(2). Retrieved September 23, 2011, from http://firstmonday.org/htbin/cgiwrap/bin/ojs/index.php/fm/article/viewArticle/3336/2767.

Christensen, H. S. (2012). Simply Slacktivism? Internet Participation in Finland. *eJournal of eDemocracy & Open Government, 4*(1), 1–23.

Coleman, S. (2007). How Democracies Have Disengaged from Young People. In B. D. Loader (Ed.), *Young Citizens in the Digital Age: Political Engagement, Young People and New Media* (pp. 166–185). Abingdon: Routledge.

Coleman, S., & Blumler, J. G. (2009). *The Internet and Democratic Citizenship: Theory, Practice and Policy*. Cambridge: Cambridge University Press.

Couldry, N. (2003). *Media Rituals: A Critical Approach*. Abingdon: Routledge.

Couldry, N. (2012). *Media, Society, World: Social Theory and Digital Media Practice*. Cambridge: Polity.

Couldry, N., Livingstone, S., & Markham, T. (2010). *Media Consumption and Public Engagement: Beyond the Presumption of Attention*. Basingstoke: Palgrave Macmillan.

Dahlgren, P. (2005). The Internet, Public Spheres, and Political Communication: Dispersion and Deliberation. *Political Communication, 22*, 147–162.

Dahlgren, P. (2009). *Media and Political Engagement: Citizens, Communication and Democracy*. Cambridge: Cambridge University Press.

Dalton, R. J. (2008). *Citizens Politics: Public Opinion and Political Parties in Advanced Industrial Democracies* (5th ed.). Washington, DC: CQ Press.

Davison, P. (2012). The Language of Internet Memes. In M. Mandiberg (Ed.), *The Social Media Reader* (pp. 120–134). London: New York University Press.
Delli Carpini, M. X., & Williams, B. A. (2000). Let Us Infotain You: Politics in the New Media Environment. In W. L. Bennett & R. Entman (Eds.), *Mediated Politics: Communication in the Future of Democracy* (pp. 160–181). Cambridge: Cambridge University Press.
Delli Carpini, M. X., Cook, F. L., & Jacobs, L. R. (2004). Public Deliberation, Discursive Participation and Citizenship Engagement: A Review of the Empirical Literature. *Annual Review of Political Science, 7*(1), 315–344.
Deuze, M. (2012). *Media Life.* Cambridge: Polity.
Drumbl, M. A. (2012). Child Soldiers and Clicktivism: Justice, Myths, and Prevention. *Journal of Human Rights Practice, 4*(3), 481–485.
Eliasoph, N. (1998). *Avoiding Politics: How Americans Produce Apathy in Everyday Life.* Cambridge: Cambridge University Press.
Ellison, N. B., Steinfield, C., & Lampe, C. (2007). The Benefits of Facebook "Friends:" Social Capital and College Students' Use of Online Social Network Sites. *Journal of Computer-Mediated Communication, 12*(4), 1143–1168.
Engelhardt, J. v., & Jansz, J. (2014). Challenging Humanitarian Communication: An Empirical Exploration of Kony 2012. *The International Communication Gazette, 76*(6), 464–484.
Entman, R. (2004). *Projections of Power: Framing News, Public Opinion, and U.S. Foreign Policy.* Chicago, IL: Chicago University Press.
Eveland, W. P., & Hively, M. H. (2009). Political Discussion Frequency, Network Size, and "Heterogenity" of Discussion as Predictors of Political Knowledge and Participation. *Journal of Communication, 59*(2), 205–224.
Fletcher, R., & Nielsen, R. K. (2017a). Are News Audiences Increasingly Fragmented? A Cross-National Comparative Analysis of Cross-Platform News Audience Fragmentation and Duplication. *Journal of Communication, 67*(4), 476–498.
Fletcher, R., & Nielsen, R. K. (2017b). Are People Incidentally Exposed to News on Social Media? A Comparative Analysis. *New Media & Society.* Retrieved from https://doi.org/10.1177/1461444817724170.
Fox, S. (2014). Is It Time to Update the Definition of Political Participation? Political Participation in Britain: The Decline and Revival of Civic Culture. *Parliamentary Affairs, 67*(2), 495–505.
Freelon, D., McIlwain, C., & Clark, M. (2016). Beyond the Hashtags: #Ferguson, #BlackLivesMatter, and the Online Struggle for Offline Justice. *Center for Media and Social Impact, American University.* Retrieved April 24, 2018, from https://papers.ssrn.com/sol3/papers.cfm?abstract_id=2747066.
Fung, A. (2006). Varieties of Participation in Complex Governance. *Public Administration Review, 66,* 66–75.

Gallagher, R. J., Reagan, A. J., Danforth, C. M., & Dodds, P. S. (2018). Divergent Discourse Between Protests and Counter-Protests: #BlackLivesMatter and #AllLivesMatter. *PLoS One, 13*(4). Retrieved from https://doi.org/10.1371/journal.pone.0195644.

Gallucci, N. (2018, March 27). America's Youth Could Put Slacktivism Behind Us Once and for All. *Mashable*. Retrieved April 24, 2018, from https://mashable.com/2018/03/27/trump-era-end-of-slacktivism.

Garcia, A. (2013, March 26). The Best Going Red for Equality Equal Signs from Social Media Today. *The Gaily Grind*. Retrieved August 5, 2013, from http://www.thegailygrind.com/2013/03/26/the-best-going-red-for-equality-equal-signs-from-social-media-today.

Giddens, A. (1991). *Modernity and Self-Identity: Self and Society in the Late Modern Age*. Cambridge: Polity.

Gil de Zúñiga, H., Molyneux, L., & Zheng, P. (2014). Social Media, Political Expression, and Political Participation: Panel Analysis of Lagged and Concurrent Relationships. *Journal of Communication, 64*(4), 612–634.

Gladwell, M. (2010, October 4). Small Change: Why the Revolution Will Not Be Tweeted. *The New Yorker*. Retrieved November 3, 2010, from https://www.newyorker.com/magazine/2010/10/04/small-change-malcolm-gladwell.

Goffman, E. (1990). *The Presentation of Self in Everyday Life*. London: Penguin.

Goffman, E., Lemert, C. C., & Branaman, A. (1997). *The Goffman Reader*. Cambridge, MA: Blackwell.

Goodin, R. E., Rice, J. M., Parpo, A., & Eriksson, L. (2008). *Discretionary Time: A New Measure of Freedom*. Cambridge: Cambridge University Press.

Graber, D. A. (2004). Mediated Politics and Citizenship in the Twenty-First Century. *Annual Review of Psychology, 55*, 545–571.

Graham, T., & Wright, S. (2014). Discursive Equality and Everyday Talk Online: The Impact of "Superparticipants." *Journal of Computer-Mediated Communication, 19*(3), 625–642.

Graham, T., Jackson, D., & Wright, S. (2015). From Everyday Conversation to Political Action: Talking Austerity in Online 'Third Spaces'. *European Journal of Communication, 30*(6), 648–665.

Granovetter, M. S. (1973). The Strength of Weak Ties. *American Journal of Sociology, 78*(6), 1360–1380.

Gregory, S. (2012). Kony 2012 Through a Prism of Video Advocacy Practices and Trends. *Journal of Human Rights Practice, 4*(3), 463–468.

Hall, N. (2017). Innovations in Activism in the Digital Era. In Hertie School of Governance (Ed.), *The Governance Report 2017* (pp. 143–156). Oxford: Oxford University Press.

Halupka, M. (2014). Clicktivism: A Systematic Heuristic. *Policy and Internet, 6*(2), 115–132.

Halupka, M. (2018). The Legitimisation of Clicktivism. *Australian Journal of Political Science, 53*(1), 130–141.

Hardy, B., & Scheufele, D. A. (2006). Examining Differential Gains from Internet Use: Comparing the Moderating Role of Talk and Online Interactions. *Journal of Communication, 55*(1), 71–84.

Hargittai, E., Neuman, W. R., & Curry, O. (2012). Taming the Information Tide: Perceptions of Information Overload in the American Home. *The Information Society: An International Journal, 28*(3), 161–173.

Hay, C. (2002). *Political Analysis: A Critical Introduction.* Basingstoke: Palgrave Macmillan.

Hensby, A., Sibthorpe, J., & Driver, S. (2011). Resisting the 'Protest Business': Bureaucracy, Postbureaucracy and Active Membership in Social Movement Organizations. *Organization, 19*(6), 809–823.

Hooghe, M., & Dejaeghere, Y. (2007). Does the 'Monitorial Citizen' Exist? An Empirical Investigation into the Occurrence of Postmodern Forms of Citizenship in the Nordic Countries. *Scandinavian Political Studies, 30*(2), 249–271.

Hotz, A. (2012, September 17). Newsweek 'Muslim Rage' Cover Invokes a Rage of Its Own. *The Guardian.* Retrieved August 12, 2013, from http://www.theguardian.com/media/us-news-blog/2012/sep/17/muslim-rage-newsweek-magazine-twitter.

Inglehart, R. (1990). *Culture Shift in Advanced Industrial Society.* Princeton, NJ: Princeton University Press.

Jarvis, J. (2009). *What Would Google Do?* New York: Collins Business.

Jarvis, J. (2011). *Public Parts: How Sharing in the Digital Age Improves the Way We Work and Live.* London: Simon & Schuster.

Jasper, J. M. (1997). *The Art of Moral Protest: Culture, Biography, and Creativity in Social Movements.* London: University of Chicago Press.

Jenkins, H. (2006). *Convergence Culture: Where Old and New Media Collide.* New York: New York University.

Jenkins, H., & Carpentier, N. (2013). Theorizing Participatory Intensities: A Conversation About Participation and Politics. *Convergence: The International Journal of Research into New Media, 19*(3), 265–286.

Jones, J. P. (2005). *Entertaining Politics: New Political Television and Civic Culture.* Oxford: Rowman & Littlefield.

Jordan, G., & Maloney, W. (2007). *Democracy and Interest Groups: Enhancing Participation?* Basingstoke: Palgrave.

Jurgenson, N. (2011, September 13). *Digital Dualism and the Fallacy of Web Objectivity.* Retrieved February 25, 2013, from http://thesocietypages.org/cyborgology/2011/09/13/digital-dualism-and-the-fallacy-of-web-objectivity.

Jurgenson, N. (2012, October 24). Speaking in Memes. *The New Inquiry*. Retrieved August 13, 2013, from http://thenewinquiry.com/essays/speaking-in-memes.

Kahne, J., Middaugh, E., Lee, N. J., & Feezell, J. (2012). Youth Online Activity and Exposure to Diverse Perspectives. *New Media & Society, 14*(3), 492–512.

Kaplan, A. M., & Haenlein, M. (2010). Users of the World, Unite! The Challenges and Opportunities of Social Media. *Business Horizons, 53*(1), 59–68.

Karpf, D. (2010). Online Political Mobilization from the Advocacy Group's Perspective: Looking Beyond Clicktivism. *Policy and Internet, 2*(4), 7–41.

Karpf, D. (2012). *The MoveOn Effect: The Unexpected Transformation of American Political Advocacy*. Oxford: Oxford University Press.

Karpf, D. (2016). *Analytic Activism: Digital Listening and the New Political Strategy*. Oxford: Oxford University Press.

Keen, A. (2008). *The Cult of the Amateur: How Blogs, Myspace, YouTube, and the Rest of Today's User-Generated Media Are Destroying Our Economy, Our Culture, and Our Values*. New York: Random House.

Kettell, S. (2006). *Dirty Politics? New Labour, British Democracy and the Invasion of Iraq*. London: Zed Books.

Khazan, O. (2013, April 30). UNICEF Tells Slacktivists: Give Money, Not Facebook Likes. *The Atlantic*. Retrieved August 2, 2013, from http://www.theatlantic.com/international/archive/2013/04/unicef-tells-slacktivists-give-money-not-facebook-likes/275429.

Kirkpatrick, D. D. (2012, September 17). Newsweek's 'Muslim Rage' Cover Mocked Online. *The New York Times*. Retrieved August 12, 2013, from http://thelede.blogs.nytimes.com/2012/09/17/newsweeks-muslim-rage-cover-mocked-online/.

Knibbs, K. (2013, March 26). The Birth of Marriage Equality Meme. *Digital Trends*. Retrieved August 5, 2013, from http://www.digitaltrends.com/social-media/red-equal-signs-take-over-facebook-the-birth-of-a-marriage-equality-meme.

Kreiss, D. (2012). *Taking Our Country Back: The Crafting of Networked Politics from Howard Dean to Barack Obama*. Oxford: Oxford University Press.

Kristofferson, K., White, K., & Peloza, J. (2014). The Nature of Slacktivism: How the Social Observability of an Initial Act of Token Support Affects Subsequent Prosocial Action. *Journal of Consumer Research, 40*(6), 1149–1166.

Kümpel, A. S., Karnowski, V., & Keyling, T. (2015). News Sharing in Social Media: A Review of Current Research on News Sharing Users, Content, and Networks. *Social Media + Society, 1*(2). Retrieved from https://doi.org/10.1177/2056305115610141.

Lessig, L. (2008). *Remix: Making Art and Commerce Thrive in the Hybrid Economy*. New York: Penguin Press.

Liddle, R. (2013, March 10). Placards? They're So Last Year. Make Way for the Mighty Mouse. *The Sunday Times*. Retrieved March 10, 2013, from http://www.thesundaytimes.co.uk/sto/Magazine/Features/article1225047.ece?shareToken=1eb4425e171e4a1ecda5d2c956c0540d.

Livingstone, S. (2011). Digital Learning and Participation Among Youth: Critical Reflections on Future Research Priorities. *International Journal of Learning and Media, 2*(2–3), 1–13.

Lotan, G. (2012, March 14). [Data Viz] Kony2012: See How Invisible Networks Helped a Campaign Capture the World's Attention. *SocialFlow*. Retrieved December 31, 2012, from http://blog.socialflow.com/post/7120244932/data-viz-kony2012-see-how-invisible-networks-helped-a-campaign-capture-the-worlds-attention.

Lukes, S. (2005). *Power: A Radical View*. Basingstoke: Palgrave Macmillan.

Madianou, M. (2013). Humanitarian Campaigns in Social Media: Network Architectures and Polymedia Events. *Journalism Studies, 14*(2), 249–266.

Margetts, H., John, P., Hale, S., & Yasseri, T. (2015). *Political Turbulence: How Social Media Shape Collective Action*. Princeton, NJ: Princeton University Press.

Marwick, A. E., & boyd, d. (2011). I Tweet Honestly, I Tweet Passionately: Twitter Users, Context Collapse, and the Imagined Audience. *New Media & Society, 13*(1), 114–133.

McLeod, J. M., Scheufele, D. A., & Moy, P. (1999). Community, Communication, and Participation: The Role of Mass Media and Interpersonal Discussion in Local Political Participation. *Political Communication, 16*(3), 315–336.

Meraz, S., & Papacharissi, Z. (2013). Networked Gatekeeping and Networked Framing on #Egypt. *The International Journal of Press/Politics, 18*(2), 138–166.

Mirkinson, J. (2012, September 17). Newsweek's 'Muslim Rage' Cover Draws Angry Protest. *The Huffington Post*. Retrieved August 12, 2013, from http://www.huffingtonpost.com/2012/09/17/newsweek-muslim-rage-cover_n_1890124.html.

Morozov, E. (2009, May 19). The Brave New World of Slacktivism. *Foreign Policy*. Retrieved April 18, 2011, from http://neteffect.foreignpolicy.com/posts/2009/05/19/the_brave_new_world_of_slacktivism.

Morozov, E. (2011). *The Net Delusion: How Not to Liberate the World*. London: Penguin.

Morozov, E. (2013). *To Save Everything, Click Here: The Folly of Technological Determinism*. London: Allen Lane.

Mossberger, K., Tolbert, C. J., & Stansbury, M. (2003). *Virtual Inequality: Beyond the Digital Divide*. Washington, DC: Georgetown University Press.

Nasr, R. (2012, September 18). Newsweek Muslim Rage Cover: Someone at Newsweek Needs to Get Fired for This. *PolicyMic*. Retrieved August 12,

2013, from http://www.policymic.com/articles/14908/newsweek-muslim-rage-cover-someone-at-newsweek-needs-to-get-fired-for-this.

Negroponte, N. (1995). *Being Digital.* London: Hodder and Stoughton.

Norris, P. (2011). *Democratic Deficit: Critical Citizens Revisited.* Cambridge: Cambridge University Press.

O'Loughlin, B. (2011). Information Overload, Paradigm Underload? The Internet and Political Disruption. *Global Policy, 2*(3), 349–351.

O'Loughlin, B., Vaccari, C., Dennis, J., & Aslan Ozgul, B. (2017). Twitter and Global Political Crises: Cycles of Insecurity in #PrayforParis and #PrayforSyria. *Middle East Journal of Culture and Communication, 10*(2–3), 175–203.

Obar, J. A., Zube, P., & Lampe, C. (2012). Advocacy 2.0: An Analysis of How Advocacy Groups in the United States Perceive and Use Social Media as Tools for Facilitating Civic Engagement and Collective Action. *Journal for Information Policy, 2,* 1–25.

Olson, M. (1971). *The Logic of Collective Action: Public Goods and the Theory of Groups.* Cambridge, MA: Harvard University Press.

Papacharissi, Z. (2010). *A Private Sphere: Democracy in a Digital Age.* Cambridge: Polity.

Papacharissi, Z. (2012). Without You, I'm Nothing: Performances of the Self on Twitter. *International Journal of Communication, 6,* 1989–2006.

Papacharissi, Z. (2014). *Affective Publics: Sentiment, Technology, and Politics.* Oxford: Oxford University Press.

Pattie, C., Seyd, P., & Whiteley, P. (2004). *Citizenship in Britain: Values, Participation and Democracy.* Cambridge: Cambridge University Press.

Procter, R., Vis, F., & Voss, A. (2013). Reading the Riots on Twitter: Methodological Innovation for the Analysis of Big Data. *International Journal of Social Research Methodology, 16*(3), 197–214.

Putnam, R. D. (2000). *Bowling Alone: The Collapse and Revival of American Community.* London: Simon & Schuster.

Rainie, L., & Smith, A. (2012). *Social Networking Sites and Politics.* Washington, DC: Pew Research Centre.

Rainie, L., & Wellman, B. (2012). *Networked: The New Social Operating System.* Cambridge: MIT Press.

Rickett, O. (2013, November 22). Want to Change the World? It Won't Happen via Your Mouse Button. *The Guardian.* Retrieved March 20, 2014, from http://www.theguardian.com/commentisfree/2013/nov/22/change-the-world-charity-facebook-e-petition.

Rotman, D., Vieweg, S., Chi, E. H., Preece, J., Shneiderman, B., Pirolli, P., et al. (2011). *From Slacktivism to Activism: Participatory Culture in the Age of Social Media.* Paper presented at the Conference of Human Factors in Computing Systems, Vancouver, Canada.

Ryan, D. (2007). Getting the Word Out: Notes on the Social Organization of Notification. *Sociological Theory, 24*(3), 228–254.

Scheufele, D. A. (2001). Democracy for Some? How Political Talk Both Informs and Polarizes the Electorate. In R. P. Hart & D. Shaw (Eds.), *Communication and U.S. Elections: New Agendas* (pp. 19–32). Lanham, MD: Rowman & Littlefield.

Schudson, M. (1999). *The Good Citizen: A History of American Public Life.* Cambridge, MA: Harvard University Press.

Shifman, L. (2013). *Memes in Digital Culture.* Cambridge: MIT Press.

Shirky, C. (2008). *Here Comes Everybody: The Power of Organizing Without Organizations.* London: Allen Lane.

Shirky, C. (2010). *Cognitive Surplus: Creativity and Generosity in a Connected Age.* London: Allen Lane.

Shirky, C. (2011, January/February). The Political Power of Social Media: Technology, the Public Sphere and Political Change. *Foreign Affairs.* Retrieved March 15, 2011, from http://www.foreignaffairs.com/articles/67038/clay-shirky/the-political-power-of-social-media.

Shulman, S. (2009). The Case Against Mass E-Mails: Perverse Incentives and Low Quality Public Participation in U.S. Federal Rulemaking. *Policy and Internet, 1*(1), 23–53.

Skoric, M. M., & Kwan, G. (2011). Do Facebook and Video Games Promote Political Participation Among Youth? *Journal of eDemocracy, 3*(1), 70–79.

Stoker, G. (2006). *Why Politics Matter: Making Democracy Work.* Basingstoke: Palgrave Macmillan.

Sunstein, C. R. (2007). *Republic.Com 2.0.* Princeton, NJ: Princeton University Press.

Svensson, J. (2011). Theorizing Citizenships in Late Modern ICT Societies. *Triple C: Cognition, Communication, Co-operation, 9*(2), 644–656.

The Simpsons Against the Conservatives. (2017, June 11). 'Perhaps This Pamphlet Will Prove Helpful'. *Facebook Update.* Retrieved April 25, 2018, from https://www.facebook.com/TheSimpsonsAgainstTheConservatives/photos/a.1405074764868l9.1073741827.1399085398800046/168792716991628.

Theocharis, Y. (2012). Cuts, Tweets, Solidarity and Mobilisation: How the Internet Shaped the Student Occupations. *Parliamentary Affairs, 65*(1), 162–194.

Theocharis, Y., & van Deth, J. W. (2018). The Continuous Expansion of Citizen Participation: A New Taxonomy. *European Political Science Review, 10*(1), 139–163.

Toff, B., & Nielsen, R. K. (2018). "I Just Google It": Folk Theories of Distributed Discovery. *Journal of Communication.* Retrieved from https://doi.org/10.1093/joc/jqy009.

Tufekci, Z. (2012). We Were Always Human. In N. L. Whitehead & M. Wesch (Eds.), *Human No More: Digital Subjectivities, Unhuman Subjects, and the End of Anthropology* (pp. 33–47). Boulder: University of Colorado.

Vaccari, C. (2013). *Digital Politics in Western Democracies: A Comparative Study*. Baltimore, MD: Johns Hopkins University Press.

Vaccari, C., Chadwick, A., & O'Loughlin, B. (2015a). Dual Screening the Political: Media Events, Social Media, and Citizen Engagement. *Journal of Communication, 65*(6), 1041–1061.

Vaccari, C., Valeriani, A., Barberá, P., Bonneau, R., Jost, J. T., Nagler, J., et al. (2015b). Political Expression and Action on Social Media: Exploring the Relationship Between Lower- and Higher-Threshold Political Activities Among Twitter Users in Italy. *Journal of Computer-Mediated Communication, 20*(2), 221–239.

Valenzuela, S., Kim, Y., & Gil de Zúñiga, H. (2011). Social Networks That Matter: Exploring the Role of Political Discussion for Online Political Participation. *International Journal of Public Opinion Research, 24*(2), 163–184.

Valeriani, A., & Vaccari, C. (2016). Accidental Exposure to Politics on Social Media as Online Participation Equalizer in Germany, Italy, and the United Kingdom. *New Media & Society, 18*(9), 1857–1874.

van Dijck, J. (2013). 'You Have One Identity': Performing the Self on Facebook and LinkedIn. *Media, Culture and Society, 35*(2), 199–215.

Vegh, S. (2003). Classifying Forms of Online Activism: The Case of Cyberprotests Against the World Bank. In M. D. Ayers & M. McCaughey (Eds.), *Cyberactivism: Online Activism in Theory and Practice* (pp. 71–96). Abingdon: Routledge.

Vromen, A. (2017). *Digital Citizenship and Political Engagement: The Challenge from Online Campaigning and Advocacy Organisations*. Basingstoke: Palgrave Macmillan.

Wahl-Jorgensen, K. (2018). The Emotional Architecture of Social Media. In Z. Papacharissi (Ed.), *A Networked Self and Platforms, Stories, Connections*. Oxon: Routledge.

White, M. (2010, August 12). Clicktivism Is Ruining Leftist Activism. *The Guardian*. Retrieved January 31, 2012, from http://www.guardian.co.uk/commentisfree/2010/aug/12/clicktivism-ruining-leftist-activism.

White, M. (2011). *Activism vs. Slacktivism*. Paper presented at the FairSay eCampaigning Forum 2011, University of Oxford. Retrieved from https://www.youtube.com/watch?v=sHN4JNW9Yx8.

Willingham, A. J. (2018, March 26). Slacktivism Is Over. The #NeverAgain Movement Is About What's Next. *CNN*. Retrieved April 24, 2018, from https://edition.cnn.com/2018/03/25/us/march-for-our-lives-slacktivism-trnd.

Wright, S. (2012). Politics as Usual? Revolution, Normalization and a New Agenda for Online Deliberation. *New Media & Society, 14*(2), 244–261.

Yacobi, B. G. (2012). The Limits of Authenticity. *Philosophy Now, 92*(September/October), 28–30.

Yang, H., & DeHart, J. L. (2016). Social Media Use and Online Political Participation Among College Students During the US Election 2012. *Social Media + Society, 2*(1). Retrieved from https://doi.org/10.1177/2056305115623802.

Zuckerman, E. (2008, March 8). *The Cute Cat Theory Talk at Etech.* Retrieved August 23, 2013, from http://www.ethanzuckerman.com/blog/2008/03/08/the-cute-cat-theory-talk-at-etech.

Zuckerman, E. (2012, August 3). *Unpacking Kony 2012.* Retrieved March 11, 2012, from http://www.ethanzuckerman.com/blog/2012/03/08/unpacking-kony-2012.

CHAPTER 3

Operationalising the Continuum of Participation

The continuum of participation is designed to empirically observe the personalised political attitudes and behaviours that characterise contemporary citizenship. This chapter outlines the foundations of this approach, the methodological challenges that come with analysing political engagement across media, and maps a number of complementary theories to the different stages across the continuum. Firstly, I review the debates within political science and communication studies surrounding the definition of citizenship and political participation. Much of the literature focuses on a static conceptualisation of citizenship, which prioritises state-centric forms of participation and overlooks the structural transformations evident in everyday political behaviour. As Sloam (2012: 4) argues, "if we are to understand political participation at all, we must explore how each new generation comes to develop its own conceptions of citizenship and expresses itself through civic and political engagement." By referring to scholars that argue that our definitions of citizenship should evolve with the attitudes, behaviours, and practices of citizens in day-to-day life (Bennett 2008; Dalton 2008; Graber 2004; Papacharissi 2010), I describe how political identity has become increasingly personalised, leading to a diffusion of what constitutes political engagement. Secondly, I outline how these alternate forms of engagement can be captured empirically by providing an overview of the indicators used in the fieldwork. While these provide some transparency on the behaviours that will be examined across the continuum of participation,

J. Dennis, *Beyond Slacktivism*,
Interest Groups, Advocacy and Democracy Series,
https://doi.org/10.1007/978-3-030-00844-4_3

I describe why the qualitative traditions that inform the research design are vital in illustrating the complex processes that connect personalised political attitudes, participatory behaviours, and media practices. Finally, through an amalgamation of theoretical contributions from Bennett (2008), Chadwick (2012), and Papacharissi (2010), I offer a deductive framework that challenges the hypotheses derived from the slacktivist critique.

The Rationale for the Continuum: Defining Citizenship and Participation

Citizenship is a concept with many competing definitions. Pattie et al. (2004: 22) define citizenship as, "[a] set of norms, values and practices designed to solve collective action problems which involve the recognition by individuals that they have rights and obligations to each other if they wish to solve such problems." As such, citizenship is enacted in relation to the authority of a political community. Traditional accounts of citizenship generally refer to a legalistic and rights-based definition; the community is defined as the nation state, in which citizens are represented by political parties, trade unions, and religious cleavages (Bellamy 2008). However, the political community is no longer restricted to just the nation state but includes a diverse range of associations at the local, national, and global level (Cammaerts and Van Audenhove 2005; Svensson 2011). A void exists between these bounded notions of citizenship, which often underpin popular discussion around slacktivism, and the reality of life in advanced industrialised democracies. Increasingly, citizens have more control over their political identity, more choice over the political communities they join, and are more creative in the political acts that they undertake. To justify the empirical relevance of the continuum of participation model, this section offers an overview of the debates surrounding the definition and measurement of citizenship and democratic engagement.

To analyse citizenship, it must be deconstructed into two constituent parts; the attitudinal, an individual's sense of norms, rights, and values, and the behavioural, how an individual participates within their respective political community (Pattie et al. 2004: 129). The attitudinal and behavioural form a reciprocal relationship, as a citizen's political identity shapes how they engage, while the norms of a political community are formed and established by the participation of its members

(Svensson 2011: 644). Therefore, political attitudes and behaviours are in a constant state of evolution, and the way in which citizenship is defined should reflect the normative desires of the citizenry at the time of inquiry.

Numerous scholars have described this evolution, pointing to new sources of identity and the growth of unconventional forms of political engagement (Bennett 2008, 2012; Cammaerts and Van Audenhove 2005; Dalton 2008; Pattie et al. 2004; Zukin et al. 2006). A distinct transformation has occurred from the dominance of ideologies to a state of relative individuation, where individual autonomy and self-expression are sacrosanct. A number of developments have facilitated this shift.

Firstly, the location of where "politics" takes place has become more diffuse due to the "information society," as the mass adoption of new communication technologies undermines the monopoly the state holds over the spread of information (Castells 2000, 2001). Citizens are no longer restricted by the limitations of physical proximity but are instead connected to transnational political events and issues, with global ramifications in an abstract global space. Through real-time, interactive, and global communication, a time-space compression has occurred, facilitating information flows between the local, national, and global spheres with relative ease. As Howard (2011: 72) notes, "digital media create a space of cultural flows that makes territorially distant places feel nearby." Subsequently, the boundaries between foreign territories and their respective political issues and identities have become blurred. Under this diffusion, the locus of power shifts from government and elected representatives to new actors, such as those in the commercial sector and non-governmental organisations. Therefore, citizens may see the need to achieve public goals through cooperative work that engages or targets institutions other than the government.

In alignment with the structural evolution of politics, the monolithic national culture often associated with individual nation states has broken down into a state of cultural pluralism. This has resulted in the diversification of identity and the development of alternative sociocultural frameworks (Bennett 2012; Dahlgren 2009; Dalton 2008; Giddens 1991). Castells (2000: 128) traces the evolution of sociocultural frameworks over time. Primary networks, those concentrated around the family and religious identity, were the first to form. Secondary networks followed, in which citizens were bound together through group-based political associations. Finally, contemporary society is typified by tertiary networks, those centred around an individual's personally defined political identity. This breakdown of uniformity can be linked to gradual cultural changes within society. As Inglehart (1990: 3) notes, "what people want out of life is changing." As basic economic needs have been met and educational standards have improved, new issues have become politicised. Inglehart describes this as a value change from "materialism," and the need to secure physical and economic necessities, to "post-materialism," and the pursuit of autonomy through self-expression (Inglehart 1990: 68).

As a result of these changes, traditional representative associations have experienced a decline in their influence on political identity in Britain (Dahlgren 2009; Pattie et al. 2004). Despite a significant increase in membership of the Labour Party following the election of Jeremy Corbyn as its leader in 2015, just 1.6% of the UK electorate is a member of a political party (Audickas et al. 2018). As grass-roots party activism has become increasingly subjugated by centralisation, public support for parties has become much more conditional, often dependent on specific issues (Denver 2006; Dunleavy 2005; Hay 2007; Stoker 2006). Instead, citizens increasingly identify with new emergent forms of group-based politics that are organised around personal identity and offer opportunities for self-actualisation.

As a result of these structural and sociocultural changes, democratic engagement is increasingly personally defined and focused on issues of importance to the individual rather than institutionally derived and patterned by older, more coherent ideologies of modernity (Bauman 2001; Dalton 2008; Giddens 1991; Inglehart 1990; Norris 2011; Pattie et al. 2004; Zukin et al. 2006). This decentralisation has enabled individuals to form political communities over shared interests, even niche commonalities, rather than being limited to geographical restrictions or hierarchical institutions (Bennett et al. 2011; Bennett and Segerberg 2013; Karpf 2012a; Papacharissi 2010). Changes in citizenship are therefore facilitated, but not determined, by technological advancement as new communication technologies enable these alternate, networked forms of political organisation to prosper. Described by some scholars as "networked individualism," citizens can join and form networked communities, constructing their collective experience around issues in which they have an emotional investment (Castells 2001; Rainie and Wellman 2012).[1]

A shift has therefore occurred away from structural models of citizenship, such as "civic voluntarism," in which macro-level social forces are responsible for participation (Verba and Nie 1972; Verba et al. 1995), to "choice-based citizenship," where the personal identity of each citizen shapes their participation (Dalton 2008; Norris 2011; Pattie et al. 2004). Personal efficacy is key to understanding this choice-based model; if a citizen believes that their participation has little impact on outcomes, whether political, social, or psychological, then there is little incentive to get involved. These outcomes are not limited to policy impact or material self-interest, but also include the symbolic rewards and sense of empowerment that citizens can accrue through participation.

Individual autonomy is central to modern citizenship. As traditional avenues of influence fail to diversify and evolve, alternative modes of self-expressive participation seem to form and thrive. Citizens seek new methods of influence that are reflexive to the different spatial domains in which political decisions take place. As Neuman et al. (2011: 32) argue, if we look beyond formal, institutionalised politics, it is evident that citizens are not apathetic:

> [A] leading problem in this literature involves what constitutes political participation. Most research so far has focused on very traditional outcomes… but there are good reasons to think that many citizens, especially younger ones, are more interested in civic engagement, lifestyle politics, and citizen-directed advocacy than they are in institutionalised forms of participation.

A more nuanced understanding of participation is therefore required to account for the growth of alternative forms of political behaviour.

Political participation has been traditionally defined as those activities that aim to influence the selection of government personnel and the actions they take (Verba et al. 1978: 2). Acts typically include voting in elections, contacting representatives, party membership, and involvement in the policy process, such as through public consultations (Verba et al. 1995: 2). In the backdrop of decreasing voter turnout and declining trust in elected representatives (see Apostolova et al. 2017), there has been notable interest in the level of political disengagement in the UK in recent years. Although evidence from the *Audit of Political Engagement*—the Hansard Society's annual "health check" on British democracy—shows a significant increase in those willing to vote compared to previous years, the public's sense of efficacy in formal modes of participation is still relatively low (Hansard Society 2018: 42). While the causes of this disengagement are disputed, Norris (2011: 8) links these trends to growing dissatisfaction with the democratic performance of political institutions.

Two conflicting schools of thought contest the ramifications of this democratic deficit. Firstly, those advocating the "generational replacement" thesis argue that democracy is in crisis, as older, politically active citizens are replaced by an increasingly apathetic and disengaged youth (Putnam 2000; Putnam et al. 2004; Whiteley 2012). However, the validity of this interpretation depends on how democratic engagement is conceptualised. Minimalist approaches to democracy confine participation to mere representation and elite influence within institutionalised politics. As such, active citizenship becomes synonymous with the institutions that govern. However, as Fox (2014) asks, should we focus on established "conventional" forms of behaviour, or do we need to take account of "unconventional" modes of engagement?

I argue that democratic systems are dynamic; they are based on a loose set of ideals that are subject to interpretation and renewal. Although traditional forms of engagement may be on the decline, this does not account for claims of holistic political disengagement. Instead, our frameworks for understanding political participation have become outdated. As Stanyer (2005: 19) observes:

> Public political attitude expression is undergoing a transformation. It is no longer confined to certain events such as elections nor does it necessarily require the co-presence of others. The public can articulate its views on political matters via a greatly expanded series of protest repertoires and media outlets, and via new technologies. As the number of issues coming to the public's attention has increased, attitude expression is less and less confined to national issues and conventional politics.

The second school of thought, "post-modern citizenship," has a very different evaluation of these trends. While recognising the decline in these conventional acts, others argue that democracy is not under threat due to the rise of new forms of participation (Amnå and Ekman 2014; Dahlgren 2009; Dalton 2008; Pattie et al. 2004; Papacharissi 2010). A growing appetite for self-actualisation has fundamentally altered how citizens participate. As Norris (2011: 219) notes, "traditional political activities that arose and flourished in industrial societies during the late 19th and early 20th centuries are often thought to have peaked in the post-war era and waned in popularity today." Participation is shifting to new, non-institutional forms of action, which are based on post-materialist values (Bennett 2008, 2012; Sloam 2012). Citizens increasingly prioritise issues that relate to their political identity. Giddens (1991: 214) describes this as "life politics," "political issues which flow from processes of self-actualisation in post-traditional contexts, where globalizing influences intrude deeply into the reflexive project of the self, and conversely where processes of self-realisation influence global strategies." As life politics drives social and political identity, micropolitical engagement becomes more common and, thus, empirically significant.

Academic research on political participation predominantly focuses on macro-political activities, those actions that aim to influence rules, laws, or policies. However, given the evolution from structural definitions of citizenship to choice-based models, micropolitical participation is equally important. Micropolitics refers to the day-to-day experiences that shape and form our political preferences. As Hay (2002: 3) argues, it is imperative that research adapts, exploring the political significance of these seemingly non-political behaviours:

> …the political should be defined in such a way as to encompass the entire sphere of the social. The implication of this is that events, processes and practices should not be labelled 'non-political' or 'extra-political' simply by virtue of the specific setting or context in which they occur. All events, processes and practices which occur within the social sphere have the potential to be political and, hence, to be amenable to political analysis. The realm of government is no more innately political, by this definition, than that of culture, law or the domestic sphere.

This emphasis on personal attitudes and private behaviours opens up new spaces for democratic involvement.

Adopting such an approach means that less visible, "passive" forms of engagement become empirically relevant. Framing participation as active or passive has normative implications. Passivity is often synonymous with disillusionment or a lack of effort, when seemingly passive political behaviours may be beneficial to democracy (see Amnå and Ekman 2014; Schudson 1999). Bucy and Gregson (2001: 359) argue that, while passivity invokes a certain sense of detachment, activities such as news consumption, opinion formulation, and interpersonal discussion, represent important expressive behaviours that require time and effort.

These activities are examples of "cognitive engagement," broadly defined as "paying attention to politics and public affairs" (Zukin et al. 2006: 54), and they are a necessary precondition of instrumental forms of action (Carpentier 2011). These behaviours are particularly significant when we consider political efficacy. Traditional forms of engagement can lack the same observable and immediate symbolic rewards as these forms of micro-level engagement.

The growing popularity of these expressive forms of engagement means that the conventional–unconventional distinction is no longer relevant. We are not witnessing holistic political disengagement or the erosion of British civic culture, but the birth of a new one that emphasises self-actualisation. The following section outlines the methodological challenges for empirical research on choice-based citizenship online and the steps that this book takes to overcome them.

Measuring Across the Continuum: Indicators and Research Design

The conceptual foundation on which a researcher constructs their study has an essential impact on one's methodological design and, subsequently, the conclusions reached, given the often deterministic nature of those variables under review. This is especially true of research exploring political participation. How a researcher conceptualises engagement can shape their conclusions on the health of a political system. For example, Whiteley (2012) warns that Britain is teetering on the edge of becoming a flawed democracy, given the declining membership of political parties, waning voter turnout, and decreasing engagement with community organisations. However, as Fox (2014) highlights, these conclusions are inexorably tied to Whiteley's definition of participation.

Whiteley loosely bases his prognosis on the definition of participation derived from the seminal works of Verba and Nie (1972; Verba et al. 1978). Such a definition is bound to political institutions and does not reflect the evolution of citizenship and subsequent diversification of participatory styles. Studies that adopt this approach often emphasise the importance of macro-level indicators of participation, like voting, at the expense of micro-level acts, the type which prosper within online environments (Bennett et al. 2011: 836). It should not come as a surprise that findings of this nature often support claims that the Internet sustains pre-existing patterns of participatory inequality (Brundidge and

Rice 2009). However, such a conclusion is problematic as political disconnection in this context refers to the disjuncture between citizens and political institutions, rather than a disconnection with politics more broadly. As Fox (2014) notes, there is no "true" definition of political participation; researchers must construct and adopt a definition that fits their research context. Therefore, it is important to highlight why analysing conventional, macro-level indicators in isolation is not appropriate for this book, before explaining the type of micropolitical acts, both online and offline, that this study observes across the continuum of participation.

It is necessary to recognise that some studies on digital participation focus on the effect of the Internet on a narrow selection of offline political acts, rather than other forms of online activism (Boulianne 2009). These studies operationalise macro-level indicators of political participation, those acts that are explicitly aimed at political institutions or public policy, rather than micro-level measurements, which track everyday political experiences. As such, some studies have found evidence of a relationship between Internet use and political disengagement through measures such as party membership or voting (see Coleman 2007 for an overview). However, this does not represent *holistic* political disengagement as these indicators lack measurement validity in this context; they do not embody the changes to political identity and citizenship in Britain. As Vaccari (2013: 222–223) observes, the way researchers conceptualise engagement must take into account this evolution in participatory styles:

> That political actions of many kinds—often aimed more at expressive than instrumental goals—occur constantly at the intersection between digital media, mass media, and people's social lives does not necessarily mean that citizens will participate more, or more effectively. It does, however, imply that people's definition of what it means to engage with politics and their understanding of how it can—and, perhaps, should—be done have changed substantially compared to the standard definitions employed in political science research.

This book defines participation as a process, exploring the relationships between different acts across the continuum of participation. As such, I did not draw arbitrary parameters between the value of different acts before the data collection. This would contradict the emphasis on individual-level sense-making that forms the focus of this study. Every citizen has a certain degree of political sophistication, but this varies depending on personal issue interest and everyday experiences. The most effective way to capture this dissimilarity is through thick description, a technique that allows for self-reflection. By using diaries and interviews, this research encourages participants to describe what they perceive to be political or non-political and to reflect on their engagement from this perceptive (see Couldry et al. 2010; Eliasoph 1998, for example).

Participation is measured through an amalgamation of indicators from other studies (Bennett et al. 2011: 842; Bucy and Gregson 2001: 357; Pattie et al. 2004: 78; Zukin et al. 2006: 57). For example, this research emulates the approach used by Zukin et al. (2006) in measuring participation as a process, from information dissemination to action, as shown in Table 3.1.

This list of indicators provides a useful platform on which to build, albeit with some alterations. Primarily, the diversity of political behaviour

Table 3.1 The core indicators of engagement

Modes of participation	*Indicators of engagement*
Cognitive engagement	Following government and public affairs
	Talking with friends and family about politics
	Political knowledge
	Attention to news media
Public voice	Contacting officials
	Contacting the print media
	Contacting the broadcast media
	Protesting
	Email petitions
	Written petitions
	Boycotting
	Canvassing
Civic action	Community problem solving
	Regular volunteering for a non-electoral organisation
	Active membership in a group or association
	Participation in fundraising run/walk/ride
	Other fundraising for charity
Political action	Regular voting
	Persuading others
	Displaying buttons, signs, stickers
	Campaign contributions
	Volunteering for candidate or political organisations

Source Zukin et al. (2006)

on social media significantly blurs the different modes of participation, making the use of discrete categories somewhat redundant. The continuum of participation is therefore used as a solution to harness the complex diffusion of personally expressive political engagement online, as illustrated in Table 3.2. Civic and political forms of engagement are merged within this list, as participants determine the parameters of what constitutes political or civic involvement.

It is important to note that this list of indicators acts as a descriptive aid, rather than a definitive list. The ordering mimics the four stages on the continuum of participation but, as discussed in Chapter 2, these acts are fluid and can correlate with different categories depending on the context of use; this list is not prescriptive. This research observes how citizens envisage participation through their experiences, rather than the researcher imposing a mandatory definition through a rigid set of indicators.

A similar approach is taken in relation to the forms of digital engagement that are analysed. As outlined in Chapter 1, this study focuses on

Table 3.2 Example indicators of political participation

Indicators of engagement
• Attention to news media
• Attention to information created and shared by peers
• Following "political" interests (including government, public affair, issues)
• Opinion formulation
• Interpersonal political discussion
• Contacting the broadcast or print media
• Mediated interactions or face-to-face contact with an elected representative
• Mediated interactions or face-to-face contact with other political actors
• Expressions of civic or political orientation
• Self-produced forms of digital media
• Membership of peer defined networks and groups
• Membership of traditional, hierarchical organisations
• Organising and mobilising future civic and political actions
• Donating to civic or political causes
• Signing a petition
• Voting in an election
• Consumer activism (boycotting and buycotting)
• Political party activities (canvassing, campaigning)
• Campaigning and advocacy work (including raising awareness, fundraising for a civic or political cause, and self-produced forms of digital media)
• Volunteered time for a civic or political cause
• Taken part in a legal public demonstration
• Taken part in illegal protest activities

two social networking sites in depth, Facebook and Twitter. A difficulty with the empirical study of social media is what Karpf (2012b: 640) labels as "internet time," the rapid speed with which digital technologies develop and change. This unpredictability can make life difficult for those trying to analyse media effects in a digital environment. As service functionality evolves and changes, research can quickly go from cutting edge to irrelevant. This book attempts to overcome this potential pitfall through thick description of holistic service use, exploring each platform in relation to other online and offline behaviour, rather than isolating specific functions. In doing so, the findings offer a snapshot of how Facebook and Twitter integrate within broader media and engagement practices at the individual level.

In measuring the attitudinal context for these actions, participants were given the opportunity to define and discuss politics, and their political motivations, on their own terms. Demographic factors, including age, income, geographical background, and level of education, are significant when we consider how citizens construct and understand these experiences (Verba and Nie 1972; Verba et al. 1995). As such, it is important to note that the sampling frame used within this book does not form a representative sample of the target population, that is those British citizens who share the characteristics of so-called slacktivists. Instead, this study relies on convenience samples that are discussed in detail in the Research Appendix. Other structural factors, such as time demands and technical competencies, were recorded during data collection as a means of contextualising the findings.

Time and its relationship with effort is a relevant measurement in contextualising this snapshot of user behaviour. Effort has long been considered a core indicator in assessing the depth of an individual's political participation (Verba et al. 1978: 55). The slacktivist critique operationalises effort in terms of the time expended when undertaking a political act. Citizens are deemed lazy when the action itself—such as the click of a button (Morozov 2013)—only takes a small amount of time. As a result, the often unseen processes that may precede such an act, such as cognitive mobilisation and private deliberation, are ignored. A similar logic can be applied to voting.

The time expended to vote physically can be a matter of seconds, especially when we consider the growing popularity of the postal vote (Cracknell 2014). However, unlike low-threshold acts online, this does not mean voting is perceived to be a lazy or insignificant act. Such an assessment underplays the time a citizen spends considering which candidate to vote for. This process may involve a range of mediated and face-to-face interactions. If a citizen turns up to the polling booth and chooses a candidate at random, then he or she may be deemed to be "lazy." However, we cannot assume that *all* of those who vote are lazy based on the costs associated with the action in isolation; the same should also apply to digitally mediated expression and micro-activism.

This book operationalises time as a measure of the depth of one's engagement. The amount of time that a participant devotes to political actions across the continuum of participation is compared to their perception of their spare time; the amount of time available after bodily, financial, and household necessities is accounted for (Goodin et al. 2008). It is important to recognise that the amount of spare time available to an individual depends on their personal context. The time-pressure illusion—the gap between actual spare time and potential discretionary time—is an increasingly important factor when accounting for the nature of contemporary citizenship.

Ultimately, the research design used in this book is based on Karpf's (2012b) concept of "kludginess," using experimental workarounds to generate empirically based observations in a fast-changing, spatially diffuse, and subsequently chaotic media environment. The fluid and rapidly evolving nature of the Internet poses methodological challenges (Bimber and Copeland 2013; Gerodimos and Ward 2007; Karpf 2012b). Gerodimos and Ward (2007) pinpoint two problems in particular that call for a re-evaluation of how we research political participation online; the diffusion of "what" encompasses political acts and "where" they take place. This combination of the growth of new forms of political behaviour and the porous spatial characteristics of the Internet creates difficulties for the researcher, as it is near impossible to define the parameters of precisely where political behaviour takes place online. It is intrinsically difficult to record who accesses online content, and what they do with it post-consumption, especially if they leave no digital trace. This makes for a messy landscape, one in which isolated variables and measurement precision can be tricky (Karpf 2012b: 645). As such, Gerodimos and Ward (2007) advocate an in-depth qualitative approach, as this can provide observation of online political behaviour across different spaces and offer a sense of the motivational context on which these acts are predicated. This is adopted within this research through an ethnography of 38

Degrees and by using media diaries to capture detailed self-reflection of an individual's political experiences and media use. The methods used in each study are highlighted in the corresponding chapter.

Mapping Theory onto the Continuum: A Deductive Framework

The way a researcher operationalises citizenship within empirical research can typically take one of two approaches (Svensson 2011: 645). One may adopt an inductive approach, in which an observation of political attitudes and behaviours forms new sociopolitical theory, or a deductive approach, where a study's findings are compared against existing citizenship theory. This book combines elements of both by way of observing how social media affects how citizens envisage their citizenship and then act upon it. By mapping some theoretical contributions from political communication research onto the continuum of participation—as shown in Table 3.3—an alternative prognosis to slacktivism is offered.

Firstly, the conditions of information consumption on social networking sites have been hypothesised by some to be beneficial for political citizenship. Building on Downs' (1957) theory of by-product learning, in which citizens can acquire political information as a by-product of everyday activities in seemingly non-political environments, Chadwick (2012) proposes that social media users are accidentally exposed to political

Table 3.3 The continuum of participation model

Stage of the continuum of participation	*Description*
Access	Cognitive engagement and the ways by which citizens pay attention to politics and public affairs
Expression	Users post a variety of personally expressive content on social media as a means of political participation The effects of expression can vary across the continuum depending on the motivations of the user, the composition of the audience, and how receivers use this information
Connection	The processes of political organisation, as citizens use social media to establish and join networks for a range of purposes
Action	Goal-orientated, public political acts, or those behaviours that complement other online and/or offline political acts as part of engagement repertoires

information through their everyday use. Although users may perceive Facebook and Twitter to be apolitical spaces, political expression, and civic discussion can occur organically, as users reflect on events and issues impact experiences that occur within everyday life. In doing so, users—intentionally or unintentionally—contribute political material for others. Therefore, Chadwick offers an alternative prognosis to that presented by Prior (2007) and Sunstein (2007), who suggest that digital media enable the user to filter out political material in favour of entertainment.

The hypothesis that social media create the conditions for by-product learning has been tested empirically in large-N studies (see Fletcher and Nielsen 2017b; Vaccari 2014). However, there is still uncertainty about the cognitive and discursive processes that occur following this point of consumption. We cannot assume that every user pays the same attention to each piece of political content that they are exposed to. We know very little of the processes that an individual undertakes once they have consumed this information. For instance, do they discuss this with others? Do they verify or contextualise the material by researching the topic more broadly? This book examines whether Facebook and Twitter users are accidentally exposed to political information as a by-product of everyday use and, if so, what happens after the initial point of consumption.

Secondly, due to the porous boundaries between content production and consumption embedded within the design of social media, a number of studies have illustrated how political conversation is fostered by virtue of access to this political material (Bennett et al. 2011; Brundidge 2010; Chadwick 2012; Valenzuela et al. 2011). Users can discuss and share content with others as they consume it, fostering an active, rather than passive, consumption experience (Jenkins 2006). For instance, as part of their study on the use of Twitter during the topical debate television programme *Question Time*, Anstead and O'Loughlin (2011: 441) found evidence of "viewers who use online publishing platforms and social tools to interpret, publicly comment on, and debate a television broadcast while they are watching it." With this in mind, this book explores the dynamics of political conversation on Facebook and Twitter.

Thirdly, existing empirical research has shown how users post a variety of personally expressive content on social media as a means of political engagement (Bennett 2008; Bennett and Segerberg 2013; Papacharissi 2010; Stanyer 2005). However, ascertaining the democratic value of this behaviour is not straightforward due to how these acts blur what is considered private—and normatively separate from institutionally bound definitions of citizenship—and what is considered public. In *The Private Sphere* (2010), Papacharissi describes how this convergence has been triggered, in part, by technological developments. As a result, how individuals envisage and act upon their citizenship is fundamentally changing, as public political acts emerge from the confines of one's personal, privatised space. Papacharissi (2010: 166–167) offers the "private sphere" as a descriptive tool for understanding these new sites of identification:

> The meaning of the political lies in the ability to express dissent, to think differently. To the extent that the private sphere affords the autonomy, control, and expressive capabilities that enable dissent, it effectively reconciles the personal with the political in a way that enables connection with like-minded individuals. The private sphere, as metaphor, describes and explains the mechanisms for civic connections in contemporary democracies. Its value is descriptive and explanatory, but not prescriptive. Far from a recipe for democracy, the private sphere is an attempt at new space and a new sociality.

The notion of the private sphere challenges the long-standing assumption that collective action requires a public face (Olson 1971). Instead, as political acts increasingly represent and fulfil a personalised political identity that is both reflexive and fluid, "citizens feel more secure in preserving their individual autonomy and the integrity of their civic identity, and in control of their civic fate" (Papacharissi 2010: 22).

Social media acts as a structural facilitator for these actions, providing the familiarity of a seemingly private space, but with a diverse range of public and semi-public audiences that are—to some extent—controlled by the user. Facebook and Twitter are examples of networked platforms on which users can tailor their information consumption, community membership, and engagement to suit their personal preferences. As such, Papacharissi (2010: 131) argues that self-expression, once confined to private spaces for many citizens, can have public implications:

> Participating in a MoveOn.org online protest, expressing political opinion on blogs, viewing or posting content on YouTube, or posting a comment in an online discussion group represents an expression of dissent with a public agenda… It stands as a private, digitally enabled, intrusion on a public agenda determined by others.

Drawing on Papacharissi's (2010) notion of the private sphere, this book analyses the context and conditions of these seemingly private forms of political expression, ascertaining the public political impact of these behaviours, if any.

Fourthly, rather than replacing tried-and-tested activist repertoires as hypothesised by the slacktivist critique, digital micro-activism replaces equivalent low-effort behaviours, such as postcard campaigns and paper petitions (Chadwick 2007; Karpf 2010, 2012a). As Karpf (2010: 7) notes, "[they] represent a difference-of-degree rather than difference-in-kind." By observing the political behaviour at both the individual level—through media diaries—and the organisational level—through an ethnography of the political group 38 Degrees—this study explores the role digital micro-activism plays in relation to other modes of participation.

Finally, this study considers the motivational context for so-called slacktivism. Drawing on the rich literature on political citizenship discussed in this chapter, Bennett (2008; Bennett et al. 2011) has outlined a cultural shift in political identity, as individual autonomy is replacing duty and obligation. This evolution from the "dutiful citizen" to the "actualizing citizen" encapsulates the critique of state-centric citizenship and embraces new, alternative forms of citizen culture. Bennett (2008) argues that citizens now have more freedom to define and manage their identities. This is in contrast to the experience of past generations, who were assigned broad social identities based on religious affiliations or social cleavages. In the actualising citizen framework, political behaviour is increasingly focused on generating feelings of self-efficacy, as personally expressive forms of engagement that represent an individual's social and political identity become more commonplace (Bennett 2008: 14). As such, citizens act according to personal preferences and lifestyle choices, illustrated by growing levels of support for issues that reflect a post-materialist value orientation, such as environmentalism and consumer activism.

One may argue that the actualising citizen framework establishes a rigid dichotomy between citizenship styles similar to those discussed in Chapter 2. However, Bennett et al. (2011: 839) dismiss this, arguing that the categories are fluid, as citizens mix both actualizing and dutiful citizenship styles. For example, voting is still a significant form of democratic engagement for many young people, but the motivations for casting a vote are changing. Rather than advocating that duty-bound citizenship has been wholly replaced, the framework describes a gradual shift in contemporary citizenship. Citizens increasingly shape and define their political identity due, in part, to the structural freedoms afforded by the Internet. This study assesses the motivational logics that underpin behaviours across the continuum of participation, investigating the viability of the actualizing citizen framework in Britain.[2]

Taken collectively, these theoretical contributions offer a remarkably different picture of digital citizenship, disputing the hypotheses of the slacktivist critique. This book evaluates the extent to which these attitudinal and behavioural traits are shared by a sample of participants who share media habits with so-called slacktivists. This deductive framework is reviewed in the conclusion (Chapter 7).

Conclusion: Investigating a New Civic Vernacular

> The emerging political conscience is not collective, but privatized—both by virtue of its connection to consumer culture and in terms of the private spaces it occupies. The contemporary citizen adopts a personally devised definition of the political, and becomes emancipated in private, rather than public, spaces, thus developing a new civic vernacular.
>
> (Papacharissi 2010: 19)

By observing how Facebook and Twitter are embedded within an individual's everyday political experiences, this book explores what Papacharissi (2010: 161) describes as a new "civic vernacular." This conceptualisation of digital engagement is based around the very same behaviours that the slacktivist critique dismisses as ineffective and inauthentic: signing an e-petition, sharing a politically charged status update, changing a profile picture to support a cause. What links these two opposed judgements is the sense that political citizenship has become increasingly focused around the individual, rather than the collective. This personalisation, outlined in this chapter, is characterised by the values of autonomy, individual efficacy, and self-expression. For the likes of Gladwell (2010) and Morozov (2011), these values are detrimental to democracy. These low-threshold acts are examples of narcissism, providing psychological, reputational, and social benefits for the individual at the expense of the causes they claim to support. For Bennett (2008), Chadwick (2012), and Papacharissi (2010), these behaviours are legitimate forms of democratic involvement and provide evidence of active citizenship. Together, this dual set of hypotheses act as a guide for analysing the findings generated through the primary research. I now move onto these empirical findings, starting with an ethnographic study of the political activist group, 38 Degrees.

Notes

1. I do not suggest that these changes necessarily result in transnational citizenship, whereby identity is no longer tied to national or territorial boundaries. Rather, the nation state, as well as social factors like class, gender, and race, acts as a foundation for the construction of this identity (Bellamy 2008; Dalton 2008: 25; Pattie et al. 2004: 21). Political socialisation is still important. I draw on Dalton's (2008: 25) "hierarchical model of beliefs" under which personal political identity is formed on the basis of these attitudinal orientations.
2. Although this framework is based on the attitudes and behaviours of young people, it is important to note that this study will not focus on them in isolation. Instead, the actualising citizen framework will be applied to a wider age range to explore if these trends reflect a more general phenomenon.

References

Amnå, E., & Ekman, J. (2014). Standby Citizens: Diverse Faces of Political Passivity. *European Political Science Review, 6*(2), 261–281.

Anstead, N., & O'Loughlin, B. (2011). The Emerging Viewertariat and BBC Question Time: Television Debate and Real-Time Commenting Online. *International Journal of Press/Politics, 16*(4), 440–462.

Apostolova, V., Uberoi, E., & Johnston, N. (2017). *Political Disengagement in the UK: Who Is Disengaged?* (Briefing Paper Number CBP7501). Retrieved from http://researchbriefings.parliament.uk/ResearchBriefing/Summary/CBP-7501.

Audickas, L., Dempsey, N., & Keen, R. (2018). *Membership of UK Political Parties* (Briefing Paper Number SN05125). Retrieved from https://researchbriefings.parliament.uk/ResearchBriefing/Summary/SN05125.

Bauman, Z. (2001). *The Individualized Society.* Cambridge: Polity.

Bellamy, R. (2008). Evaluating Union Citizenship: Belonging, Rights and Participation with the E.U. *Citizenship Studies, 12*(6), 597–611.

Bennett, W. L. (2008). Changing Citizenship in the Digital Age. In W. L. Bennett (Ed.), *Civic Life Online: Learning How Digital Media Can Engage Youth* (pp. 1–24). Cambridge: MIT Press.

Bennett, W. L. (2012). The Personalization of Politics: Political Identity, Social Media, and Changing Patterns of Participation. *The ANNALS of the American Academy of Political and Social Science, 644*(20), 20–39.

Bennett, W. L., & Segerberg, A. (2013). *The Logic of Connective Action: Digital Media and the Personalization of Contentious Politics*. Cambridge: Cambridge University Press.

Bennett, W. L., Wells, C., & Freelon, D. (2011). Communicating Civic Engagement: Contrasting Models of Citizenship in the Youth Web Sphere. *Journal of Communication, 61*(5), 835–856.

Bimber, B., & Copeland, L. (2013). Digital Media and Traditional Political Participation Over Time in the U.S. *Journal of Information Technology & Politics, 10*(2), 125–137.

Boulianne, S. (2009). Does Internet Use Affect Engagement? A Meta-Analysis of Research. *Political Communication, 26*(2), 193–211.

Brundidge, J. (2010). Toward a Theory of Citizen Interface with Political Discussion and News in the Contemporary Public Sphere. *International Journal of Communication, 4*, 1056–1078.

Brundidge, J., & Rice, R. E. (2009). Political Engagement Online: Do the Information Rich Get Richer and the Like-Minded Get More Similar? In A. Chadwick & P. N. Howard (Eds.), *Routledge Handbook of Internet Politics* (pp. 144–157). Abingdon: Routledge.

Bucy, E. P., & Gregson, K. S. (2001). Media Participation: A Legitimizing Mechanism of Mass Democracy. *New Media & Society, 3*(3), 357–380.

Cammaerts, B., & Van Audenhove, L. (2005). Online Political Debate, Unbounded Citizenship, and the Problematic Nature of a Transnational Public Sphere. *Political Communication, 22*(2), 179–196.

Carpentier, N. (2011). *Media and Participation: A Site of Ideological-Democratic Struggle*. Bristol: Intellect.

Castells, M. (2000). *The Rise of the Network Society*. Oxford: Blackwell.

Castells, M. (2001). *The Internet Galaxy: Reflections on the Internet, Business, and Society*. Oxford: Oxford University Press.

Chadwick, A. (2007). Digital Network Repertoires and Organizational Hybridity. *Political Communication, 24*(3), 283–301.

Chadwick, A. (2012). Recent Shifts in the Relationship Between the Internet and Democratic Engagement in Britain and the United States: Granularity, Informational Exuberance, and Political Learning. In E. Anduiza, M. Jensen, & L. Jorba (Eds.), *Digital Media and Political Engagement Worldwide: A Comparative Study* (pp. 39–55). Cambridge: Cambridge University Press.

Coleman, S. (2007). How Democracies Have Disengaged from Young People. In B. D. Loader (Ed.), *Young Citizens in the Digital Age: Political Engagement, Young People and New Media* (pp. 166–185). Abingdon: Routledge.

Couldry, N., Livingstone, S., & Markham, T. (2010). *Media Consumption and Public Engagement: Beyond the Presumption of Attention*. Basingstoke: Palgrave Macmillan.

Cracknell, R. (2014, May 1). 'First Class the Post': The Rise of Postal Voting. *House of Commons Library*. Retrieved July 21, 2015, from http://commonslibraryblog.com/2014/05/01/postal-voting-in-the-uk/.

Dahlgren, P. (2009). *Media and Political Engagement: Citizens, Communication and Democracy*. Cambridge: Cambridge University Press.

Dalton, R. J. (2008). *Citizens Politics: Public Opinion and Political Parties in Advanced Industrial Democracies* (5th ed.). Washington, DC: CQ Press.

Denver, D. (2006). *Elections and Voters in Britain* (2nd ed.). Basingstoke: Palgrave Macmillan.

Downs, A. (1957). *An Economic Theory of Democracy*. New York: Harper.

Dunleavy, P. (2005). Facing Up to Multi-party Politics: How Partisan Dealignment and PR Voting Have Fundamentally Changed Britain's Party Systems. *Parliamentary Affairs, 58*(3), 503–532.

Eliasoph, N. (1998). *Avoiding Politics: How Americans Produce Apathy in Everyday Life*. Cambridge: Cambridge University Press.

Fletcher, R., & Nielsen, R. K. (2017b). Are People Incidentally Exposed to News on Social Media? A Comparative Analysis. *New Media & Society*. Retrieved from https://doi.org/10.1177/1461444817724170.

Fox, S. (2014). Is It Time to Update the Definition of Political Participation? Political Participation in Britain: The Decline and Revival of Civic Culture. *Parliamentary Affairs, 67*(2), 495–505.

Gerodimos, R., & Ward, J. (2007). Rethinking Online Youth Civic Engagement: Reflections on Web Content Analysis. In B. D. Loader (Ed.), *Young Citizens in the Digital Age: Political Engagement, Young People and New Media* (pp. 114–126). Abingdon: Routledge.

Giddens, A. (1991). *Modernity and Self-Identity: Self and Society in the Late Modern Age*. Cambridge: Polity.

Gladwell, M. (2010, October 4). Small Change: Why the Revolution Will Not Be Tweeted. *The New Yorker*. Retrieved November 3, 2010, from https:// www.newyorker.com/magazine/2010/10/04/small-change-malcolm-gladwell.

Goodin, R. E., Rice, J. M., Parpo, A., & Eriksson, L. (2008). *Discretionary Time: A New Measure of Freedom*. Cambridge: Cambridge University Press.

Graber, D. A. (2004). Mediated Politics and Citizenship in the Twenty-First Century. *Annual Review of Psychology, 55*, 545–571.

Hansard Society. (2018). *Audit of Political Engagement 15: The 2018 Report*. London: Hansard Society.

Hay, C. (2002). *Political Analysis: A Critical Introduction*. Basingstoke: Palgrave Macmillan.

Hay, C. (2007). *Why We Hate Politics.* Cambridge: Polity.
Howard, P. N. (2011). *Castells and the Media.* Cambridge: Polity.
Inglehart, R. (1990). *Culture Shift in Advanced Industrial Society.* Princeton, NJ: Princeton University Press.
Jenkins, H. (2006). *Convergence Culture: Where Old and New Media Collide.* New York: New York University.
Karpf, D. (2010). Online Political Mobilization from the Advocacy Group's Perspective: Looking Beyond Clicktivism. *Policy and Internet, 2*(4), 7–41.
Karpf, D. (2012a). *The MoveOn Effect: The Unexpected Transformation of American Political Advocacy.* Oxford: Oxford University Press.
Karpf, D. (2012b). Social Science Research Methods in Internet Time. *Information, Communication and Society, 15*(5), 639–661.
Morozov, E. (2011). *The Net Delusion: How Not to Liberate the World.* London: Penguin.
Morozov, E. (2013). *To Save Everything, Click Here: The Folly of Technological Determinism.* London: Allen Lane.
Neuman, W. R., Bimber, B., & Hindman, M. (2011). The Internet and Four Dimensions of Citizenship. In R. Y. Shapiro & L. R. Jacobs (Eds.), *The Oxford Handbook of American Public Opinion and the Media* (pp. 22–42). Oxford: Oxford University Press.
Norris, P. (2011). *Democratic Deficit: Critical Citizens Revisited.* Cambridge: Cambridge University Press.
Olson, M. (1971). *The Logic of Collective Action: Public Goods and the Theory of Groups.* Cambridge, MA: Harvard University Press.
Papacharissi, Z. (2010). *A Private Sphere: Democracy in a Digital Age.* Cambridge: Polity.
Pattie, C., Seyd, P., & Whiteley, P. (2004). *Citizenship in Britain: Values, Participation and Democracy.* Cambridge: Cambridge University Press.
Prior, M. (2007). *Post-broadcast Democracy: How Media Choice Increases Inequality in Political Involvement and Polarizes Elections.* Cambridge: Cambridge University Press.
Putnam, R. D. (2000). *Bowling Alone: The Collapse and Revival of American Community.* London: Simon & Schuster.
Putnam, R. D., Feldstein, L., & Cohen, D. (2004). *Better Together: Restoring the American Community.* London: Simon & Schuster.
Rainie, L., & Wellman, B. (2012). *Networked: The New Social Operating System.* Cambridge: MIT Press.
Schudson, M. (1999). *The Good Citizen: A History of American Public Life.* Cambridge, MA: Harvard University Press.
Sloam, J. (2012). Introduction: Youth, Citizenship and Politics. *Parliamentary Affairs, 65*(1), 4–12.

Stanyer, J. (2005). The British Public and Political Attitude Expression: The Emergence of a Self-Expressive Political Culture? *Contemporary Politics, 11*(1), 19–32.

Stoker, G. (2006). *Why Politics Matter: Making Democracy Work*. Basingstoke: Palgrave Macmillan.

Sunstein, C. R. (2007). *Republic.Com 2.0*. Princeton, NJ: Princeton University Press.

Svensson, J. (2011). Theorizing Citizenships in Late Modern ICT Societies. *Triple C: Cognition, Communication, Co-operation, 9*(2), 644–656.

Vaccari, C. (2013). *Digital Politics in Western Democracies: A Comparative Study*. Baltimore, MD: Johns Hopkins University Press.

Vaccari, C. (2014, November 9). *Response to the Consultation Themes Set Forth by the Digital Democracy Commission*. Retrieved August 8, 2015, from http://www.parliament.uk/documents/speaker/digital-democracy/VaccariSCDDresponsefinal.pdf.

Valenzuela, S., Kim, Y., & Gil de Zúñiga, H. (2011). Social Networks That Matter: Exploring the Role of Political Discussion for Online Political Participation. *International Journal of Public Opinion Research, 24*(2), 163–184.

Verba, S., & Nie, N. H. (1972). *Participation in America: Political Democracy and Social Equality*. London: Harper & Row.

Verba, S., Nie, N. H., & Kim, J. (1978). *Participation and Political Equality: A Seven-Nation Comparison*. Cambridge, MA: Cambridge University Press.

Verba, S., Schlozman, K., & Brady, H. (1995). *Voice and Equality: Civic Voluntarism in American Politics*. Cambridge, MA: Harvard University Press.

Whiteley, P. (2012). *Political Participation in Britain: The Decline and Revival of Civic Culture*. Basingstoke: Palgrave Macmillan.

Zukin, C., Keeter, S., Andolina, M., Jenkins, K., & Delli Carpini, M. X. (2006). *A New Engagement: Political Participation, Civic Life, and the Changing American Citizen*. Oxford: Oxford University Press.

CHAPTER 4

People. Power. Change. 38 Degrees and Digital Micro-Activism on Social Media

38 Degrees is a non-profit, political activist group based in the UK. Since their foundation in 2009, the group has amassed a "membership" of over 3 million people (Chadwick and Dennis 2017), with donations totalling over £4.5 million in 2016 (Sayer Vincent 2017).[1] The organisation boasts an impressive track record across a range of political issues, most notably their campaign against the Conservative-Liberal Democrat coalition government's plans to sell off public forests in 2011. However, what is most striking about the group is their organisational ethos, "People. Power. Change." Named after the angle at which snowflakes come together to form an avalanche, individual autonomy is central to the group's modus operandi. In doing so, they are representative of a new generation of digital advocacy organisations. Like MoveOn in the USA (Karpf 2012, 2016) and GetUp! in Australia (Vromen 2017; Vromen and Coleman 2013), 38 Degrees is a member of the Online Progressive Engagement Network (OPEN), a set of multi-issue advocacy groups that use digital technologies to offer member-driven campaigns.

A critique frequently levelled at OPEN organisations is that their style of campaigning encourages slacktivism (Davies 2014; Rickett 2013; James 2014). Drawing upon a three-month participant observation, ethnographic data from interviews with staff and members, as well as campaign emails, social media data, and online news articles, this chapter examines how 38 Degrees seek to avoid slacktivism through their mobilisation strategy. I explore whether the group's use of Facebook and

J. Dennis, *Beyond Slacktivism*,
Interest Groups, Advocacy and Democracy Series,
https://doi.org/10.1007/978-3-030-00844-4_4

Twitter create new opportunities for political learning, discursive engagement, and political action, or if inefficient online tactics compromise offline activism?

The chapter proceeds as follows. Firstly, I offer an overview of 38 Degrees at the organisational level, describing its structure and the role that the leadership play. The popularity of the group comes from its member-centric approach. Through the use of digital technologies, members can shape and influence campaign strategy. However, while the organisation is member driven, it is not leaderless. As the campaign to halt the proposed limits to GP visits shows, the staff in the London office translates the priorities established by the membership—through communications over email, Facebook, and Twitter—into campaign actions. These leaders draw on their political expertise to design online and face-to-face engagement repertoires.

Investigating the organisational level may seem contradictory to the calls for further empirical research at the individual level made throughout this book. However, researchers can often learn more by exploring the links *between* different units of analysis (Howard 2011: 2). Throughout this chapter, I explore the attitudes and behaviours of individual members within the engagement repertoires that are crafted at the organisational level.[2] I argue that we can only understand how members make use of social media in this activist context by examining the relationships formed between ordinary members and the leadership. In doing so, I illustrate when a 38 Degrees campaign transforms into substantive forms of instrumental engagement and when their activism fulfils some of the hypotheses derived from the slacktivist critique.

Secondly, I analyse how the leadership at 38 Degrees uses social media to craft opportunities for member involvement across the continuum of participation. This study challenges the attitudinal and behavioural claims of the slacktivist critique on the role of seemingly low-effort political behaviours on social media. In what I describe as the organisational management of digital micro-activism, the leadership of 38 Degrees use social media to provide democratic shortcuts for substantive political involvement for their membership. On Facebook, staff draw on comments and metrics to guide the strategic direction of the group. On Twitter, they identify opportunities where a rapid and targeted mobilisation will result in reputational damage and public pressure. When members engage in emotive forms of self-expression, this fulfils a number of functions that go beyond the self-gratification hypothesised by the slacktivist critique. These forms of personalised communication can raise awareness of political issues amongst wider publics, form bonds between the geographically dispersed and ideologically disparate membership, and under certain conditions, they can represent a form of digital activism in their own right. Through the organisational management of digital micro-activism, the leadership offers granular campaign actions based on the priorities set by their membership. This digital engagement can act as a participatory shortcut, providing a bridge to the processes of policymaking for time-poor citizens. Therefore, in this activist context, political behaviour on social media is not deemed to be ineffective by virtue of technological design, as their strategic deployment by political professionals gives these actions value.

This chapter also contributes to the growing literature on OPEN organisations (Chadwick and Dennis 2017; Hall 2017; Vromen 2017), offering further empirical support to Karpf's (2016) concept of "analytic activism," in which advocacy groups can better represent their members by drawing on feedback from digital channels. I develop this approach by exploring analytic activism from the perspective of those citizens involved. Rather than acting on the basis of reputation management or as a way of avoiding high-cost political activism, as hypothesised by the slacktivist critique, members mobilise around issues of personal relevance. They recognise and value the digital feedback loops offered by the group's use of Facebook and cite this as a key reason for involvement.

Method Notes

This chapter draws upon data collected through interviews, participant observation, campaign emails, social media content, and online news articles. From April to July 2013, I worked at the headquarters of 38 Degrees and visited a variety of locations around Britain. During this time, I acted as a "participant as observer," contributing to the day-to-day running of campaigns as a volunteer. To minimise my impact on the study, these tasks were predominantly administrative. This was an overt observation, with clearance forms outlining the project distributed to all interviewees. This ethnographic approach was adopted as it provides the researcher with unique access to their object of study on which to build a contextual understanding of their actions (see Eliasoph 1998).

I also conducted 22 interviews, seven with staff members based in the organisation's London office and 15 with members (see the Research

Appendix). All interviews were semi-structured to provide opportunities for interviewees to discuss political issues in their own terms. Initially, members were sampled on the basis of individuals that I met during the participant observation period. This included contacts made at an informal members meal and during a protest in London. However, given that these individuals were from a relatively small geographical area and had chosen to attend these events—a sign of their dedication to the group—I also contacted individuals who had posted public contributions relating to 38 Degrees on Facebook and Twitter. Therefore, this sample is not representative of the membership of 38 Degrees, as it omits those who do not engage with the group on social media. However, given the focus of this book, all those interviewed share the characteristics of the slacktivist critique, having engaged in some form of digital micro-activism.

A limitation of ethnographic research is that the researcher must interpret and construct their object of study for others (Geertz 1975). Overt observation also runs the risk that the objects of study may change their conduct. I try to minimise these concerns by complimenting the ethnographic data with evidence of member behaviour. Posts were collected from the group's Facebook page on a daily basis during the observation. Twitter data was gathered using Sysomos MAP, a text mining platform which grants access to the full Twitter "firehose" archive. All emails sent during this period were gathered through 38 Degrees' Blue State Digital (BSD) suite of campaigning tools, to which I was given access. Finally, online news articles relating to 38 Degrees were collected daily using Cutbot, a media monitoring service that collects news articles according to search criteria.

By drawing on this combination of data sources, this chapter has two aims. Firstly, what role does digital micro-activism play within the group's campaigns? By triangulating interview data from staff and members, social media content from campaigns, and first-hand observation notes, I examine whether 38 Degrees avoids slacktivism with its mobilisation strategy. Secondly, I analyse how individual members view digital micro-activism in relation to their role within the organisation.

The Role of Leaders in an OPEN Organisation

Before analysing how Facebook and Twitter are used within the group's campaigns, I offer a contextual overview of 38 Degrees at the organisational level. This is necessary, as the significance of digital micro-activism only becomes apparent through an evaluation of the role that the leadership plays. Much has been written about the group's influence on British politics, but this is often anecdotal or politically motivated (Liddle 2013; Rickett 2013). By offering clarity on the organisational structure and by determining how its member-centric philosophy operates in practice, this section will highlight the factors that set apart OPEN organisations from other advocacy groups (see Karpf [2012] on "organizing with different organizations").

38 Degrees bears little resemblance to the organisational models that scholars in political science have become accustomed to. Unlike political parties or traditional pressure groups, 38 Degrees operates on a more level playing field. Members play an important role in directing the group's day-to-day decision making. The organisation tries to foster what Amy describes as a "culture of mutuality" between the leadership team and the members (Interview 4, May 2013). Primarily, the organisation is designed to act as a conduit for its membership, removing some of the layers of elite-level decision making that characterised political groups of the late twentieth century.

Members are responsible for many decisions made throughout each campaign. By using digital tools that are diffused widely amongst its membership, grass-roots activists can express their opinion and set the group's priorities very quickly on an impressive scale. These priorities are generated through a number of qualitative and quantitative data sources, the most important of which are the results from a weekly online survey of a random sample of members, the analysis of email feedback, and the collection of communications on Facebook and Twitter (Interview 7, June 2013). By drawing on these data sources, forms of low-threshold, digital micro-activism are linked to substantive forms of political participation.

Alongside their use of social media, which I examine in the following section, the leadership use ad hoc surveys so that members can influence key decisions. As Amy (Interview 4, May 2013) notes, "we talk to our members about tactics… we regularly poll on key pivots within a campaign." During a campaign to lobby a leading energy provider to pay more corporation tax, members were consulted on whether the organisation should launch the campaign. Their ideas were sought for potential campaign tactics and, as shown in Fig. 4.1, members were given the final say as to whether or not 38 Degrees should try to organise a mass, "people-powered" switch away from the energy provider to alternative

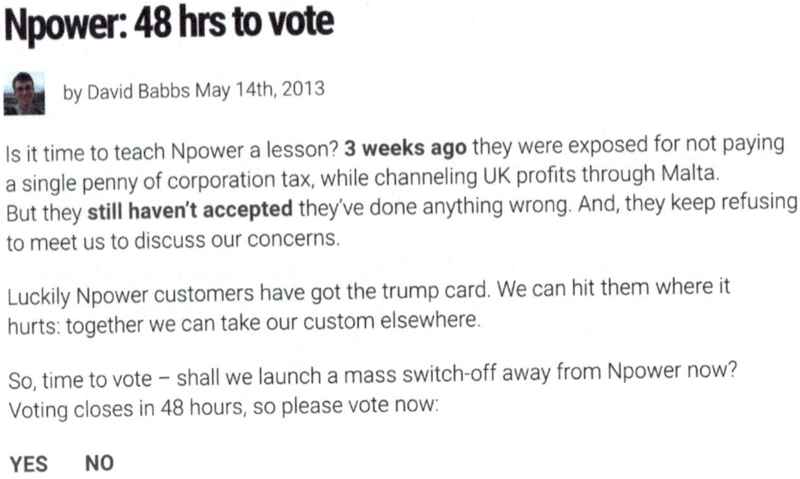

Npower: 48 hrs to vote

by David Babbs May 14th, 2013

Is it time to teach Npower a lesson? **3 weeks ago** they were exposed for not paying a single penny of corporation tax, while channeling UK profits through Malta.
But they **still haven't accepted** they've done anything wrong. And, they keep refusing to meet us to discuss our concerns.

Luckily Npower customers have got the trump card. We can hit them where it hurts: together we can take our custom elsewhere.

So, time to vote – shall we launch a mass switch-off away from Npower now? Voting closes in 48 hours, so please vote now:

YES **NO**

Fig. 4.1 A poll for members of 38 Degrees to decide on a campaign tactic (*Source* Babbs [2013])

suppliers (see Chadwick and Dennis 2017). Outside of these specific requests during a campaign, the leadership also seeks feedback on the group's overarching strategy. Members shape the long-term direction of the group through detailed surveys, such as in the run-up to a new calendar year (38 Degrees 2014a), or before an election (38 Degrees 2014b). For those involved, this is a clear and visible way of exerting their influence.

This member-centric approach was evident from the moment that I arrived at the group's London office. The leadership function performed by the office was immediately downplayed. A number of statements stood out during my induction for the role of volunteer: "use we, as opposed to us or them"; "talk about the movement and not the office"; and "never answer questions on a policy position as the central office does not make a position—members do." At first, I was sceptical about the feasibility of this in practice, but throughout my time observing the group it became clear that the leadership does try to design actions with the will of their members in mind.

However, 38 Degrees is not an example of "organizing without organizations" (Shirky 2008). The relationships formed within OPEN organisations are less hierarchical than their traditional counterparts, but they are not flat. As Jenkins argues, "leadership is a very necessary condition for participatory organizations to function" (Jenkins and Carpentier 2013: 15). The staff, based in the organisation's central London office, performs a gatekeeping role. They have an enhanced level of influence over the design and selection of campaign actions. Equally, this is not an elite-dominated hierarchy pretending to be member driven. The organisation relies on the central office to assimilate the priorities of its members and then offers repertoires of engagement. As such, the group's overall direction is decided by its membership. Gerbaudo (2012) describes this as "soft leadership," as the staff organises and structures the group's campaigns while minimising encroachment on the will of each member. The central team provides the technological capacity and campaigning expertise to realise the priorities established by the membership.

The terms of membership in an OPEN organisation are very different to those in legacy advocacy groups. Traditionally, one would become a member of a political organisation, be it a political party or a trade union, by opting into a shared, collective identity. The terms of membership were relatively straightforward: one paid a membership fee, received some formal recognition, often by way of a card, and signed up to a broad set of shared ideological principles. In this way, membership was deemed to be a reflection of one's character. By comparison, 38 Degrees operationalise a much more flexible definition of membership. From the leadership's perspective, one becomes a member by signing up to become an email recipient. In his analysis of MoveOn, Karpf (2012: 31) suggests that many email recipients may not be aware that they are in fact deemed to be members. However, what may appear disingenuous—after all, many political parties have substantial mailing lists—is a distinctive feature of the organisation and part of its attraction for citizens.

The imprecise parameters of this definition speak to the attachment formed between a citizen and the organisation, a relationship that is in constant flux. Some may seldom open the emails that they receive marked "38 Degrees," while others may take part in each and every action. By defining membership in this way, those involved are not tied to one fixed ideology but have the freedom to choose those campaigns they wish to be involved in. "Mike," a 24-year-old engineer from London, cites this self-determination as the primary reason for his association with the organisation (Interview 9, June 2013). Likewise, "George," a 63-year-old retired journalist from Birmingham, appreciates that the leadership does not pressure supporters to get involved (Interview 13, June 2013). Members value this control over the conditions of their participation.

In providing this choice, members can personalise and adapt their engagement to fit their own interests. Some of those that I spoke to drew on their own personal experiences when justifying why they initially got involved with 38 Degrees. For "Mary," this was a campaign to stop the impending closure of her local hospital (Interview 16, June 2013). For "Liam," his involvement grew out of his concern for members of his family who are public sector employees (Interview 19, October 2013). By campaigning on issues that have relevance in day-to-day life, the bond between the participant and the cause is intensified.

Perhaps where the significance of this new form of identification is most evident is when it is juxtaposed against a traditional custom of group-based politics. During my observation of the organisation, I arranged a members' meal in Wallington, South London. In this conventional, face-to-face setting the fundamental divides that exist between different supporters soon became apparent, be it on climate change, same-sex marriage, or one's right to privacy. However, following the lively debates that ensued, what was made abundantly clear to me was that what united my dinner guests was how much they all valued the freedom to act collectively, but on their terms.

Rickett (2013) has criticised these forms of engagement, arguing that they only require a shallow commitment from participants. It is true that the actions designed by the central office often require small amounts of effort, or more precisely time, but they are designed with this in mind. By making campaign actions granular, the leadership seeks to lower the barrier of entry to political participation. As Amy (Interview 4, May 2013) argues, lowering the costs associated with participation is part of the group's commitment to "people power," as the leadership tries to involve those citizens who may have been marginalised in the past:

> Time, who has time? As a rule, people with money and people without care and responsibilities, so that has a massive impact on class and politics, a massive impact on gender and politics, a massive impact on the way in which people who have a disability can engage with politics, etc. etc. You make it the preserve of people who are time-rich and who are

often also money-rich. To me, it isn't the kind of political system that I am very interested in perpetuating. So, do we make it easier for people to get involved? Absolutely, and I am massively proud of that.

The members that I interviewed also value this granularity (Interview 8, June 2013; Interview 22, November 2013).

Furthermore, 38 Degrees is not an "online-only" campaigning organisation. The leadership does not offer these forms of digital micro-activism in isolation, but, as the next section illustrates, connects them to different forms of participation as part of interconnected engagement repertoires. As "Adam," a technology manager at 38 Degrees, explains, each campaign will involve a range of ways a member can get involved, from an e-petition to more "high bar" actions, such as organising a local meeting or attending a demonstration (Interview 5, May 2013).

Therefore, I identify three factors that the leadership consider when designing a campaign, as shown in Fig. 4.2. Firstly, is this based on the

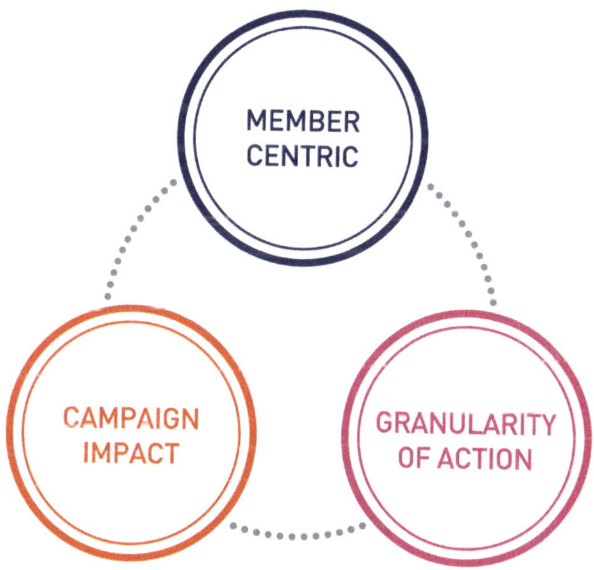

Fig. 4.2 Three factors that guide the organisational management of digital micro-activism

priorities established by the membership? As previously discussed, the central team use a range of digital technologies to track these priorities. Secondly, is the request for involvement inclusive? In other words, is it granular in a way that anyone could get involved, regardless of their comprehension of the subject matter, their campaigning experience, or the amount of time that they can offer to the cause? Finally, is there a clear theory of change (Vromen 2017)? Can members see why taking a specific action could lead to the desired result? What motivates members to devote more effort to a campaign is the belief that the group can produce substantive change. Ultimately, these three factors underpin what I describe as the organisational management of digital micro-activism, as the leadership of 38 Degrees craft opportunities for meaningful participation through the use of low effort, widely diffused forms of digital media.

Given its role in providing these opportunities, it is necessary to ask whether there is an ideological grounding that underpins the leadership. I found limited evidence to suggest that the staff share a cohesive set of ideals. Just like the discussions I witnessed at the members' meal, there were often fundamental differences amongst the leadership over campaign strategy. Instead, I argue that the underlying principles that guide the group are the mechanism and form of 38 Degrees as an OPEN organisation and its commitment to repertoires of action that are based on these three factors.

In using low-effort forms of digital communication to influence the way in which members act together, the leadership possesses significant agency over the group. However, contrary to liquid forms of leadership in other leaderless movements, where those who influence group behaviour wish to be seen as "anti-leaders" (Gerbaudo 2012: 13–14), the staff at 38 Degrees are very transparent about their role in the organisation. As David Babbs (Interview 7, June 2013) notes, the relationship between the staff in London and ordinary members is one of mutual dependency; the members provide the legitimacy and overall direction of the group, while the leaders bring the campaigning expertise and technological platforms that make their activism possible. This member-driven model of political mobilisation marks a significant development in the ongoing evolution of democratic engagement. What follows is a series of examples that I observed that illustrate how the central team uses Facebook and Twitter to craft these opportunities for member involvement across the continuum of participation.

Access: Political Learning and Priority Setting

"Access," as defined in Chapter 2, refers to cognitive engagement, the process that we experience when faced with new information. At first glance, one would not categorise 38 Degrees as a news provider, but it often fulfils this function for its members. Before launching a campaign, the leadership will post information relating to an issue on their Facebook Page (Interview 4, May 2013). For some members, this acts as an educative space, as they are exposed to new information as a by-product of their routine use of the platform.

In our interview, "Danni," a 24-year-old account manager at an advertising firm, spoke of the difficulty of following news on the issues that she cares about (Interview 22, November 2013). Although she visits the BBC News website daily, she feels that the selection of political information on offer is limited. By following 38 Degrees on Facebook, members feel that they can keep track of "alternative" perspectives that they would not otherwise be exposed to. As "Claire" describes, "I think it makes a lot of people aware of issues which they would not really know existed" (Interview 8, June 2013). In this way, the group's social media accounts act as a site of political learning.

Facebook, alongside questionnaires shared over email, is also used to determine the level of support for a new campaign or a specific tactic. By posting news items on the group's page, the central office can obtain qualitative and quantitative data from members in a short space of time. For example, before launching their campaign in response to allegations of tax avoidance by npower, a member of staff posted an article from the *Sun* onto their Facebook page, asking the membership to "Click LIKE and SHARE if you think 38 Degrees should campaign on this. Comment and let npower know what you think of them" (38 Degrees 2013b). The post received 2042 likes and 1254 shares, deemed by the leadership to be a sign of approval from the membership. Reflecting on this process, David Babbs, Executive Director of 38 Degrees (Interview 7, June 2013), notes, Facebook offers a vital consultative space, in which the leadership can ascertain the level of member support for an issue and how a potential campaign should be framed and conducted:

> Facebook is a real-time conversation space… I think it gives us two forms of input. It gives us a sense of energy levels around something, which helps us to decide whether we should campaign on this or not, but also when we

are communicating with our members about an issue, it gives us insights into the language they are using and the tone that they would expect us to adopt.

While one may question whether these digital interactions are valid and reliable measures of opinion for the wider membership[3] (Anstead and O'Loughlin 2015), members are aware and value the use of these metrics to approximate their level of support quickly. For Mike, Facebook Likes and comments are an "easy way of showing your feelings towards an issue" (Interview 9, June 2013). Similarly, "Helen" recognises the importance of these digital feedback loops to the group's style of campaigning; "I think its strength is the speed with which it can measure public opinion across a broad number of issues" (Interview 14, July 2013).

The immediacy of this coordinated response to professional news media coverage is a key feature of OPEN organisations. While other studies have highlighted the use of surveys and petitions for this function (Chadwick and Dennis 2017; Karpf 2016), expressive, low-threshold interactions on Facebook also diffuse some agency over decision making away from the central staff to members.

Connection and Expression: Network Building

"Connection," the second stage on the continuum of participation, refers to the relationships and networks formed by citizens. Due to the episodic involvement that members have with the group, selecting their participation on an issue-by-issue basis, the leadership must craft ways to foster bonds swiftly amongst these sedimentary networks. Although email is an essential tool for mass organisation-to-member communication, it has little value in facilitating member-to-member communication due to the mailing list being closed. As an alternative, member-to-member conversation on Facebook is encouraged. By using the service to interact with others, or even by observing these conversations on the group's Facebook page, the leadership aim for the geographically dispersed membership base to develop connections and a sense of collective identity around ad hoc issue campaigns (Interview 4; Interview 7, June 2013).

"Expression," the third stage of the continuum of participation, signifies the variety of ways in which citizens share their opinions. While members recognise the value of social media in "raising awareness"

(Interview 9, June 2013), "capturing a wider audience" (Interview 20, October 2013), and "building a movement" (Interview 10, June 2013), many of those that I interviewed were not willing to discuss political issues on the group's Facebook Page. "Ian," a 60-year-old teacher from Brighton, suggests that Facebook is not the right forum for "thrusting" one's opinions onto others, instead preferring to talk to people about politics face-to-face (Interview 17, October 2013). Others, like Mike, express their views to selected sub-groups through private messaging platforms (Interview 9, June 2013; Interview 22, November 2013). Furthermore, some recognise specific limitations when building support for campaigns on the group's Page. As Helen observes, "occasionally I'm not happy with the way a campaign's message has been worded on Facebook… I find it a bit simplistic" (Interview 14, July 2013). This tension between providing inclusive forms of digital participation that appeal to wider audiences on the platform, while also presenting the complexity of an issue, was evident throughout my observation of the central office.

Despite this unease with the group's Page, and Facebook more generally as a platform for political conversation, members were willing to share campaign material and express their opinions with their networked contacts on those issues that have personal relevance. As "Daniela" reflects, "if I feel strongly about it, then I share it with my friends" (Interview 10, June 2013). She frequently shares petitions and calls to action that relate to the environment or humanitarian disasters. These are issues that she noted were important to her. This personal activation was present across the sample. Liam's motivation was activism around health care (Interview 19, October 2013). For Claire, it was women's rights (Interview 8, June 2013). It is this choice over the campaigns that a member supports—a central feature of OPEN organisations—that provides the conditions to overcome technical and social reservations when posting political material on Facebook.

For the leadership, this self-expression forms a key role in their campaigns. The group's digital infrastructure is built upon a suite of technologies provided by BSD. These campaign management tools have a set of norms embedded within their design (see McKelvey and Piebiak 2016). Figure 4.3 illustrates a standard user journey for a 38 Degrees campaign on BSD, in which members are encouraged to share evidence of their behaviour with others.

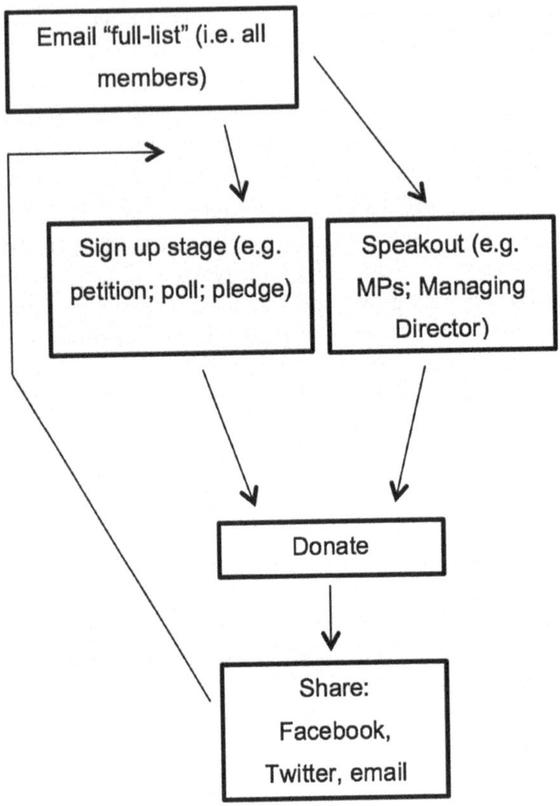

Fig. 4.3 A flowchart of a typical user journey for a 38 Degrees campaign on Blue State Digital

In isolation, sharing evidence of one's opinion or political action may seem ineffective. However, this ignores wider network effects. Expressive engagement can be fulfilling for the participant but can also educate and mobilise others in their network. Many of those members that I spoke to recognise the value of raising awareness amongst their peers (Interview 10; Interview 11, June 2013). A smaller number also noted how social media could be a trigger for further action, a way of enabling others "who are aware of an issue but may not know how to act" (Interview 11, June 2013). These network effects were demonstrated within the sample. Both Claire and "Siobhan" became members after seeing a petition on Facebook, while Danni had only been involved in campaigns as a result of the passionate engagement of her networked contacts (Interview 22, November 2013).

What makes this amplification an effective form of network building is the nature of the contacts who make up these networks, as members share personally expressive campaign material on social media with other users who, to a varying degree, depending on the nature of the relationship, have a vested interest in them. For example, during the campaign to influence the Transparency of Lobbying, Non-Party Campaigning and Trade Union Administration Bill in 2013, referred to as the "Gagging Law" due to the restrictions the bill proposed for political campaigning in general, the leadership provided a poster that members were asked to print off. Those involved personalised the images, indicating a cause of deep concern to them that would be restricted under the bill. Members were then asked to upload a photograph of their poster to social media. In doing this, the staff recognise the importance of expressive forms of engagement within their mobilisation strategy. They often encourage members to express how a specific issue impacts them personally. This not only provides symbolic empowerment and psychological rewards, such as enhanced feelings of efficacy for the individual but also represents a powerful tool for the mobilisation of others.

Action: A Service-Specific Logic

"Action," the final stage of the continuum of participation, refers to goal-orientated, public-political acts and those behaviours that complement other online and/or offline acts. During my time spent observing 38 Degrees, it was evident that the leadership uses social media for both purposes. What follows is a snapshot of two case studies, a campaign to gain support for an amendment to the Energy Bill to decarbonise the UK's electricity generation by 2030, and a series of local level efforts to galvanise resistance to the government's 2012 healthcare reforms. Facebook and Twitter are explored independently, as each service performs a different function.

In reading this chapter, the lack of discussion of the group's use of Twitter might be surprising; this is a significant observation. For 38 Degrees, the service has clearly defined roles. There was little evidence to suggest that the members that I met used the platform for political discussion with other members, outside of amplifying campaign actions through retweets (Interview 10; Interview 11, June 2013). Furthermore, based on data collected by the leadership team, Twitter is not as effective as email or Facebook in supporting further engagement (Interview 2; Interview 5, May 2013).

Twitter is predominantly used by members to lobby corporations, journalists, and political representatives, on the instruction of the leadership. The #vote4cleanpower campaign, conducted as part of a coalition of interest groups and NGOs, illustrates this. After initially taking to Facebook to ask members for their views on the Energy Bill and how to respond to it, the leadership decided to focus on gaining support for an amendment to decarbonise the UK's electricity generation by 2030. Initially, this campaign was coordinated over email, with a web tool created that enabled members to lobby their local MP by providing their postcode. This tactic is typical of the digitally enabled campaigning techniques used by OPEN organisations. It had some success, with 17 MPs, whom the group had identified as being undecided on the issue, committing to vote in support of the amendment. However, as the vote on the amendment drew closer the leadership switched their attention to Twitter, mobilising members to send tweets to undecided MPs in a strategic fashion. As Fig. 4.4, the email sent to members, illustrates, the rationale behind this action is that communication on Twitter is more instantaneous, responsive, and—crucially—public (Interview 5, May 2013).

The speed of this mobilisation is significant. Although the amendment was narrowly defeated by 23 votes, over 2000 tweets were sent by members over the course of the two hours between the call for participation and the parliamentary vote (Interview 7, May 2013).

Encouraging members to use Twitter fulfils multiple functions. Firstly, given the prominence of MPs on Twitter, with 544 of the 650 elected representatives now using the service,[4] the leadership use the social networking site as a way of providing a means of elite contact. Using a practice described by Zuckerman (2012) as "tweetbombing," the leadership organises members to send a tweet to at a specific time, targeting an elected representative as a way of drawing attention to an issue.

Secondly, this technique is strategically significant, as MPs seek to preserve and strengthen their reputation while using the service. Members were provided with pre-formatted tweets that included the Twitter username for their MP. This enabled each member to share their outrage with their MP directly, while also providing a public record of the controversial Energy Bill for others to see. As a tweet from the then Liberal Democrat MP for Bradford East shows (Ward 2013), some representatives responded to this pressure by outlining their intention to support the amendment. This example shows how Twitter is used by 38 Degrees as a platform for direct action.

At 4pm today, MPs will vote on whether to have a clean energy target to tackle climate change. **The result's on a knife edge, with the Telegraph predicting the government winning by just one vote.** [1] With the vote so close, **some wavering MPs really could have the deciding vote.** Their vote could decide between a future of dirty fossil fuels or clean energy.

If we can put enough pressure on them right now, we can still persuade them to vote the right way. **They may not check their emails before the vote, but they're on twitter.**

If enough voters tweet at the right MPs straight away then it might just be enough to push them to vote against dirty fossil fuels. They'll walk in to vote with the voices and wishes of the public ringing in their ears, and buzzing in their pocket.

Can you send a tweet to one of the undecided MPs right now and ask them to support clean energy?

Tweet : ., please #vote4cleanpower in this afternoon's vote

Fig. 4.4 A Twitter mobilisation targeted at undecided MPs (*Source* action@38degrees.org.uk, 2013. Just 1 vote for our climate [email]. Sent June 4, 2013. Retrieved June 4, 2013)

In contrast, Facebook is deployed by the leadership to support other forms of activism. This strategy in itself is not new. Several studies have outlined how digital technologies are used by OPEN organisations to support other tactics (Chadwick and Dennis 2017; Hall 2017; Karpf 2012; Vromen 2017). However, what is unique about the way in which 38 Degrees use Facebook is how it underpins structural transformations, as the membership displace the leadership's role in the design and implementation of campaign strategy.

The Health and Social Care Bill, which became UK law in 2012, radically overhauled local healthcare governance, as Primary Care Trusts (PCTs) and Strategic Health Authorities—responsible for the design of local healthcare services—were replaced by Clinical Commissioning Groups (CCGs). The bill enabled CCGs, formed of local General Practitioners (GPs), to tender local health services to providers from the private sector. In response to member demand, the leadership initially organised an e-petition. However, through further member communications and expert professional and legal advice, they later reshaped the spatial focus of the campaign.

The staff at 38 Degrees used Facebook to assist a structural shift, moving from a nationally coordinated, digitally networked action to a local-level, face-to-face mobilisation. Over 150 local groups were created that met face-to-face and were, crucially, semi-autonomous. Karpf (2012: 19) offers three distinct models to describe how netroots organisations use the Internet to organise, two of which are evident in this case study. In the initial phase, when the membership was encouraged to fund an event with GPs, to fund legal work, and to sign a localised e-petition, a "hub and spokes model" was in use. Here, I observed a large amount of organisation-to-member communication between the small central staff and the large membership base.

In contrast, the localised efforts reflect what Karpf (2012) describes as a "neo-federated model," in which digital tools were used to take control of campaign strategy. Facebook Groups became the organisational foundation for many of these local campaigns. George, who was involved with efforts in the Midlands, describes how they were used for internal communication, where members would discuss strategy, organise events, and arrange meetings with representatives from the CCG (Interview 15, August 2013). Likes, comments, and shares—dismissed by those advocating the slacktivist critique—provided the basis to form what George describes as a "coherent voice… an understanding amongst the group that reflects the various voices" (Interview 15, August 2013). As such, Facebook can act as an organisational tool for 38 Degrees, enabling the group to switch its structural form rapidly.

Understanding Micro-Level Motivations: Participatory Shortcuts with Influence

So far, this chapter has illustrated *how* 38 Degrees uses the low-threshold functionality of social media to mobilise its membership. But *why* do members decide to take part in these forms of digital micro-activism? Are 38 Degrees able to avoid the tokenistic, minimal commitment hypothesised by the slacktivist critique?

A primary reason that members give for their involvement in 38 Degrees is the participatory shortcuts described. Those that I interviewed stressed their value in providing opportunities for involvement for citizens excluded from traditional forms of activism. As Ian (Interview 17, August 2013) reflects, "[38 Degrees] provide a voice that otherwise would not be heard. Voices of people who may be stuck at home or be very busy and have relatively little time to get out there." Many spoke of the struggles of balancing political involvement with family (Interview 13, June 2013), work (Interview 19, August 2013), and social commitments (Interview 17, October 2013).

"Geraldine," a 68-year-old member from Liverpool, is emblematic of this marginalisation. She spoke of the difficulties in remaining politically active while also caring for her husband. For her, 38 Degrees "reach people who don't normally get involved in political issues. People like myself who can't get out and get on the bandwagon… they are reaching the ordinary people" (Interview 13, June 2013). Members recognise the value of digital micro-activism in achieving this. "Joan," a 73-year-old artist from London, stresses the importance of 38 Degrees as a "campaigning tool", one that offers a host of tactical shortcuts; "they make it easy for you to choose campaigns, easy for you to email your MP, easy to shape your own letter from the points and the information that they give you" (Interview 21, October 2013). These forms of digital micro-activism provide democratic shortcuts for members who may lack the expertise, technical skills, and/or time to do these acts independently (Interview 15, August 2013; Interview 19, October 2013).

When considering the democratic value of these shortcuts, the slacktivist critique suggests that these quick and easy fixes may satisfy one's desire for political involvement, reducing the desire to engage further. Despite the theory of change approach used by the leadership, in which member involvement is scaled (Vromen 2017), some feel that they cannot commit to campaigns as they progress. For Danni, this is due to a perceived lack of time for follow-up activities, despite her support for an issue (Interview 22, November 2013). George (Interview 15, August 2013) experienced this reluctance to commit to higher threshold activities first hand when he took a leading role in local efforts to minimise the impact of the Health and Social Care Act:

> There members that have been signatories to what we've been about for a long time. I haven't actually seen them at a meeting, but I know that they open the newsletters and I know that they go on to sign petitions and things like that. I think 38 Degrees' needs to be addressing them as well, making them feel, if they want to, they can do just a little bit more.

This can have a detrimental effect on morale amongst those highly involved members, as Helen indicated to me following a disappointing turnout at a protest (Interview 14, July 2013).

However, this is not to say that the members that I interviewed at various campaign events deem this digital engagement to be lazy or insignificant. Rather, it is this expression of digital preferences that underpins the legitimacy of the group. As George (Interview 15, August 2013) observes, "they may not all be totally active, in fact, chances are that they're not, but even if a third of them or a fifth of them are engaged, that's a substantial body of people." Volume here is key. A single Facebook Like may seem insignificant, but collectively, thousands of Likes can help represent the priorities of the wider membership.

It is this sense of involvement in the internal decision-making processes of the group that helps to explain its attraction. Whether it be through the visible metrics embedded within Facebook, ad hoc surveys on key decisions within a campaign, or detailed questionnaires about the long-term direction of the group, members *feel* that they play a decisive role in formulating and shaping campaigns. This relates to an individual's sense of personal efficacy. The digital feedback loops that staff at 38 Degrees deploy in their campaigning provide members with the feeling that their participation has value. For Liam, it is the perception that the leadership listen to members: "it has given me a platform in which I feel like my opinion is being acknowledged and registered" (Interview 19, October 2013). Others extend this logic, reflecting how they feel that members are responsible for key decisions, and not the leadership. Danni explains this by describing the staff team in London as "facilitators," providing the technological capacity and campaigning expertise to realise the priorities established by the membership (Interview 22, November 2013). George argues that it is this sense of autonomy and influence that explains the group's popularity: "this is where 38 Degrees' strength lies… in giving people tools that they can use to pursue campaigns" (Interview 15, August 2013). By using forms of digital listening, members feel like they wield some influence over key decisions within the selection, design, and execution of each campaign.

Just as members value their influence within the organisation, they also place significant emphasis on political outcomes, and the ability to initiate political change. As one may expect given the sampling frame, all members that I spoke to felt strongly that 38 Degrees are a powerful campaigning group in British politics. While some listed examples of policy impact (Interview 8, June 2013), others noted the symbolic influence the group had in ensuring that elected representatives and corporations "acknowledge the discontent of citizens" (Interview 9, June 2013). The leadership recognises the importance of this perception of real-world impact and uses social media platforms to involve the membership when the group succeeds. When a 38 Degrees campaign achieves its stated objective, the leadership takes to social media to celebrate. Figure 4.5 illustrates how

Fig. 4.5 An example of 38 Degrees using Facebook to involve members in a campaign victory (*Source* 38 Degrees [2013a])

contributions from members had led to Cumbria County Council voting against building a nuclear waste facility (38 Degrees 2013a). This generates feelings of self-efficacy amongst members and helps to strengthen their attachment to the group (Interview 8, June 2013).

Conclusion: The Organisational Management of Digital Micro-Activism

> A 'like' or retweet can be either powerful or pointless—it depends on the broader strategic context of these acts of digital communication.
>
> (Karpf 2016: 1)

Several findings from this chapter challenge the slacktivist critique, illustrating how OPEN organisations avoid slacktivism with their mobilisation strategy. Firstly, digital micro-activism can be effective under certain conditions. When used strategically, Facebook provides feedback loops for 38 Degrees, enabling the leadership to diffuse some decision-making responsibilities to members. In doing so, this study offers further empirical support to what Karpf (2016) describes as "analytic activism," as the leadership of 38 Degrees use social media data to listen and respond to the priorities of its members. When determining the level of support behind an issue or generating ideas for a specific campaign, low-effort forms of digital micro-activism—such as liking, commenting, and sharing on social media—provide a means for members to shape and influence campaign strategies. In isolation, these acts may seem trivial. However, when examined at scale across a continuum of participation, Facebook provides opportunities for members to shape the direction of the organisation.

This has significant implications when we consider the debates around slacktivism. Integral to this critique is the claim that low-threshold digital interactions have no material impact; they do not form a link to institutional decision making or the policymaking process. On first glance, the group's membership does seem to share the defining characteristics of slacktivists. They share political views to their networks on social media by way of self-gratification, and the actions designed by the leadership require very little time from those involved. However, by embedding myself within the organisation, and by contextualising the behaviours derided as slacktivism within the group's broader campaign strategies, the findings from this study suggest that these behaviours amount to more than just banal self-expression. Instead, in what I describe as the organisational management of digital micro-activism, the leadership deploys these mundane tools in political contexts in which they are symbolically empowering *and* have a material impact.

This study also illustrates how the citizens involved understand this analytic activism. Amongst those members that I interviewed, the digital feedback loops provided by emails, petitions, and Facebook, are a key justification for their involvement. The legitimacy of the organisation comes directly from these forms of digital micro-activism, and the perception that one's preferences and actions have value. They recognise the strategic context of this digital listening and cite this as a reason for their involvement with 38 Degrees, rather than a political party (Interview 15; Interview 17, August 2013). As Hensby et al. (2011: 820) argue, citizens increasingly seek to be more than "surrogate participants," relied upon for donations. These feedback loops are important for their sense of personal efficacy.

Secondly, this chapter supports the findings of survey-based studies (Bode 2017; Christensen 2012; Vaccari et al. 2015) in challenging the substitution thesis; digital participation compliments tried-and-tested activist repertoires. Some of the innovative forms of on-the-ground activism organised by 38 Degrees are only made possible by the technological affordances of Facebook. The "Save Our NHS" campaign illustrates how the platform can be used to support a rapid structural transformation, from a national, centrally managed e-petition, to over 150 semi-autonomous local groups. Emotive self-expression within personalised networks on Facebook is integral to the amplification of a cause.

Thirdly, these forms of digital micro-activism are, as the slacktivist critique suggests, easy; they are deliberately designed this way to lower the costs associated with participation (Interview 4, May 2013). The context here is key. Irrespective of scale, metrics are meaningless to campaigners without a clear theory of change. For 38 Degrees, the central team in London draw on their campaigning expertise to give strategic value to these actions. When these low-threshold behaviours form part of organisational feedback loops (Facebook) or are deployed at tactically significant moments (Twitter), digital micro-activism can act as a democratic shortcut. Rather than being an easy way of avoiding political involvement, this organisational management of digital micro-activism acts as a bridge to sites of power for ordinary members.

However, there are inherent tensions between the democratic shortcuts provided and collective action that requires strong-tie relationships. The localised activism formed in response to the UK government's healthcare reforms illustrates how Facebook can be used to support a rapid structural shift from a leader-led digital mobilisation to a more traditional form of organisational politics (Chadwick 2007). However, as George identified, this can lack scale, with declining levels of participation as the campaign progressed. Therefore, there is an important distinction to be made between mobilisation and organisation.

This study offers some support to those who argue that social media limits some forms of organisational politics (Gladwell 2010; Morozov 2011). When a campaign requires strong-tie relationships that are built around a collective identity, these democratic shortcuts are less useful. Their strategic utility is dependent on how members use Facebook. Fostering such close connections is difficult given the reluctance of some members to engage in conversation on the group's public Facebook page. The complex social and reputational dynamics of public-political expression mean that many would rather discuss campaigns within semi-public or private spaces. Furthermore, while democratic shortcuts may provide pathways to engagement for previously marginalised citizens (Bode 2017), they do not guarantee further involvement. By examining the group's campaigning across a continuum of participation, it is evident that some members are unable or unwilling to engage in an extended repertoire of actions. This drop-off in supporters can impact morale for the most engaged.

Finally, this study challenges the hypothesis that reputation management underpins digital micro-activism on social media. 38 Degrees activists mobilise around issues that are personally relevant. In itself, this finding is not new; this is a defining feature of OPEN organisations (Chadwick 2007; Karpf 2012; Vromen 2017). What this chapter adds is a starting point for understanding how this self-determination influences the political behaviour of 38 Degrees activists on social media. When members do participate in public forms of self-expression and digital micro-activism, these acts are not triggered by inauthentic reputational management or the ease of the act itself, but by issues that resonate with their own privately held beliefs. The conditions of this personalised activation are examined in detail in the following two chapters, as I analyse the political information and news that citizens are exposed to on Facebook and Twitter during everyday use.

Notes

1. Members do not have to pay a membership fee but can donate to the organisation if they wish. As with MoveOn in the United States, 38 Degrees "redefines membership from 'small donor' to 'message recipient'" (Karpf 2012: 31).
2. The term "craft" refers to the processes in which campaign staff design opportunities for citizen engagement using digital technologies. This

concept originates from Kreiss' (2010: 23) study of Howard Dean's campaign for the Democratic presidential nomination in 2004.

3. There is a significant discrepancy between the total number of members included on the group's mailing list, at over 3 million, and the 389,255 Facebook users who follow the 38 Degrees page. However, given that anyone who has signed a petition on the organisation's website is included on their mailing list, this total is not an accurate measure of active members. These figures are correct as of March 2018.
4. Figure correct as of May 2018, see http://twitter.com/tweetminster/lists/ukmps.

References

38 Degrees. (2013a, January 31). Success! *Facebook Update*. Retrieved May 20, 2018, from https://www.facebook.com/peoplepowerchange/photos/a.457255765787.382103.200006375787/10152483133555788/?type=3.

38 Degrees. (2013b, April 17). Are Npower the New Starbucks? *Facebook Update*. Retrieved September 15, 2015, from https://www.facebook.com/peoplepowerchange/posts/10152754455415788.

38 Degrees. (2014a, January 7). *New Year Survey*. Retrieved January 7, 2014, from https://secure.38degrees.org.uk/new%C2%ADyear%C2%ADsurvey.

38 Degrees. (2014b, July 7). *Choose Your Priority Issues*. Retrieved July 9, 2014, from https://secure.38degrees.org.uk/page/s/priorities-your-most-important-issues.

Anstead, N., & O'Loughlin, B. (2015). Social Media Analysis and Public Opinion: The 2010 UK General Election. *Journal of Computer-Mediated Communication, 20*(2), 204–220.

Babbs, D. (2013, May 14). Npower: 48 Hrs to Vote. *38 Degrees*. Retrieved May 22, 2013, from http://blog.38degrees.org.uk/2013/05/14/npower-48-hrs-to-vote/.

Bode, L. (2017). Gateway Political Behaviors: The Frequency and Consequences of Low-Cost Political Engagement on Social Media. *Social Media + Society, 3*(4). Retrieved from https://doi.org/10.1177/2056305117743349.

Chadwick, A. (2007). Digital Network Repertoires and Organizational Hybridity. *Political Communication, 24*(3), 283–301.

Chadwick, A., & Dennis, J. (2017). Social Media, Professional Media and Mobilisation in Contemporary Britain: Explaining the Strengths and Weaknesses of the Citizens' Movement 38 Degrees. *Political Studies, 65*(1), 42–60.

Christensen, H. S. (2012). Simply Slacktivism? Internet Participation in Finland. *eJournal of eDemocracy & Open Government, 4*(1), 1–23.

Davies, D. T. C. (2014). HC Deb 11 March 2014, Vol 577, Col 256.

Eliasoph, N. (1998). *Avoiding Politics: How Americans Produce Apathy in Everyday Life*. Cambridge: Cambridge University Press.

Geertz, C. (1975). Thick Description: Toward an Interpretive Theory of Culture. In C. Geertz (Ed.), *The Interpretation of Cultures: Selected Essays* (pp. 3–32). New York: Basic Books.

Gerbaudo, P. (2012). *Tweets and the Streets: Social Media and Contemporary Action*. London: Pluto Press.

Gladwell, M. (2010, October 4). Small Change: Why the Revolution Will Not Be Tweeted. *The New Yorker*. Retrieved November 3, 2010, from https://www.newyorker.com/magazine/2010/10/04/small-change-malcolm-gladwell.

Hall, N. (2017). Innovations in Activism in the Digital Era. In Hertie School of Governance (Ed.), *The Governance Report 2017* (pp. 143–156). Oxford: Oxford University Press.

Hensby, A., Sibthorpe, J., & Driver, S. (2011). Resisting the 'Protest Business': Bureaucracy, Postbureaucracy and Active Membership in Social Movement Organizations. *Organization, 19*(6), 809–823.

Howard, P. N. (2011). *Castells and the Media*. Cambridge: Polity.

James, S. B. (2014, January 22). Tory MP Brands 38 Degrees Campaign as 'Stupid'. *Third Sector*. Retrieved from http://www.thirdsector.co.uk/Policy_and_Politics/article/1228234/tory-mp-brands-38-degrees-campaign-stupid/.

Jenkins, H., & Carpentier, N. (2013). Theorizing Participatory Intensities: A Conversation About Participation and Politics. *Convergence: The International Journal of Research into New Media, 19*(3), 265–286.

Karpf, D. (2012). *The MoveOn Effect: The Unexpected Transformation of American Political Advocacy*. Oxford: Oxford University Press.

Karpf, D. (2016). *Analytic Activism: Digital Listening and the New Political Strategy*. Oxford: Oxford University Press.

Kreiss, D. (2010). *Taking Our Country Back? Political Consultants and the Crafting of Networked Politics from Howard Dean to Barack Obama* (Doctoral dissertation, Stanford University).

Liddle, R. (2013, March 10). Placards? They're so Last Year. Make Way for the Mighty Mouse. *The Sunday Times*. Retrieved March 10, 2013, from http://www.thesundaytimes.co.uk/sto/Magazine/Features/article1225047.ece?shareToken=1eb4425e171e4a1ecda5d2c956c0540d.

McKelvey, F., & Piebiak, J. (2016). Porting the Political Campaign: The Nationbuilder Platform and the Global Flows of Political Technology. *New Media & Society, 20*(3), 901–918.

Morozov, E. (2011). *The Net Delusion: How Not to Liberate the World*. London: Penguin.

Rickett, O. (2013, November 22). Want to Change the World? It Won't Happen Via Your Mouse Button. *The Guardian*. Retrieved March 20, 2014, from http://www.theguardian.com/commentisfree/2013/nov/22/change-the-world-charity-facebook-e-petition.

Sayer Vincent. (2017, January 31). *38 Degrees: Report and Financial Statements for the Year Ended 30 September 2016*. Retrieved May 20, 2018, from https://files.38degrees.org.uk/items/files/000/000/097/original/38_Degrees_final_accounts_2016_%281%29.pdf.

Shirky, C. (2008). *Here Comes Everybody: The Power of Organizing Without Organizations*. London: Allen Lane.

Vaccari, C., Valeriani, A., Barberá, P., Bonneau, R., Jost, J. T., Nagler, J., & Tucker, J. (2015). Political Expression and Action on Social Media: Exploring the Relationship Between Lower- and Higher-Threshold Political Activities Among Twitter Users in Italy. *Journal of Computer-Mediated Communication, 20*(2), 221–239.

Vromen, A. (2017). *Digital Citizenship and Political Engagement: The Challenge from Online Campaigning and Advocacy Organisations*. Basingstoke: Palgrave Macmillan.

Vromen, A., & Coleman, W. (2013). Online Campaigning Organizations and Storytelling Strategies: Getup! in Australia. *Policy and Internet, 5*(1), 76–100.

Ward, D. [DWard]. (2013, June 4). Having Considered All Arguments & Listened to Debate Today, I Will Be Voting for #vote4cleanpower and the #2030decarb Target in #energybill. *Tweet*. Retrieved May 20, 2018, from https://twitter.com/DWard/status/341906513117474816.

Zuckerman, E. (2012, April 20). *The Tweetbomb and the Ethics of Attention*. Retrieved April 25, 2012, from http://www.ethanzuckerman.com/blog/2012/04/20/the-tweetbomb-and-the-ethics-of-attention/.

CHAPTER 5

An Informed Public? News Consumption on Social Media

A key feature of slacktivism is a critique of the type of issues that result in large-scale mobilisation on social media. As outlined in Chapter 2, a handful of viral campaigns have been used to argue that the networked characteristics of these platforms result in users being swayed by the popularity of an issue, rather than its normative value (Morozov 2011; Sunstein 2007). This leads to widespread support for flawed campaigns at the expense of other more deserving or urgent causes. As the selection of examples used to explain the concept on Wikipedia illustrates,[1] there are two distinct observations about political behaviour present within this critique.

Firstly, the political issues that slacktivists prioritise on social media are driven by narcissism, rather than genuine intent. As users are aware that their online behaviour is visible, they engage in digital micro-activism as a form of self-presentation, showing their friends and followers that they are politically active and care about significant social issues. The #BringBackOurGirls campaign, formed following the kidnapping of 276 schoolgirls in Chibok, Nigeria, by the extremist organisation Boko Haram, is a commonly cited example of this. As the now iconic image of the then US First Lady Michelle Obama in Fig. 5.1 illustrates, politicians, celebrities, and citizens took to Twitter in their droves to raise awareness of the issue and campaign for the girls' release. The hashtag went viral, recording over four million mentions in 2014 (Olson 2016). However, like the aforementioned #Kony2012 campaign, the depth of

J. Dennis, *Beyond Slacktivism*,
Interest Groups, Advocacy and Democracy Series,
https://doi.org/10.1007/978-3-030-00844-4_5

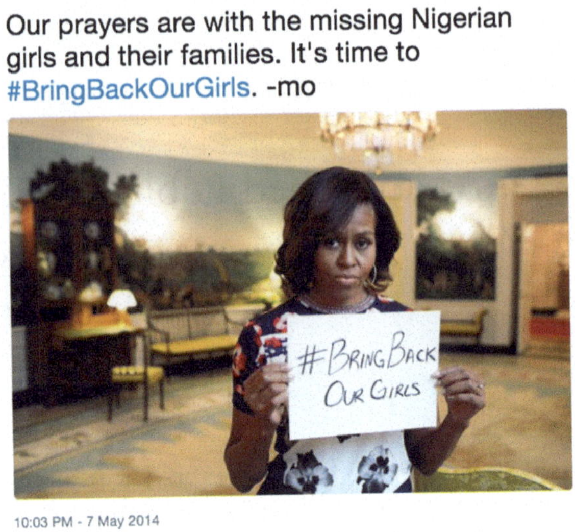

Fig. 5.1 A tweet in support of #BringBackOurGirls by Former First Lady Michelle Obama (*Source* Obama [2014])

involvement required from supporters was questioned, with many highlighting the lack of practical, offline actions undertaken to secure the release of the girls (Chiluwa and Ifukor 2015). Given such seemingly low levels of engagement, some argued that this was not a genuine commitment, but a form of virtue signalling, an expression of moral values done primarily with the aim of enhancing standing within a social group. In this way, digital micro-activism is individualistic, as those involved select issues on the basis of reputational benefits, rather than collective rewards.

Secondly, the slacktivist critique claims that the credibility of viral campaigns can vary substantially. As users navigate platforms that are characterised by fast information dissemination and affective expression (see Wahl-Jorgensen 2018), quick emotional triggers may take precedence over thoughtful and rational critique. This can lead to political attitudes and behaviours being formed on misinformation. Figure 5.2 shows a tweet from the now defunct Twitter account, @AmazingPicz, in which users were asked to share an image of cats seemingly in distress by way of indicating their opposition to animal testing. Over 5000 users did this, despite it being a hoax. The photography was taken from an article in a local US newspaper, the *Gainsville Sun*, which explained that

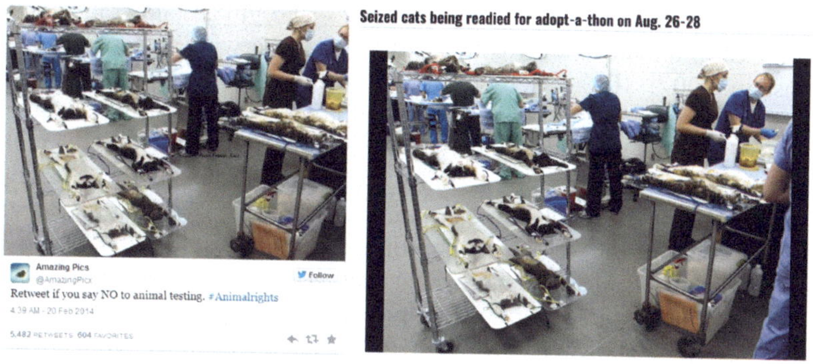

Fig. 5.2 A hoax tweet on animal testing and the original news story it misrepresents (*Source* Amazing Pics [2014] and Swirko [2011])

the cats were not being tested on, but spayed in advance of an adoption drive (Speaking of Research 2014). What was presented as a cruel act was in fact a form of charity, as the cats were rescued from an abusive sanctuary. Such deception is often associated with digital micro-activism.

But are these cases actually representative of day-to-day news consumption on social media? Do they reflect the kind of political issues that users pay attention to and reflect upon during everyday use? The critique certainly connects with wider concerns about the growing dependency on social networking sites for news. Popular commentary around recent seismic political events in the UK has firmly placed Facebook and Twitter in the spotlight. Whether it is the suggestion that Russian bots on Twitter tried to swing the 2017 general election in favour of the Labour Party (*Sunday Times* 2018), or the claim that echo chambers on Facebook contributed to the shock decision to leave the European Union (Bell 2016), social media is increasingly presented as an impediment to the ideal of an informed public.

Classical theories of democracy are based on the belief that citizens should be reasonably well informed about public affairs (see Chapter 3). For Sunstein (2007), collective exposure to a discrete set of news stories, events, and issues is vital in this aim. Drawing on the example of the Super Bowl, the annual championship game of the National Football League (NFL), he argues that it is through shared experiences like this that communal identity is formed and maintained. These common experiences provide what he describes as "social glue," allowing people to find commonalities with others who may otherwise seem unfamiliar (Sunstein 2007: 103). Such social interactions can help build mutual trust and respect across dissimilar communities. While it is unrealistic to expect all citizens to prioritise hard news within their normal media consumption, in an era of limited choice, accidental exposure to news and civic information was relatively common (Downs 1957; Neuman et al. 1992). Consider the sports fan waiting for the latest results during a televised news broadcast. This citizen may acquire political information as a by-product of a seemingly non-political activity. With digital media providing more choice and control to citizens, Sunstein warns of the risks of audience fragmentation. If citizens can avoid certain perspectives (Powers 2017), or common experiences, or even ignore politics entirely (Iyengar et al. 2008; Prior 2005, 2007), then society risks becoming more polarised, as diverse groups share fewer reference points on which to form relationships. Therefore, the opportunities for selective exposure presented by social media can be seen as a direct threat to democracy itself.

This personalisation can come in two forms. Firstly, audiences exert substantially more control over their news intake (Negroponte 1995). Existing research shows that citizens use digital media to personally tailor the information they consume around niche topics (Anderson 2004; Tewksbury and Rittenberg 2012). With the growth of online news organisations, such as BuzzFeed, the Huffington Post, and VICE (Küng 2015), and the increasing popularity of user-generated content and citizen journalism (Barnes 2016), audiences have a much greater variety of sources to choose from. Practically, this manual personalisation occurs through the decisions that someone takes to filter this information. The seemingly simple choices about the websites we choose to visit and the Facebook Pages and Twitter accounts that we choose to follow have significant implications for our awareness and understanding of civic issues.

Secondly, devices, software, and platforms that use machine-learning to share personally relevant content are becoming increasingly popular. Many of the digital products and services that we use day-to-day feature some element of algorithmic personalisation, drawing on rich data sets on a user's habits, preferences, and identity categorisations to personalise the experience provided (Kant 2016). The example most relevant to this book is the News Feed, the constantly updating list of posts that feature on a user's home page on Facebook. In 2014, Mark Zuckerberg, CEO of Facebook, described his vision for the News Feed: "our goal is to build the perfect personalised newspaper for every person in the world. We're trying to personalise it and show you the stuff that's going to be most interesting to you" (Flynn 2018). In order to prioritise posts from the wealth of content produced by a user's Friends, the Pages they follow, and those organisations that target them with advertisements, the News Feed algorithm draws on over 100,000 highly personalised factors (Constine 2016). While little is known about the precise make-up of this algorithm, behavioural signals, such as the volume of likes and shares on a post and the history of interactions with the author, are key factors in determining a user's top posts.[2]

As more news organisations are enticed by the potential audience they can reach through distributed content, outputs that publishers create to be consumed natively on another platform (e.g. Facebook Instant Articles; Google Accelerated Mobile Pages), some warn that personalisation will result in filter bubbles, whereby citizens become separated from information they disagree with or do not find interesting. Building on Sunstein's (2007) concerns over selective exposure, Pariser (2011) warns that algorithmic personalisation will ultimately lead to users consuming a much narrower selection of news and information. In effect, companies like Facebook adopt a gatekeeping function. Where in the past journalists would take the lead on editorial decisions about the news that we consume, these choices are increasingly being made by algorithms (Powers 2017: 1316–1317).

This argument is exemplified in the dissemination of news relating to the 2014 protests in Ferguson, USA, which followed the fatal shooting of Michael Brown by a police officer. Tufekci (2014) highlighted how, on August 14 with the unrest at its peak, her Twitter feed provided a constant stream of updates from both journalists and citizens on the ground. However, she found that the story received very little coverage on Facebook. This is what Tufekci describes as "algorithmic censorship," as content personalisation supersedes more pressing political and social issues. Crucially, these are topics that an editor of a newspaper would prioritise. Instead, Facebook users were inundated with videos of the Ice Bucket Challenge, a fundraising activity in which someone is filmed pouring ice and water onto their head to raise money for research into Motor Neurone Disease (Zuckerman 2014). Therefore, the role that algorithms play in determining news prioritisation and subsequent attention is significant.

The next two chapters analyse how 29 digitally active citizens use social media in their day-to-day lives. By drawing on a mixed-method research design, in which evidence of citizen behaviour on Facebook and Twitter is contextualised with interviews and reflective weekly diary entries collected over three months, I analyse the effect of routine social media use on political engagement. In this chapter, I focus on how citizens consume news from these platforms within their day-to-day lives. Given the fears that personalisation may result in audience fragmentation and acts of slacktivism, I explore the issues and events that these users are exposed to. By producing rich accounts of media use at the individual level, this research examines how Facebook and Twitter shape perceptions of public issues.

I argue that media habits are considerably more complex—and potentially less damaging—than these critiques assume. By comparing the content of the diaries with the lead stories of four British newspapers, I show that personal identity increasingly drives more individualised forms of news consumption. Both Twitter and, to a lesser extent, Facebook are used to tailor updates around a user's own interests. However, the implications of this personalisation for democratic engagement do not reflect the ominous forecasts of the slacktivist critique; in this study, there was no evidence of selective exposure leading to harmful audience fragmentation. The comparison between the diaries and newspaper coverage illustrates that this personalisation was balanced by moments of collective exposure, as citizens focused their attention on public issues. These shared experiences are sometimes triggered by accidental exposure on social media.

Method Notes

> The problem of 'effects' is one of the oldest and most intractable in media research: the way forward is to avoid trying to show what people *believe* changes as a result of *particular* media content. We are interested instead in what people *regularly do*, and the conditions under which they are able to act.
>
> (Couldry 2012: 84, emphasis in original)

Two conceptual realities pose methodological difficulties when trying to examine contemporary news consumption. Firstly, given the emphasis on personalised political identity within contemporary studies of citizenship (Bennett 2012; Dalton 2008; Norris 2011), it is necessary that empirical work engages with a citizen's own understanding of what constitutes the "political," and how this influences the news that they consume and, crucially, prioritise (see Chapter 3). If we are to understand the empirical relevance of popular theories like slacktivism and the filter bubble phenomenon, we need to go beyond an examination of the news that people see on social media; exposure does not equal understanding. As Couldry (2012: 84) observes above, researchers must examine the context of news consumption. For instance, what information is taken away from a story? How does this relate to broader attitudes and beliefs? Does this shape political behaviour?

Secondly, these attitudinal and behavioural reflections must also be explored in relation to media use within a hybrid media system (Chadwick 2013), where online and offline informational stimulants converge and overlap in unpredictable ways. As such, the data required to analyse the effect of social media on political learning and on the formulation of attitudes is fragmented. The interactions that shape these often take place across a range of overlapping public, semi-public, and private spaces. This requires new methodological approaches that observe and analyse political communication across media (Bode and Vraga 2017).

I seek to overcome these challenges through a multi-method research design, combining personalised diary data, interviews, and evidence of participant behaviour collected from Facebook and Twitter. This research design, adapted from the approach used by Couldry, Livingstone, and Markham in *Media Consumption and Public Engagement* (2010), provides a basis to track a participant's reflections on political news across online and offline spaces. In total, 29 diarists completed weekly, free-form diary updates over a period of three months between October 2013 and March 2014. Participants were asked to reflect on how they use different forms of media, but were not given direction over the length or structure of the diary. This was done purposefully to encourage reflection on whatever political issues participants deemed to be important and to track the different spaces in which participants consume news.

A semi-structured interview was conducted with each participant before they began the project. This provided a sense of each participant's background and the issues that they had an existing interest in. Following this, all public posts on Facebook (561 posts) and Twitter

(1008 tweets) were collected to explore what topics were discussed on social media.

Alongside the diaries, I also maintained a database of the cover stories from the front pages of four British newspapers: the *Sun*, the *Daily Mail*, *The Times*, and the *Guardian*. This data is used to compare the relative prominence of news stories in the press with those reported in the diaries, exploring the hypothesis that diarists use Facebook and Twitter to personalise their news consumption and avoid the communal experiences deemed necessary to form societal bonds.

This study uses a non-random, convenience sampling frame based on the target population: British citizens that use Facebook and/or Twitter. As such, this study is not representative of the wider British public or the user base of each platform (boyd and Crawford 2012; Sloan 2017). This convenience sample was designed intentionally to identify participants with media habits and a political interest that was reflective of the slacktivist critique. Of the 29 diarists, 24 had a Facebook account and 20 used Twitter, with two diarists included who do not use either service, as a control. Political interest was calculated through a measure of political activity, which, when compared to the findings of the *Audit of Political Engagement* (Hansard Society 2014), suggested that participants were generally representative of the target population. Further information on this sampling frame, the methodology more generally, and its limitations, is provided in the Research Appendix.

Accessing News: Personalisation and Increasing Diversity

This study is inspired by the work of Couldry et al. (2010), and their use of diaries to analyse "public connection" in Britain. Rather than focusing on an impossible ideal of a society that gives full and continuous attention to news and current affairs, public connection refers to "a basic level of orientation that can reliably, particularly at times such as elections, be translated into attention" (Couldry et al. 2010: 3). Undertaken between February and July 2004, their research found that most diarists displayed such a connection, but did so as a result of more conventional forms of media consumption. While regular engagement with broadcast and print media provided the necessary preconditions for democratic engagement, they found little evidence to suggest that regular Internet use could fulfil the same role (Couldry et al. 2010: 181–183).

Over a decade later, the public's media habits have changed greatly. In their study, just four of the 21 diarists used the Internet as a source of news (Couldry et al. 2010: 98). In this project, 19 of the 26 participants use online media as their primary source, as shown in Fig. 5.3.[3] Although the extent of this shift is somewhat indicative of the sampling frame used,[4] the Reuters Institute for the Study of Journalism found that 41% of those British citizens with Internet access use it as their main source of news (Newman et al. 2017). These changes pose questions about the information that users are exposed to online, and whether this impacts how citizens perceive public issues.

There was great variety in the sources that diarists turn to for news, as participants often combined digital sources with traditional media within their daily routines. As we may expect, the digital versions of a number of legacy news media outlets were very popular. Almost every diarist (26) accessed BBC News Online in some form during the study, most commonly by directly accessing the organisation's website. For "Angela," "Danny," and "Sam," the BBC was their first port of call when seeking the latest updates on current affairs. Others were less dependent but still relied on the public service broadcaster at key moments. For instance, "Will" (pre-diary interview) would only access the BBC News website

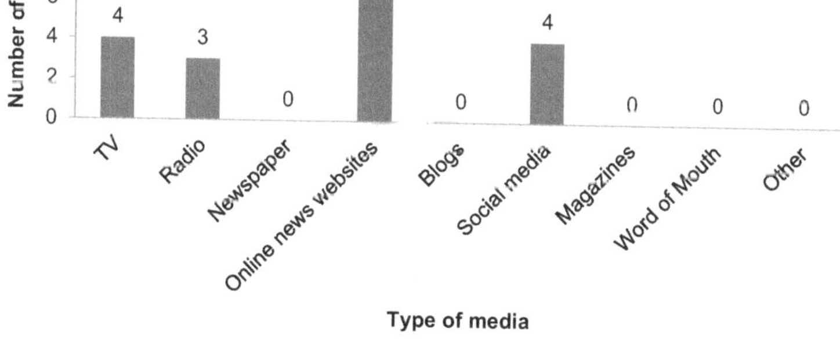

Fig. 5.3 The main source of news for participants (*Source* During the diary period where did you get the majority of your news from? [$n = 26$])

if triggered by "a big news event." Such high usage levels correspond with other studies that highlight the strength of the BBC within the UK media environment (Newman et al. 2017: 54).

The Mail Online, the digital arm of the British newspaper the *Daily Mail*, was also frequently mentioned in the diaries (42 references), albeit in a markedly different context. A number of diarists found that links to the website were often posted on social media as a reaction to the content itself, and it was this controversy that captured their attention (Marco, entry 6; Zoey, entry 9). For example, "Christian" (entry 1) expressed his anger at a story that his friend shared on Facebook. He argued that the piece deliberately distorted the lyrics of the recently deceased musician Lou Reed to claim that he glamorised drug use. Others, like "Andrea" (entry 4; 5; 9) and "Joshua" (entry 4; 5) visit the Mail Online directly for its showbiz coverage, with Abbey noting that the "sidebar of shame," the right-hand column on the website that specialises in celebrity news, is a guilty pleasure (entry 5). Rather than consulting the website for hard news, for many, browsing the site represented a form of procrastination. Even though the publication was described as "badly written" (Amy, entry 6) and "misleading" (Marco, entry 6), and compared to Nazi propaganda (Joshua, entry 4), participants would often discuss issues raised by the publication in their weekly reflections.

A number of diarists also drew upon digital-born news publishers. One such provider was VICE News. Founded in Montreal in 1994 as an underground counterculture magazine, VICE has since morphed into a leading producer of online video for younger audiences (Küng 2015). Specialising in investigative journalism, it has developed a reputation for opposing conventional approaches to journalism. This includes offering alternative perspectives on current affairs, such as its abrasive and controversial coverage of the UK general election (Dennis and Sampaio-Dias 2017), and shedding light on diversity issues, such as *Gaycation*, a series that examines LGBTQ rights around the globe. By following VICE on Facebook, Andrea (entry 11), a university student from the South East, felt she could maintain an interest in stories that did not receive adequate exposure in more traditional news sources, those issues that are "a bit out of the norm." "Simon" (entry 5) visited the website directly after protests emerged in Ukraine following President Yanukovych's refusal to sign a political association and free trade agreement with the European Union. He praised the coverage, noting that it amplified the voices of those citizens directly experiencing the events. Similarly, "Liz" (entry 6) began following the publisher on Twitter during the study period. Across a number of weeks (entry 6; 7; 9), she discussed how content from VICE gave her a unique perspective on "different aspects of life." In line with her interest in following news on abuses of human rights (Liz, pre-diary interview), Liz reflected on a number of documentaries that explored neglected social issues, such as deprivation in the north of England and drug use in Pakistan. This coverage represents part of the expanding choice available online.

Alongside VICE News, a number of entries also reflected on stories published by BuzzFeed (Charlie, entry 11; Louise, entry 12; Mallory, entry 11). Founded in 2006, BuzzFeed is renowned for its cat memes, quizzes, and listicles. With articles such as "18 Reasons Cats Think Humans Are Terrible at Being Cats" (Main 2013) and "11 Delightful Poems Found in Pornhub Comments" (Mallikarjuna 2013), the most fitting characterisation for BuzzFeed is perhaps "soft news," a journalistic style that blurs the lines between information and entertainment. However, over the past five years the company has invested significantly in its hard news operation. Under the stewardship of editor-in-chief Janine Gibson, the UK arm of BuzzFeed News now commands an online news audience comparable to the *Daily Mirror* and the *Telegraph* (Newman et al. 2017: 54). With this in mind, many of the stories that diarists mentioned used humour as a storytelling device to engage the reader with traditional news items. Stories included the use of humorous photographs of politicians staring at floods to highlight the ineffectiveness of the government's response to a flooding crisis (Louise, entry 12), a summary of reactions from Twitter to the exaggerated impact of freedom of movement being extended to Bulgarian and Romanian nationals (Louise, entry 12), and a list of pointlessly gendered items to highlight how visible sexism can be for children (Madeline, entry 11).

Interestingly, unlike their intentional use of BBC News Online, all of the diarists who mentioned BuzzFeed were either accidentally exposed to the digital publisher by a post from a networked contact, or they themselves shared a story on social media. This may not come as a surprise, as the digital natives such as BuzzFeed and VICE News use social media as their main vehicle for content distribution (Küng 2015: 53). As founder and current CEO Jonah Peretti (quoted in Shontell 2012) states, "I care a lot about whether we're consistently creating content that people think is worth sharing." This raises questions about the conditions of this incidental exposure; how did the diarists respond and react to this material?

"Mallory" (week 11) discussed a story her friend posted from BuzzFeed about the accusations of sexual assault against Woody Allen by his adopted daughter, Dylan Farrow. In her entry, she reflects on the juxtaposition of the fanfare surrounding the much-celebrated movie director and the treatment of other accused offenders in criminal cases of child sexual abuse. Outraged by what she perceived to be an example of holding Woody Allen to different standards because of his fame, she didn't reach this opinion on the basis of the BuzzFeed article alone. This accidental encounter triggered a series of wider searches for information, with Mallory consulting other articles in a number of newspapers. This process involved the diarist verifying the source material and developing her understanding of the issue prior to forming an opinion. "Amy" (entry 12) adopted a similar approach after a friend on Facebook shared an article from HuffPost (formally the Huffington Post), the online news website. The story explored whether money from the foreign aid budget, the legal commitment to spend 0.7% of gross national income (GNI) on overseas development, should be diverted to the UK to help victims of recent flooding. On reading this piece, Amy consulted similar stories on the BBC News website and the Mail Online in order to come to her own conclusion about the important role that foreign aid plays. Such repertoires were not uncommon and represent a more attentive and critical audience than suggested by the slacktivist critique.

While some value this by-product learning (e.g. Madeline, entry 3), others were more sceptical. Danny (entry 2) considered how posts on his personalised Facebook News Feed were prioritised, questioning whether the number of likes and comments on a story was an accurate indication of its quality. Others (Christian, entry 5) queried the reliability of those sources that use social media as their main vehicle for disseminating journalism, with "Charlie" (entry 11) considering whether the business model used by BuzzFeed is compatible with the objective ideal of journalism:

> The thing that I think I dislike about it most is that BuzzFeed will be successful at selling news, well it will when it measures its articles in clicks and shares... but what it might not be successful in is presenting balance. News isn't supposed to be clickable content, it is supposed to be news coverage.

Despite this disagreement between participants over the usefulness of accidental exposure on social media, both sets of reflections illustrate a critical awareness of the information they are consuming from their social media feeds. This was not simply a case of diarists accepting the material that they see online as fact but approaching news with caution over the way it has been selected and portrayed, what Fletcher and Nielsen (2018) describe as "generalised scepticism".

Outside of incidental exposure to digital news publishers on social platforms, other participants populated their feeds with niche content by subscribing to updates from activists, journalists, and politicians. "Marco" (entry 1; 8; 9) often discussed and re-shared tweets on foreign policy from Rolandas Kačinskas, a Lithuanian diplomat with over 34,000 followers on Twitter (Kačinskas 2018).[5] He noted how Kačinskas offered a first-hand perspective of the growing tension between Russia and the Baltic states. As Marco (entry 1) observes, the ability to access updates on this issue was important, as he felt that it was being ignored by legacy news media outlets:

> This week I have been keeping up to date on the military exercises across Europe by both NATO and Russia through a Lithuanian ambassador on Twitter. I find it particularly interesting as there have been fears that Russia will invade the Baltic states as it is carrying out large military exercises in Belarus involving 40,000 Military personnel and NATO has retaliated with Steadfast Jazz exercises yet none of this seems to be reported on the BBC, Guardian, or other news websites… I only get informed on this through tweets made and retweeted by ambassadors and other officials, especially politicians from the Baltic region where most military activities are being carried out. I follow this story because it is my civic duty to know what is happening to and around my country.

As the quote explains, Marco's interest in this story stemmed from his Lithuanian heritage. He welcomed the personalisation tools on social networking sites, as they allowed him to remain informed on these events from a distance.

Similarly, in his pre-diary interview, "Oliver" noted how he used Facebook to curate updates from various sources of left-wing news. A source that stood out from his entries (entry 5; 9) was Mark McGowan, an activist more commonly known as "The Artist Taxi Driver" (McGowan 2018). Widely known for his distinctive style of content delivery, McGowan records unscripted, provocative videos on political issues from his cab. His YouTube channel includes a mixture of passionate monologues, scathing critiques of the British press, and interviews with guests ranging from the Labour Shadow Chancellor John McDonnell to Harry Cole, a political correspondent for the *Sun*. While not always agreeing with McGowan's "at times incoherent rants" (entry 5), Oliver would draw on the topics in these videos as a starting point for broader reflections on progressive causes.

This capacity to sift, filter, and personalise news consumption from an increasingly diverse set of news sources is central to the concerns over audience fragmentation. In the next section, I explore what issues diarists prioritised within their entries, considering whether this personalisation leads to a lack of agreement over what constitutes public issues.

Issue Prominence: Newspapers vs. Diaries

In order to explore the effects of news personalisation, an analysis was undertaken of the issues included in the weekly diary entries between 2 November 2013 and 15 February 2014. These issues were coded, and cumulative values were calculated for all of the active diarists in a given week. These values were then weighted to account for the fluctuation in the number of active diarists from week-to-week. The two most frequently mentioned news items from each week were plotted onto a timeline to demonstrate their relative prominence across the sample, as shown in Fig. 5.4 (a key for this timeline is included in the Research Appendix). A second timeline was created to compare the relative prominence of news items in the diaries with those in four major British newspapers during the same time period, as illustrated in Fig. 5.5.[6] The front pages of the *Daily Mail*, the *Guardian*, the *Sun*, and *The Times* were coded over the same 16-week period and weighted values were calculated to look for evidence of issue fragmentation.[7] The front pages of these publications were chosen because they represent the stories that an editorial team have prioritised within their news output.

There was some overlap between the two most frequently mentioned issues within the diaries and the front page coverage. For example, in the week ending November 23, the use of illegal drugs by former chairman of the Co-operative Bank Paul Flowers was featured most frequently in the diaries (10.57) and on the front pages of the four newspapers (30). Likewise, in the week ending December 4, Formula One

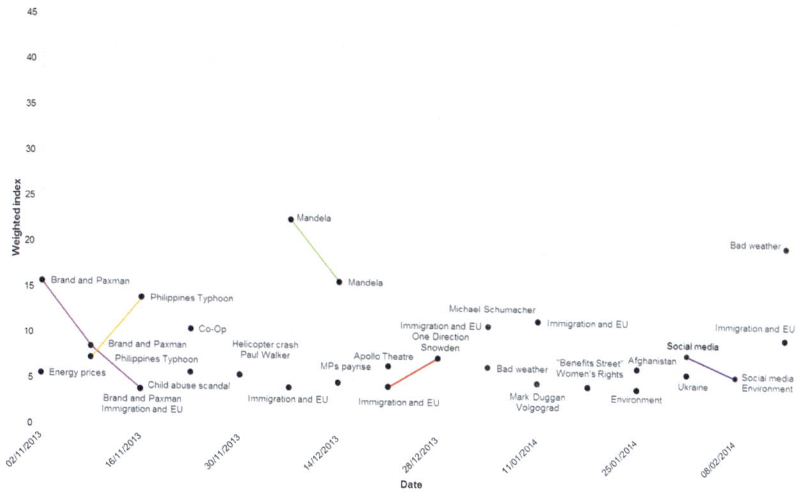

Fig. 5.4 Timeline of issues prioritised by diarists: 2 November 2013–8 February 2014

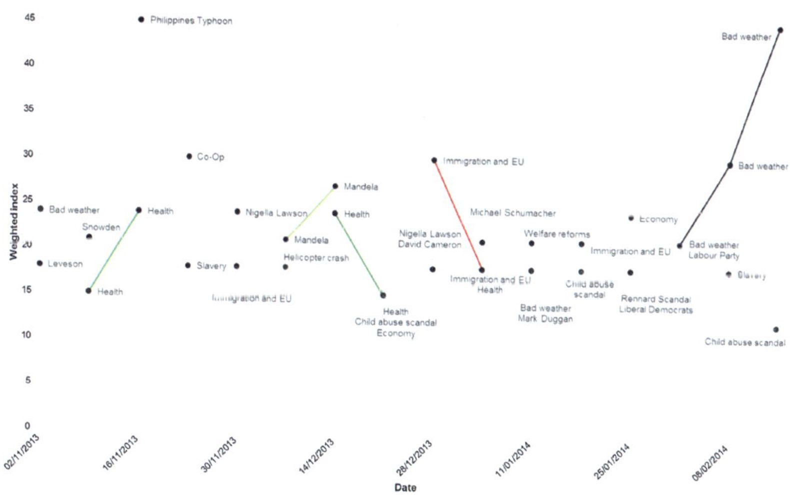

Fig. 5.5 Timeline of issues prioritised on the front pages of the four newspapers: 2 November 2013–8 February 2014

champion Michael Schumacher's skiing accident featured prominently in both. However, with only 25% of the issues mentioned in the diaries corresponding with those leading the four newspapers over the 16-week period, there was significant deviation. Furthermore, as the comparatively low-weighted values on Fig. 5.4 illustrate, there was less issue homogeneity in the weekly diary entries than in the press coverage.

Participants would instead often reflect on those issues that they deemed to be important on a personal level. Simon, a student studying Economics and based in the South East, was passionate about the rights of citizens online. He closely followed the leaks from the former Central Intelligence Agency (CIA) employee Edward Snowden, relating the revelation of the American government's extensive surveillance programme to his own concerns about online privacy (entry 1; 2; 7; 8). Drawing on news he actively sought out from BBC News Online, videos from VICE that featured on his Facebook News Feed, and a range of technology web forums, Simon personally tailored a selection of sources around an issue that resonated with his personal political identity.

Similarly, "Claudia," an employee of a charity in the education sector, would often focus on news items that related to her professional interests. Throughout her diary, she discussed the debates surrounding new performance measures for schools in England (entry 1), the challenges facing trainee teachers on the Teach First programme (entry 9)—an initiative that recruits university graduates to complete a two-year training programme in schools in low-income communities—and changes to the structure of school inspections (entry 11). While she often became aware of these issues when browsing the BBC News website (entry 2; 6; 8), watching the BBC's investigative current affairs programme, *Panorama* (entry 3), or by listening to the news updates on BBC Radio 1, she would then seek out further information from sources with a very specific remit. This included navigating to specific Twitter accounts, such as the Times Education Supplement (@TES), a publication aimed at those in the education sector, and often using the search function on Twitter to find relevant discussion around these topics (entry 1; 2; 3; 4; 7; 11; 12).

Does this personalisation lead to harmful audience fragmentation? Did participants focus on stories of importance to them at the expense of those public issues deemed vital to the health of a democracy? This study shows that, despite evidence of nuanced personalisation at the individual level, there are still moments of collective exposure; certain events triggered attention across the sample. As Fig. 5.6 illustrates, four examples of collective exposure can be identified. These news items are as follows: the *Newsnight* interview between the comedian-turned-activist Russell Brand and the journalist Jeremy Paxman; Typhoon Haiyan, the deadliest Philippine typhoon recorded in modern history; the death of Nelson Mandela; a period of severe weather in Britain in early 2014, in particular the flooding of the River Thames in the South West of England.

By comparing Figs. 5.5 and 5.6, it is evident that three of the four events that triggered collective attention amongst the diarists correlate with the front page news coverage. As such, the fear that social media exacerbates fragmentation seems to be unfounded in this study, as the diarists still share common experiences. Although it could be argued that a large-N study would be better suited to exploring audience fragmentation, the self-reflection within the diaries provides a basis to investigate how participants envisage and understand these public issues. Rather than simply observing collective exposure, I examine two of these news items in detail to analyse the relationship between the source of information and a diarist's interpretation of the event.

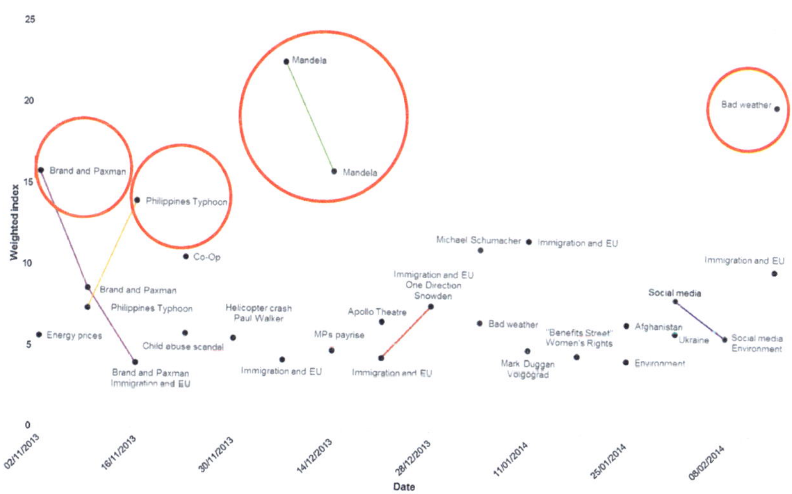

Fig. 5.6 Examples of collective exposure from the diaries

Moments of Collective Exposure in a Hybrid Media System

On 5 December 2013, Nelson Mandela, the first democratically elected President of South Africa, died. Given Mandela's imprisonment and subsequent influence on reconciling post-apartheid South Africa, his death was keenly felt around the world. Nelson Mandela's passing was the most discussed topic in this study; 23 participants mentioned it at some point within their diary. Interest in this event was sustained by the state funeral held on 15 December 2013, and the subsequent scandal that surrounded the sign language interpreter at the funeral and a selfie taken by the President of the USA, Barack Obama, the Prime Minister of Denmark, Helle Thorning-Schmidt, and the Prime Minister of the UK, David Cameron.

As with an event of this nature, diarists first learnt of the news in a number of different ways: Claudia, Will, and Danny were informed of the news face-to-face; Andrea, "Charlie," Oliver, Liz, "Matt," and Christian saw the news on social media while using it for other reasons; "Cathy" overheard a bulletin on the radio; Sam watched the breaking coverage on TV; "Leo" received a message on WhatsApp. Such diversity in communication channels is not new when one factors in the different forms of interpersonal discussion available in past media systems (Norris 2000). However, the information sources that are consulted *after* this initial point of exposure do illuminate unique behavioural shifts.

After learning of the news at her workplace Christmas party, Claudia (entry 6) then consulted BBC News Online and took to Twitter to follow subsequent updates. "Madeline" (entry 8) switched her focus away from online news websites and turned to the ongoing coverage on the BBC News Channel, while simultaneously reflecting on the news with her Mum over the phone. Christian (entry 4), who first learnt of Mandela's death on Facebook, immediately referred to a news website by way of verification:

> The first news I heard of his death was via Facebook. I quickly checked the BBC News website to verify its authenticity, I have seen numerous posts claiming that people have died when they haven't... Shortly after reading about his death on Facebook I received a notification on my iPhone from the BBC app, stating that Nelson Mandela, "the first black president and anti-apartheid icon" had died. I followed the link and watched a short

> video about his life, his imprisonment, and his achievements. Important to note that I still found out about this event via social media first, the news just slips in!

Charlie (pre-diary interview) expressed a similar sentiment in reference to Twitter: "it's probably where I find out about most things first and then I'll go over and look at it in more detail on another news website." Two themes emerge from these examples. Firstly, users can become exposed to news as a by-product of using Facebook and Twitter, just as they can learn of news accidentally in other social spaces. Secondly, the routines that diarists use to validate and understand current events are intrinsically personalised, both in terms of the tools used to access information and the level of trust placed in a particular form of media.

Despite this diversity, the way that diarists understand and give meaning to events was remarkably similar, irrespective of what form of media they relied upon. For example, for most diarists, the events acted as a learning experience regardless of the medium used to access information. Abbey (entry 6) and "Deborah" (entry 8) commented on Mandela's life, and how they were not aware of the significance of his role in providing democratic rights to the citizens of South Africa. Others, such as Angela (entry 7), Danny (entry 7), and Matt (entry 7), used the event to reflect on the inequalities still rife in South Africa today.

A number of diarists also discussed the way in which death should be treated in mediatised spaces. Angela (entry 9), Cathy (entry 5), and Sam (entry 9) posed questions about the appropriateness of the live TV coverage of Mandela's funeral, citing the need for privacy for his family and loved ones. Others, like Oliver (entry 7), were critical of the public displays of grief on Facebook. Joshua (entry 8), a recruiter from the East Midlands, complained that people were simply "jumping on the bandwagon" despite lacking any real knowledge of the significance of Mandela's life. Similarly, Abbey (entry 6) felt her networked contacts were posting updates on the service to gain reputational benefits:

> It felt a little like a competition as to who could let everyone know that they found out first. I understand its human nature to express sadness when someone dies, but why must people do it so publicly... The way social media is making people attention-hungry oversharers pains me. Live your life for you, not a virtual thumbs up.

Despite diarists drawing on different media in relation to Mandela's passing, their reactions had a number of similarities. Therefore, the information source seemingly had little bearing on how participants interpreted the event itself. For all intents and purposes, this event shares many of the same civic qualities as those that occurred in an era of relative media scarcity.

One event that triggered reflection across the sample but did not correlate with the front page coverage was the interview between Russell Brand and Jeremy Paxman on the BBC current affairs programme *Newsnight*. Undertaken following public interest in Brand's comments on voting in the British political magazine the *New Statesman* (Brand 2014: 19), the interview marked his first steps into political campaigning. The interview covered a number of topics, most controversially Brand's call for a "revolution" and a rejection of traditional political structures.[8] Unlike the other moments of collective exposure, only the *Guardian* (6 November 2013) featured the interview on its front page during the period of analysis. This lack of press coverage can be partially explained by the fact the interview itself took place prior to the start of this analysis, originally broadcast on 23 October 2013. Even so, the presence of this event across much of the sample over a week after its transmission suggests that this represents a qualitatively different kind of common experience.

This case exemplifies what Chadwick (2013) describes as hybrid media logic, in which older and newer media logics interact and cross-fertilise in unpredictable ways. The momentum of this story was helped by a response to the interview from the actor Robert Webb (2013), who took issue with Brand for actively dissuading young people from voting. However, Facebook and Twitter also played a key role in generating, sustaining, and transforming the controversy over the weeks that followed. As Fig. 5.6 indicates, the interview had the longest lifespan of any event within the diaries, featuring as one of the two most frequently mentioned news items for three consecutive weeks. It is noteworthy that of the 13 participants who discussed this news item in their diaries, not a single one watched the interview when it when originally broadcast. Instead, all bar one diarist watched the interview on YouTube, with the video becoming one of the most watched on YouTube in Britain in 2013.[9] "Annabeth" (entry 1), Charlie (entry 1), Christian (entry 1), Leo (entry 3), Madeline (entry 2), and Oliver (entry 1) were all exposed to the video by a networked contact sharing the video on Facebook.

As Oliver (entry 1) observed, "I would not have seen the Brand interview were it not for Facebook." As such, in comparison with the last case study, social media becomes more than just a vehicle for diffusing those issues determined to be on the public agenda by professional news media; Facebook and Twitter can bring alternative issues to collective consciousness. Although the video originated on broadcast television, its purpose was adapted and transformed by those sharing it.

These moments emerge and are sustained, in part, due to the technological affordances and associated discursive norms on Facebook and Twitter. What differentiates this event to those that overlapped with the newspaper coverage was the response of the diarists; six took to Facebook to express their opinions on the subject matter, the largest number to do so in reaction to an event during the project. Annabeth, "Joe," Madeline, Matt, and Oliver all shared or re-shared the YouTube video. "Thomas" took a different approach, posting his criticism of Brand's stance on voting.

The video resulted in wide-ranging reflections within the diaries. A number of participants felt that the interview was significant in shedding light on alternative political attitudes for a wider audience, be that new forms of participation (Madeline, entry 2), objections to party politics (Will, entry 2), or that voter apathy can represent a form of resistance in its own right (Simon, entry 2). Others debated the relative value of Brand's status as a celebrity. Charlie (entry 1) observed that celebrities have a distinctive power to generate interest in politics for those citizens who would not normally engage with political issues, and thus serve an important educative role. By her own admission, Annabeth (entry 1), a student from Sheffield, has little interest in politics, but she also felt compelled to explore the issues raised in the interview. As such, Brand's profile did seem to be an important factor in understanding the widespread interest in this story. As Joe (entry 7) observes, "If I see any stories on him, or anything orientated with his thoughts on politics, I will generally click on it and read." Some diarists were less complimentary. By using terms like revolution without any precision, "Alan" (entry 1) felt Brand was "out of his depth." Christian (entry 1) took issue with his attempt to be both funny and serious at the same time; "I wish he would make a serious point without the need to 'Brandify' and speak so flamboyantly for dramatic effect." Finally, following Robert Webb's rebuttal, a number of diarists took to Facebook to debate the relative merits of voting. Thomas offered a robust defence (entry 1), while Oliver (entry

2) offered a critique of what he felt was an outdated form of democratic engagement. In this way, this case study reflects Bennett's (2008) actualising logic, as the lines between consumption and production become blurred; diarists moved seamlessly between watching the interview and moments of self-expression. However, as I will illustrate in the next chapter, these expressive behaviours were not representative of the general habits of the Facebook and Twitter users in this study.

Despite the evidence of personalisation within this study, these four moments of collective exposure illustrate how attention can be mobilised around public issues on social media. In line with pre-existing theory (Amnå and Ekman 2014; Schudson 1999), the participants in this study were watchful, scanning political information across different media with substantive interest triggered by certain events. As "Zoey's" (pre-diary interview) quote illustrates, these news items disrupt the processes of personalisation: "I like celebrity news and things like that, but then there will be a news story that will really make me think."

Conclusion: Personalisation ≠ Audience Fragmentation

Accounts of slacktivism highlight how low-threshold digital activism is often based on emotive misinformation. In doing so, the slacktivist critique taps into similar debates over the influence of selective exposure and algorithmic personalisation on political behaviour. In the light of these concerns, this chapter examines the conditions of everyday news consumption on Facebook and Twitter. By drawing on a mixed-methods research design, in which evidence of citizen behaviour on Facebook and Twitter is contextualised with interviews and reflective weekly diary entries collected over three months, this chapter observes and documents the spaces—online and offline—in which citizens consume and make sense of political information. Crucially, despite evidence that participants use social media to personalise their news consumption around issues they have a long-standing interest it, there was little evidence to support the fear that selective exposure inevitably leads to audience fragmentation. By analysing rich accounts of media habits at the individual level against the lead stories of four British newspapers, it is clear that those participants who share the characteristics of slacktivists still identify with some of the public issues that are identified by legacy news media outlets.

There are two significant findings from this chapter. Firstly, as expected, news consumption on social media is personalised. Through selective exposure on Twitter and algorithmic prioritisation on Facebook, diarists receive personally tailored information. For some, this is the focal point of their news consumption. Marco and Oliver emphasised the value of social platforms in providing information on the issues that they are passionate about. This included using activist media, like The Artist Taxi Driver. Even amongst those participants who were sceptical of the usefulness of social networking sites for following current affairs (Sam; Thomas, pre-diary interview), there was evidence of Facebook and/or Twitter being used to monitor topics that are personally relevant. Moving beyond accounts that describe what people *see*, I show how the issues and events that people reflect on are different to those in the press. Within their weekly diary entries, participants often prioritised and discussed those stories that relate to themselves and their own interests.

However, the implications of this individualisation do not reflect the ominous forecasts of the slacktivist critique; in this study, there was no evidence of selective exposure leading to harmful audience fragmentation. The comparison between the diaries and newspaper coverage illustrates that this personalisation is balanced by moments of collective exposure, as citizens focus their attention on public issues featured in the press. The accounts of these shared experiences say something about the nature of contemporary news consumption: it is fundamentally diffuse, with evidence of exposure to news in a variety of online and offline spaces. Crucially, diarists don't rely on social media exclusively for their news. Even amongst those diarists that were the most active on Facebook and Twitter, digital sources complement more conventional approaches to staying up to date with current affairs. Therefore, this study illustrates some of the complex conditions of incidental exposure at the individual level. Social media represents just one of the many spaces in which someone may see news accidentally. This can then trigger complex repertoires of news verification and reflection, which move between public, semi-public, and private spaces. Therefore, while the dynamics of media consumption have irreversibly changed, citizens who use Facebook and Twitter for news consumption still participate in democratically beneficial shared experiences.

This collective exposure may occur conventionally, as illustrated by the three stories that were both popular with diarists and featured on the front pages of the newspapers, or may arise by cascades on social media. The interest in the interview between Russell Brand and Jeremy Paxman demonstrates how social networking sites can play a disruptive role in the formation of public issues, as many of the participants reflected on this televised event days after it was initially broadcast. This moment of disjuncture between editorial decision-making in the press and the attention of the diarists highlights the need for future research on how public issues are shaped and sustained on social media.

These findings also contribute to broader debates around the conditions of contemporary news consumption. Some of the popular commentary around slacktivism, fake news, and filter bubbles is based on the reductive assumption that exposure to information results in attitudinal and behavioural change. This study illustrates that citizens are more critical in their news consumption than these pejorative terms would have us believe. This chapter offers support to Fletcher and Nielsen's (2018: 2) notion of "generalised scepticism," which describes how people are cautious of the processes of news selection by traditional media and on social networking sites. As the diary entries on the passing of Nelson Mandela show, participants frequently question the information they receive on Facebook and Twitter, verifying news updates with other sources. Similarly, the reactions to the interview between Brand and Paxman illustrate how some social media users are, under the right circumstances, willing to contest and debate provocative content, even when it is endorsed by a celebrity. The conditions under which social media users are willing to challenge each other and offer politically expressive commentary is explored in detail in the next chapter.

Ultimately, the mere existence of misinformation and algorithmic personalisation does not explain the transformative events of the last few years. A wide range of empirical work has questioned the viability of the filter bubble critique, highlighting how social media users see content that counters their own beliefs (Barberá et al. 2015; Beam et al. 2018; Dubois and Blank 2018; Fletcher and Nielsen 2017; Mitchell et al. 2018; Möller et al. 2018). In respect of "fake news," citizens are often able to identify misinformation and are aware of how the term has become politicised and used by elites to criticise journalists and news outlets (Nielsen and Graves 2017). Furthermore, this focus on deliberate forms of deception overlooks the complexity of different types of misinformation—"the inadvertent sharing of false information"—and disinformation—"the deliberate creation and sharing of information known to be false" (Wardle 2017). As Chadwick et al. (2018) highlight, traditional media also contribute to the distribution of misleading content on Twitter. Therefore, by isolating particular cases or focusing on social platforms, as in the slacktivist critique, we get no closer to understanding the context and conditions of news consumption on social media. While these popular pejorative terms may offer a convenient explanation for increasing political polarisation within British society, they misrepresent existing findings and overlook more urgent research priorities.[10]

One way of moving beyond these limitations is by examining individual-level media habits beyond the point of consumption. If, as Vaccari (2018) suggests, "the clash of disagreeing opinions is more common on social media than ideological echo chambers," what is the impact on political behaviour? I explore this relationship between exposure and the formation of attitudes and political behaviours in the next chapter.

Notes

1. See https://en.wikipedia.org/wiki/Slacktivism#Examples.
2. This algorithmic filtering is not unique to social media but is widely used across a range of tools that citizens may use to access news. For instance, if someone conducts a search on Google while logged in with a Google account then personalised results will be produced, potentially drawing on the user's past search history, browsing activity, and location data (see "Google Personalized Search", LaFrance 2017). Likewise, news aggregators such as Apple News and Flipboard draw on a user's engagement history to recommend relevant material.
3. In total, 30 participants were originally recruited. Four diarists withdrew from the study prior to completion. Of those four, Alan, Christian, and Ron gave permission for their partially completed diaries to be included in the research, contributing five, six, and seven entries respectively. As a result, none of these diarists took part in the exit survey.
4. This convenience sample was designed intentionally, to identify participants with media habits and a political interest that was reflective of the slacktivist critique. Of the 29 diarists, 24 had a Facebook account and 20 used Twitter, with two diarists included who do not use either service as a control. Political interest was calculated through a measure of political activity, which, when compared to the findings of the *Audit of Political Engagement 11* (Hansard Society 2014), suggested that participants were generally representative of the target population. Participants were not excluded on the basis of their age, gender, or level of education, although

there was a slight over-representation of young males. See the Research Appendix for further details on the sampling frame used.
5. Follower count correct as of May 2018.
6. Please see the Research Appendix for an overview of how I coded the diaries and calculated the weighted values for both timelines.
7. These four sources were selected following the design outlined by Couldry et al. (2010: 22).
8. The interview can be watched in full here: https://www.youtube.com/watch?v=3YR4CseY9pk.
9. As of May 2018, the video has 11,757,423 views.
10. This is not to say that Facebook and Twitter are a universal good when it comes to ensuring the public is informed. Political communication between elites, journalists, and the public has never been so chaotic and decentralised. With this in mind, research on the spread of misinformation (Wardle 2017), computational propaganda (Howard et al. 2018), and algorithmic censorship (Tufekci 2014) is essential.

References

Amazing Pics [AmazingPicz]. (2014, February 20). Retweet If You Say NO to Animal Testing. #Animalrights. *Tweet*. Retrieved April 24, 2018, from https://twitter.com/amazingpicx/status/436359414820270080.

Amnå, E., & Ekman, J. (2014). Standby Citizens: Diverse Faces of Political Passivity. *European Political Science Review, 6*(2), 261–281.

Anderson, C. (2004, January 10). The Long Tail. *Wired*. Retrieved May 14, 2018, from https://www.wired.com/2004/10/tail.

Barberá, P., Jost, J. T., Nagler, J., Tucker, J. A., & Bonneau, R. (2015). Tweeting from Left to Right: Is Online Political Communication More Than an Echo Chamber? *Psychological Science: A Journal of the Association for Psychological Science, 26*(10), 1531–1542.

Barnes, R. (2016). The Ecology of Participation. In T. Witschge, C. W. Anderson, D. Domingo, & A. Hermida (Eds.), *The Sage Handbook of Digital Journalism* (pp. 149–163). London: Sage.

Beam, M. A., Hutchens, M. J., & Hmielowski, J. D. (2018). Facebook News and (De)Polarization: Reinforcing Spirals in the 2016 US Election. *Information, Communication & Society, 21*(7), 940–958.

Bell, E. (2016, July 3). The Truth About Brexit Didn't Stand a Chance in the Online Bubble. *The Guardian*. Retrieved May 13, 2018, from https://www.theguardian.com/media/2016/jul/03/facebook-bubble-brexit-filter.

Bennett, W. L. (2008). Changing Citizenship in the Digital Age. In W. L. Bennett (Ed.), *Civic Life Online: Learning How Digital Media Can Engage Youth* (pp. 1–24). Cambridge: MIT Press.

Bennett, W. L. (2012). The Personalization of Politics: Political Identity, Social Media, and Changing Patterns of Participation. *The ANNALS of the American Academy of Political and Social Science, 644*(20), 20–39.

Bode, L., & Vraga, E. K. (2017). Studying Politics Across Media. *Political Communication, 35*(1), 1–7.

boyd, d. & Crawford, K. (2012). Critical Questions for Big Data: Provocations for a Cultural, Technological, and Scholarly Platform. *Information, Communication and Society, 15*(5), 662–579.

Brand, R. (2014). *Revolution*. London: Random House.

Chadwick, A. (2013). *The Hybrid Media System: Politics and Power*. Oxford: Oxford University Press.

Chadwick, A., Vaccari, C., & O'Loughlin, B. (2018). Do Tabloids Poison the Well of Social Media? Explaining Democratically Dysfunctional News Sharing. *New Media & Society*. Retrieved from https://doi.org/10.1177/1461444818769689.

Chiluwa, I., & Ifukor, P. (2015). 'War Against Our Children': Stance and Evaluation in #BringBackOurGirls Campaign Discourse on Twitter and Facebook. *Discourse and Society, 26*(3), 267–296.

Constine, J. (2016, September 6). How Facebook News Feed Words. *TechCrunch*. Retrieved May 14, 2018, from https://techcrunch.com/2016/09/06/ultimate-guide-to-the-news-feed.

Couldry, N. (2012). *Media, Society, World: Social Theory and Digital Media Practice*. Cambridge: Polity.

Couldry, N., Livingstone, S., & Markham, T. (2010). *Media Consumption and Public Engagement: Beyond the Presumption of Attention*. Basingstoke: Palgrave Macmillan.

Dalton, R. J. (2008). *Citizens Politics: Public Opinion and Political Parties in Advanced Industrial Democracies* (5th ed.). Washington, DC: CQ Press.

Dennis, J., & Sampaio-Dias, S. (2017). Not Just Swearing and Loathing on the Internet: Analysing BuzzFeed and VICE During #GE2017. In E. Thorsen, D. Jackson, & D. Lilleker (Eds.), *UK Election Analysis 2017: Media, Voters and the Campaign* (pp. 66–67). Bournemouth: The Centre for the Study of Journalism, Culture and Community, Bournemouth University.

Downs, A. (1957). *An Economic Theory of Democracy*. New York: Harper.

Dubois, E., & Blank, G. (2018). The Echo Chamber Is Overstated: The Moderating Effect of Political Interest and Diverse Media. *Information, Communication & Society, 21*(5), 729–745.

Fletcher, R., & Nielsen, R. K. (2017). Are News Audiences Increasingly Fragmented? A Cross-National Comparative Analysis of Cross-Platform News Audience Fragmentation and Duplication. *Journal of Communication, 67*(4), 476–498.

Fletcher, R., & Nielsen, R. K. (2018). Generalised Scepticism: How People Navigate News on Social Media. *Information, Communication & Society*. Retrieved from https://doi.org/10.1080/1369118X.2018.1450887.

Flynn, K. (2018, January 12). Current Facebook Wants to Go Back to Being Old Facebook. *Mashable*. Retrieved May 20, 2018, from https://mashable.com/2018/01/12/zuckerberg-facebook-before-news-feed-meaningful.
Hansard Society. (2014). *Audit of Political Engagement 11: The 2014 Report*. London: Hansard Society.
Howard, P. N., Woolley, S., & Calo, R. (2018). Algorithms, Bots, and Political Communication in the US 2016 Election: The Challenge of Automated Political Communication for Election Law and Administration. *Journal of Informational Technology & Politics, 15*(2), 81–93.
Iyengar, S., Hahn, K. S., Krosnick, J. A., & Walker, J. (2008). Selective Exposure to Campaign Communication: The Role of Anticipated Agreement and Issue Public Membership. *The Journal of Politics, 70*(1), 186–200.
Kačinskas, R. [rkacinskas]. (2018). *Twitter Account*. Retrieved May 20, 2018, from https://twitter.com/rkacinskas.
Kant, T. (2016). *Making It Personal: Web Users and Algorithmic Personalisation* (Doctoral thesis, University of Sussex).
Küng, L. (2015). *Innovators in Digital News*. London: IB Tauris.
LaFrance, A. (2017, October 18). The Power of Personalization. *NiemanLab*. Retrieved May 14, 2018, from http://niemanreports.org/articles/the-power-of-personalization.
Main, S. (2013, November 21). 18 Reasons Cats Think Humans Are Terrible at Being Cats. *BuzzFeed*. Retrieved September 11, 2014, from http://www.buzzfeed.com/samimain/ways-cats-think-humans-are-terrible-at-being-cats.
Mallikarjuna, K. (2013, September 24). 11 Delightful Poems Found in Pornhub Comments. *BuzzFeed*. Retrieved September 11, 2014, from http://www.buzzfeed.com/kmallikarjuna/11-delightful-poems-found-in-pornhub-comments.
McGowan, M. [The Artist Taxi Driver]. (2018). *Facebook Account*. Retrieved May 20, 2018, from https://www.facebook.com/mark.mcgowan.969.
Mitchell, A., Simmons, K., Matsa, K. E., Silver, L., Shearer, E., Johnson, C., et al. (2018, May 14). Many Western Europeans Get News Via Social Media, but in Some Countries, Substantial Minorities Do Not Pay Attention to the Source. *Pew Research Center*. Retrieved May 14, 2018, from http://www.journalism.org/2018/05/14/many-western-europeans-get-news-via-social-media-but-in-some-countries-substantial-minorities-do-not-pay-attention-to-the-source.
Möller, J., Trilling, D., Helberger, N., & van Es, B. (2018). Do Not Blame It on the Algorithm: An Empirical Assessment of Multiple Recommender Systems and Their Impact on Content Diversity. *Information, Communication & Society, 21*(7), 959–977.
Morozov, E. (2011). *The Net Delusion: How Not to Liberate the World*. London: Penguin.
Negroponte, N. (1995). *Being Digital*. London: Hodder and Stoughton.

Neuman, W. R., Just, M. R., & Crigler, A. N. (1992). *Common Knowledge: News and the Construction of Political Meaning*. Chicago, IL: University of Chicago Press.

Newman, N., Fletcher, R., Kalogeropoulos, A., Levy, D. A. L., & Nielsen, R. K. (2017). *Reuters Institute Digital News Report 2017*. University of Oxford: Reuters Institute for the Study of Journalism.

Nielsen, R. K., & Graves, L. (2017). *"News You Don't Believe": Audience Perspectives on Fake News*. Oxford: Reuters Institute for the Study of Journalism.

Norris, P. (2000). *A Virtuous Circle: Political Communication in Postindustrial Societies*. Cambridge: Cambridge University Press.

Norris, P. (2011). *Democratic Deficit: Critical Citizens Revisited*. Cambridge: Cambridge University Press.

Obama, M. [FLOTUS44]. (2014, May 7). Our Prayers Are with the Missing Nigerian Girls and Their Families. It's Time to #BringBackOurGirls. -mo. *Tweet*. Retrieved April 24, 2018, from https://twitter.com/flotus44/status/464148654354628608.

Olson, C. C. (2016). #BringBackOurGirls: Digital Communities Supporting Real-World Change and Influencing Mainstream Media Agendas. *Feminist Media Studies, 16*(5), 772–787.

Pariser, E. (2011). *The Filter Bubble: What the Internet Is Hiding from You*. New York: Penguin Press.

Powers, E. (2017). My News Feed Is Filtered? Awareness of News Personalization Among College Students. *Digital Journalism, 5*(10), 1315–1335.

Prior, M. (2005). News vs. Entertainment: How Increasing Media Choice Widens Gaps in Political Knowledge and Turnout. *American Journal of Political Science, 49*(3), 577–592.

Prior, M. (2007). *Post-broadcast Democracy: How Media Choice Increases Inequality in Political Involvement and Polarizes Elections*. Cambridge: Cambridge University Press.

Schudson, M. (1999). *The Good Citizen: A History of American Public Life*. Cambridge, MA: Harvard University Press.

Shontell, A. (2012, December 11). Inside BuzzFeed: The Story of How Jonah Peretti Built the Web's Most Beloved New Media Brand. *Business Insider*. Retrieved September 11, 2014, from http://www.businessinsider.com/buzzfeed-jonah-peretti-interview-2012-12.

Sloan, L. (2017). Who Tweets in the United Kingdom? Profiling the Twitter Population Using the British Social Attitudes Survey 2015. *Social Media + Society, 3*(1). Retrieved from https://doi.org/10.1177/2056305117698981.

Speaking of Research. (2014, February 27). *Fact into Fiction—Why Context Matters with Animal Images*. Retrieved May 14, 2018, from https://speakingofresearch.com/2014/02/27/fact-into-fiction-why-context-matters-with-animal-images.

Sunday Times. (2018, April 29). *Exposed: Russian Twitter Bots Tried to Swing General Election for Jeremy Corbyn*. Retrieved May 14, 2018, from https://www.thetimes.co.uk/article/exposed-russian-twitter-bots-tried-to-swing-general-election-for-jeremy-corbyn-zffv8652x.

Sunstein, C. R. (2007). *Republic.Com 2.0*. Princeton, NJ: Princeton University Press.

Swirko, C. (2011, August 10). Seized Cats Being Readied for Adopt-a-Thon on August 26–28. *The Gainesville Sun*. Retrieved May 14, 2018, from http://www.gainesville.com/news/20110810/seized-cats-being-readied-for-adopt-a-thon-on-aug-26-28.

Tewksbury, D., & Rittenberg, J. (2012). *News on the Internet: Information and Citizenship in the 21st Century*. Oxford: Oxford University Press.

Tufekci, Z. (2014, August 14). *What Happens to #Ferguson Affects Ferguson: Net Neutrality, Algorithmic Filtering and Ferguson*. Retrieved September 14, 2015, from https://medium.com/message/ferguson-is-also-a-net-neutrality-issue-6d2f3db51eb0.

Vaccari, C. (2018, February 13). *How Prevalent Are Filter Bubbles and Echo Chambers on Social Media? Not as Much as Conventional Wisdom Has It*. Retrieved May 20, 2018, from https://cristianvaccari.com/2018/02/13/how-prevalent-are-filter-bubbles-and-echo-chambers-on-social-media-not-as-much-as-president-obama-thinks.

Wahl-Jorgensen, K. (2018). The Emotional Architecture of Social Media. In Z. Papacharissi (Ed.), *A Networked Self and Platforms, Stories, Connections*. Oxon: Routledge.

Wardle, C. (2017, February 16). Fake News. It's Complicated. *First Draft*. Retrieved May 11, 2018, from https://medium.com/1st-draft/fake-news-its-complicated-d0f773766c79.

Webb, R. (2013, October 30). Dear Russell, Choosing to Vote Is the Most British Kind of Revolution There Is. *New Statesman*. Retrieved April 20, 2014, from http://www.newstatesman.com/2013/10/russell-brand-robert-webb-choosing-vote-most-british-kind-revolution-there.

Zuckerman, E. (2014, September 1). *Self-segregation on Social Networks and the Implications for the Ferguson, MO Story*. Retrieved September 1, 2014, from http://www.ethanzuckerman.com/blog/2014/08/27/self-segregation-on-social-networks-and-the-implications-for-the-ferguson-mo-story.

CHAPTER 6

Civic Instigators, Contributors, and Listeners: Political Expression on Social Media

Slacktivism is based on an assumed attitudinal logic; low-effort forms of digital activism are an easy form of political fulfilment. This critique is based on the subjective interpretation of the actions of others, where the depth of one's engagement is based on the perceived difficulty of the act itself. This represents a form of technological determinism, as the characteristics of the technology shape political behaviour, rather than the intentions of the user. By using reflective diaries to observe how 29 digitally active citizens use social media within their day-to-day lives, this chapter offers a typology of citizen roles in social media environments that challenges both the attitudinal and behavioural logics that sustain the slacktivist critique.

"Civic instigators" and "contributors," those participants who most closely represent slacktivists, engage in self-expression and digital micro-activism by way of refining and honing their own political identity. They are also more likely to engage in substantive, tried and tested forms of political action; a rejection of the substitution thesis. However, this study calls into question the hypothesis that social networking sites invoke a self-expressive logic by virtue of their design (Bennett 2008; Chadwick 2012). The majority of participants in this research were "listeners," using social media to consume political information but refraining from public forms of expression. Instead, they take to private spaces to discuss politics, either online or face-to-face. When these

J. Dennis, *Beyond Slacktivism*,
Interest Groups, Advocacy and Democracy Series,
https://doi.org/10.1007/978-3-030-00844-4_6

listeners do undertake acts of digital micro-activism, they are not easy, low-threshold behaviours, but painstakingly deliberated over with the real and imagined audience in mind.

Method Notes

This chapter develops the diary study introduced in Chapter 5. By drawing on evidence of political expression collected on Facebook and Twitter, alongside interviews, survey data, and a corpus of individually completed self-reflective media diaries, this study grounds observation of participation—online and offline—within an understating of the motivational context on which these acts are predicated.

Drawing on the research design used by Couldry, Livingstone, and Markham in *Media Consumption and Public Engagement* (2010), 29 diarists were asked to track what media content they have regular access to, to reflect on political talk as it occurs in everyday life, and to keep a record of their political behaviour over a period of three months. Participants were encouraged to track their political engagement across online and offline spaces, exploring the different factors that influence political participation on Facebook, Twitter, or through more traditional means. This is an important contribution, as the current body of literature often focuses on social media in isolation from other media (see Bode and Vraga 2017). Furthermore, by requiring participants to complete the diary over a period of three months this study avoids the limitations of event-specific analysis, a trait of the slacktivist critique (see Chapter 2). The diaries offer an opportunity to analyse the relationships formed between expressive and instrumental forms of engagement across the continuum of participation.

I conducted a semi-structured interview with each participant before they began the project to establish some sense of each participant's background and the issues that they may have an existing interest in. A short survey was also conducted in June 2014, some months after the end of the study. This provided a period of reflection in which each participant could consider what they had learnt about their own media habits.

All public and semi-public posts on Facebook and Twitter were collected during the three-month period in which each individual diarist was active. On Facebook, this did not include comments or likes on the content of other users or private interactions, such as conversations on the Messenger platform.[1] The data collected from Twitter included all public interactions made by diarists during the diary period, including public responses to other accounts (@mentions).

The interviews and diaries were coded inductively using NVivo to get a sense of the diarists' priorities and the themes emerging from their experiences. I also manually read and coded 561 posts on Facebook and 1008 tweets as part of a discourse analysis to identify the service functions being used, the content of the post itself, and, if identified as political, its purpose. Moments of interest were then studied in further detail by triangulating the data from the interviews, diaries, and the body of posts. Combined together, these methods go some way towards balancing their own respective weaknesses. While the diaries are highly interpretive, by comparing them with user data from Facebook and Twitter, they provide a way to analyse the conditions in which digital micro-activism materialises. Further information, including the interview questions, questionnaire, and coding framework used, is provided in the Research Appendix.

Civic Instigators and Contributors

Despite the disagreement over the political value of such behaviours outlined in Chapter 2, there is evidence of consensus between proponents and critics of online participation that a widespread self-expressive logic exists on social media (Bennett 2008, 2012; Chadwick 2012; Gladwell 2010; Morozov 2011). Through the affordances on social platforms, the public can—and does—articulate its views on political issues. The sampling frame for this study was designed with this consensus in mind. Each participant had some level of interest in politics and most were heavy users of social media.[2] Therefore, I expected to find an abundance of examples of public political expression to analyse.

However, the majority of diarists were much more cautious than I predicted. Many were unwilling to express themselves online unless personally compelled to. These citizens are conscious of their digital identity as they move between public, semi-public, and private spaces. As a result, I argue that the slacktivist critique fails to encapsulate the nuanced motivations that underpin online forms of participation. In doing so, this chapter outlines a typology that distinguishes between the different attitudinal and behavioural traits at the individual level.

These conclusions are not immediately evident at first glance. By coding all posts on Facebook and Twitter over the duration of the project, the initial evidence seemed to support the existence of a self-expressive logic.

As Table 6.1 shows, almost a quarter of all posts on Facebook (135 posts) had a political orientation, while politics was the third most frequently mentioned topic within the Twitter data set (157 posts).

However, although the total number of politically oriented posts seems to suggest a politically active sample when compared to other subject matter, these posts were shared by a small number of participants. As Table 6.2 illustrates, a handful of diarists were responsible for a significant proportion of these updates.

Table 6.1 Volume of posts on Facebook and Twitter by topic

	Facebook		*Twitter*	
	Frequency	*% (n = 560)*	*Frequency*	*% (n = 1006)*
01 Personal	257	45.89	406	40.36
02 Humour	115	20.54	301	29.92
03 Music	67	11.96	117	11.63
04 Film	11	1.96	34	3.38
05 TV	27	4.82	80	7.95
06 Technology and video games	18	3.21	65	6.46
07 Other visual arts	8	1.43	11	1.09
08 Books and literature	9	1.61	15	1.49
09 Sports and exercise	22	3.93	41	4.08
10 Celebrity and gossip	26	4.64	90	8.95
11 Travel	50	8.93	22	2.19
12 Food and drink	40	7.14	95	9.44
13 Retail and commerce	19	3.39	60	5.96
14 Fashion	3	0.54	21	2.09
15 Religion and faith	4	0.71	32	3.18
16 Science and space	8	1.43	10	0.99
17 Environment	9	1.61	12	1.19
18 Animals and pets	7	1.25	28	2.78
19 Vehicles	6	1.07	32	3.18
20 Crime	7	1.25	18	1.79
21 Social media	5	0.89	22	2.19
22 Charity and social causes	39	6.96	14	1.39
23 Current events and news	90	16.07	125	12.43
24 Politics	135	24.11	157	15.61
25 Other	2	0.36	5	0.50
26 Health	13	2.32	25	2.49
27 Weather	3	0.54	24	2.39
28 Education	35	6.25	90	8.95

Note Frequency based on manual coding. Posts may feature multiple codes

Matt and Oliver stand out from Table 6.2, as they were the only diarists to use social media primarily for political expression and discussion. Between them, they accounted for 43% of the political posts on Facebook during the diary period. They are representative of the actualizing citizen framework discussed in Chapter 3, in that they use Facebook to share personally expressive political content (Bennett 2008; Bennett et al. 2011: 840). However, they also display a unique characteristic that differentiates them from Bennett's citizen type. As Oliver's (pre-diary interview) quote illustrates, they wish to stimulate learning and further discussion by intentionally provoking others:

Table 6.2 Participants who posted political content on Facebook and Twitter

Pseudonym	*Frequency*	*% of diarist's total updates on this service*
		Facebook (n = 135)
Oliver	58	**78.38**
Joe	18	26.47
Thomas	14	35.00
Madeline	11	9.48
Matt	10	**90.91**
Simon	10	22.22
Deborah	3	6.52
Liz	3	*27.27*
Mallory	3	*30.00*
Marco	2	13.33
Annabeth	1	2.08
Joshua	1	*20.00*
Zoey	1	2.78
		Twitter (n = 157)
Joe	90	37.50
Marco	27	17.76
Madeline	21	32.81
Zoey	10	3.68
Abbey	2	*20.00*
Liz	2	12.50
Simon	2	*66.67*
Annabeth	1	0.54
Joshua	1	1.75
Will	1	*100.00*

Note Percentages are italicised to highlight a total post count of less than 10. Percentages in bold signify diarists for whom over 50% of their updates included code 24: Politics and political events

> I use it purely and solely for finding out information about political matters, sharing information on political matters, and rubbing it in people's faces. I know that people don't like it but that's exactly why I do it… the more issues that I create for my network on Facebook, in terms of how they react to me and how do they engage with me, the better, because it's meant to be provocative.

Both Matt and Oliver are examples of what I describe as "civic instigators," citizens who actively share political material on social media and express their opinion by way of challenging others. For example, Matt shared a link to a BBC News article on the government's decision to sell public shares in the Royal Mail. He offered a robust criticism of this decision, arguing that more nationalisation was needed, not less. Likewise, Oliver shared a post from the activist group UK Uncut, which condemned the government for failing to ensure that the telecommunications company Vodafone fulfilled their tax obligations. Oliver was highly critical of this, juxtaposing it with looming cuts to the welfare budget. Both posts triggered a reaction from their networked contacts, as others contested their opinions.

At first glance, one may associate this behaviour with online trolling, disruptive forms communication that are designed to "upset as many people as possible, using whatever linguistic or behavioral tools are available" (Phillips 2015: 2). However, despite the emotionally charged responses that they received, this provocation is not done with any ill intent (see Coleman 2012: 110), but as a way of generating attention, awareness, and understanding for political issues that they deem to be important. Ultimately, they feel that their actions fulfil an educative function (Matt; Oliver, pre-diary interview).

Madeline, a 25-year-old higher education professional, shared a number of similar behavioural traits. She was also an active user of Facebook and Twitter, contributing 32 posts with a political orientation in total. She also aims to inform her family, friends, and other networked contacts through her use of both social networking sites:

> I think if you share something that's political then you're hoping that people who wouldn't know about it might see it, say people that I went to school with, worked with, or family members, those that aren't particularly politically engaged. I only really share things that are on an important

> subject. For example, something on feminism that my mum might not see but I know that she would be interested in... so it is kind of like, not to sound snobbish or bigheaded but, educating others.
>
> (Madeline, pre-diary interview)

However, she differed from Matt and Oliver as she would refrain from offering her opinion when posting updates, only doing so when personally compelled to by the content of the issue. In this way, Madeline reflects what I characterise as a "contributor," a user who shares political material but does so without including any explicit statement of one's personal opinion. Although their attitudes towards an issue may be inferred by the nature of the content shared, contributors act on the basis of a different attitudinal logic. As the quote illustrates, Madeline felt a certain sense of gratification. This came from both the fulfilment in educating others, but also in being seen as a politically articulate individual by her networked contacts. This motivation for sharing news is not new (see Gantz and Trenholm 1979), but what separates Madeline from the civic instigators in this study was her aversion to public forms of conflict on social media (Madeleine, pre-diary interview).

Joe, a student from the South East, was responsible for the largest volume of political updates in total, sharing 108 posts across Facebook (18) and Twitter (90). Like Madeline, he often refrained from explicit forms of expression. This reluctance to voice one's opinion stems from his perception of his audience. Joe (entry 8) feels that his networked contacts do not take political discussion seriously:

> Not everyone is politicised. I think that if I wrote my political thoughts I would get stupid comments that aren't worth the light of day... In terms of my friends, I have witnessed a lot of people being vilified for their thoughts on specific issues.

Joe mitigates these fears by sharing content that is politically oriented but also has an overtly humorous frame. On Twitter, he would frequently combine political comments with trending topics. By using humour, Joe felt he could entertain his audience while also making a more meaningful point. For example, he used the hashtag #JLSMemories, created by fans of the British pop group JLS in the wake of their breakup, to question the impact of austerity on society.

Furthermore, he used the hashtag #AskKingslandRoad, a question and answer session with the band Kingsland Road, to discuss immigration policy in Britain. As such, Joe's behaviour is akin to that of a contributor as he shares civically relevant material, not by way of explicit self-expression, but in an attempt to entertain his friends.

In doing so, contributors also reflect many of the characteristics of the actualizing citizen framework (Bennett et al. 2011: 840). Contributors, like civic instigators, used Facebook and Twitter to question the objectivity of legacy news media organisations. For instance, Madeline shared a meme highlighting the narrow selection of topics that feature on the front-page of the *Daily Express* (see Sturgeon 2013). These diarists also took part in new protest repertoires during the study; Oliver (entry 7) used Facebook to help organise an occupation of his university's student union, Madeline (entry 4) contributed to a blog to raise awareness of a civic issue, and Joe (entry 11) took to Twitter to lobby a company to change business practices that he deemed to be unfair. Ultimately, these citizens share an implicit understanding of the agenda-setting influence that they can wield using social media. With this in mind, these diarists are representative of a new form of digitally enabled citizen, using social networking sites for political self-expression (Bennett 2008; Chadwick 2012; Papacharissi 2010).

Listeners

They were, however, in the minority. As Will's (pre-diary interview) quote alludes to, the majority of diarists rarely discussed politics in public or semi-public spaces online:

> I rarely post… I probably post, like, once every three months or something, if that. Maybe once every six months. I'm a lurker.

Some participants, like Alan and Leo, did not post anything publicly during the study, despite their diary entries indicating that they use social media on a daily basis. They are "lurkers," regularly observing but rarely contributing, if ever. Despite the fact that past research has shown that the majority of Internet users reflect the characteristics of lurkers, and that these attributes are beneficial to the emergence and development of online communities, the term term invariably has negative connotations (Crawford 2011: 63; Nonnecke and Preece 2003). Crawford (2011: 64) presents "listening" as an alternative:

> Once the activities defined as lurking are understood as forms of listening, they shift from being vacant and empty figurations to being active and receptive processes… It reflects the fact that everyone moves between the states of listening and commenting online; *both are necessary and both are forms of participation.* [Emphasis in original]

The majority of the participants in this study reflect what I describe as "listeners," citizens who use Facebook and Twitter to learn about news and political matters, either purposefully or as a by-product of their day-to-day use, but rarely engage in any form of public political expression when using these tools.

Prior to applying this terminology to this study, it is necessary to reflect on how the process of listening differs on Facebook and Twitter as opposed to through face-to-face interactions. In a real space exchange, one is expected to listen attentively to each and every word; to not do so would be deemed socially unacceptable. However, social media users do not engage with each and every post, they are not listening in this conventional sense. Rather, they are "background listening," "allowing messages to come and go, and occasionally 'tuning in' and responding" (Crawford 2011: 68). This dynamic of tuning in is precisely what Will (entry 8), an IT consultant from London, observed when reflecting on political videos that are posted on Facebook, as different messages compete for our attention on the News Feed:

> If I don't get some instant gratification from it [a video posted on Facebook], then one or two minutes is the usual amount of time I'm prepared to waste before moving on.

This process of filtering and sifting through content represents a meaningful form of agency, suggesting that listening can be a means of political participation in its own right.

Within research on audience behaviour and media literacy, the importance of listening to democratic citizenship is well-established (see Lacey 2013). However, in studies on digital political communication, we still tend to focus on digital expression that we can easily observe. Therefore, Crawford (2011: 73) and Lacey (2013) encourage scholarly research to move beyond the reification of "voice" and instead use the theoretical device of listening to understand communication flows in and from spaces such as Facebook and Twitter. In doing so, new questions emerge in relation to political participation and civic engagement on these platforms.

Given the anxieties some feel towards any form of digital interaction and the specific cognitive load that accompanies political discussion, this categorisation has two different conditions. There are some diarists who, at first glance, do not seem to be so-called listeners. For instance, Zoey (308 posts) and Annabeth (232 posts) were two of the most expressive users during the diary period, as shown in Fig. 6.1. However, while 78% of Oliver's provocative posts and 18% of Madeline's informative contributions were political, both Zoey and Annabeth were keen to avoid this topic. Just 4% of Zoey's and 1% of Annabeth's updates had a political frame. They are instead reflective of what I describe as "active listeners,"

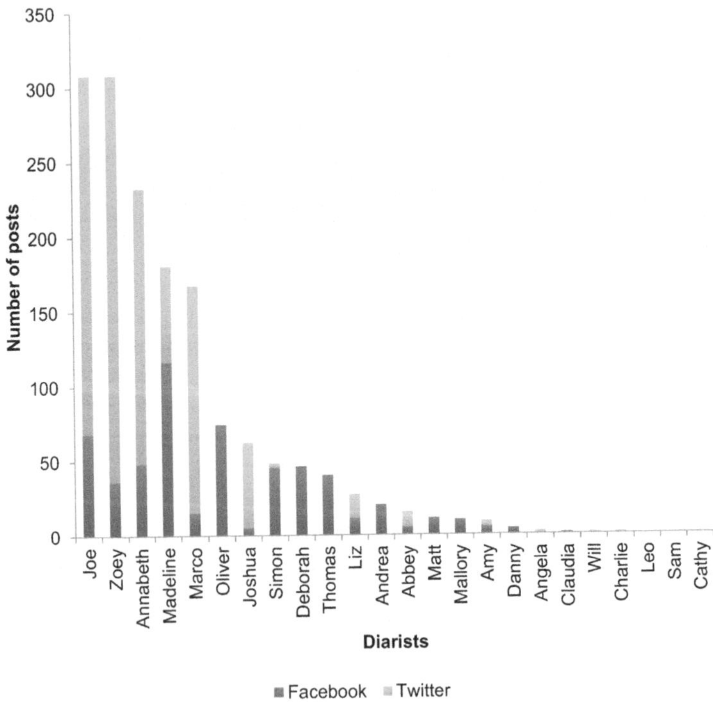

Fig. 6.1 Total number of posts on Facebook and Twitter during the diary period

those who post content and contribute to discussion on social networking sites but do not post political material with the same degree of regularity. Over half of Annabeth's contributions were personal (134 posts), as she often reflected on her first year of university. Meanwhile Zoey touched upon a range of different subjects, from celebrity gossip (33 posts) to her passion for food (34 posts).

Other participants rarely posted any form of public or semi-public update. These diarists reflect "passive listeners," users who do not post any content regardless of the subject matter. Despite their lack of activity, the diary entries suggest that these participants still use social media on a regular, often daily, basis. Sam (entry 10), a healthcare worker in the East Midlands, used Twitter to monitor discussion around radicalisation following the trial of Michael Adebolajo and Michael Adebowale, who were both found guilty of the murder of soldier Lee Rigby. Amy (entry 9) learnt of the debates surrounding the death of Mark Duggan, who was shot and killed by police in London in 2011, through a thread on her Facebook News Feed. Angela (entry 9) had a conversation with her husband about the political situation in Afghanistan after seeing a tweet that criticised an unexpected visit to Camp Bastion from the then Prime Minister, David Cameron. Therefore, these passive listeners are often interested in current affairs, but they are averse to sharing their opinions in such a public space. By focusing on observable political expression online in isolation, we ignore how these citizens may benefit from the contributions of others.

The final category in this typology refers to those citizens that have no interest in political information online. The annual *Digital News Report* (http://www.digitalnewsreport.org/), provided by the Reuters Institute for the Study of Journalism, tracks digital news consumption internationally. Their estimate suggests that around 7% of UK citizens avoid news despite the sheer amount of easily accessible content available online (Newman et al. 2015: 6). I hypothesise that these "avoiders" deliberately ignore posts on social media that have a political orientation. While some studies have found that this is a result of the negative effect the news can have on a person's mood (Newman et al. 2017: 42), I cannot draw conclusions on their motivations as no diarist displayed these characteristics in this study. This is a result of the sampling frame used in this study, as participants were recruited who had some degree of political interest (see Research Appendix).

Together, these four categories—civic instigators, contributors, listeners, and avoiders—make up the typology of citizen roles in social media environments. This describes the distinctive attitudes towards political expression on Facebook and Twitter that were present in this study. Although Chapter 5 shows that many diarists tailor news consumption around their personal interests when using these platforms, this does not lead to self-expression and discursive engagement. The absence of a self-expressive logic for those diarists categorised as listeners challenges the hypothesis that social networking sites foster public political forms of communication by virtue of their design. Instead, individual usage traits are much more nuanced than expected. As such, the typology raises a number of questions over the conditions in which listeners use these tools.

The Cognitive Load

Firstly, why do passive listeners use Facebook and Twitter, if not for self-expression and conversation? As Fig. 6.2 illustrates, over half of those involved (17) reported that they were "very busy" or "busy" for the duration of the diaries. Many participants found difficulty in balancing the competing demands on their time, be they professional responsibilities (Liz, entry 7; Sam, entry 1), family commitments (Alan, entry 2), or leisure activities (Joshua, entry 9). Furthermore, the anxieties created by this perceived lack of time can further restrict temporal autonomy. Cathy (pre-diary interview), who held a management position at a charity in the Midlands, observed how she would often stress about deadlines at work when she was trying to unwind. These time pressures can make remaining informed difficult. As a result, listeners use social media as an informational shortcut, a process in which communication can reduce the access costs associated with finding news and politically relevant information. As Amy (pre-diary interview) notes, "I just see it as a quick way of finding out about news for people who don't have enough time." This is not a new phenomenon; citizens have long been using informational shortcuts. Just as "Arnold" (entry 1), Cathy (entry 1), and Sam (entry 7) used the radio to learn about current affairs while undertaking other activities, others, like Abbey (week 3) and Simon (week 4), used social media as a bridge to political information. Alan (entry 2) and Angela (entry 8; 9) argue that this function is vital given the perceived social costs of not being informed.

Secondly, if listeners are interested and willing consumers of news and current affairs, why do they refrain from contributing to discussion online? A number of diarists felt apprehensive about how they would be judged by other networked contacts. For example, Amy (pre-diary interview) had

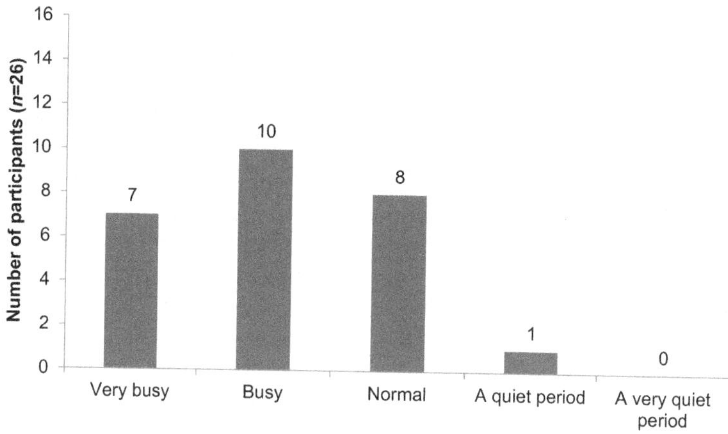

Fig. 6.2 How busy participants were during the diary period (*Source* Thinking back to the period of time when you were completing your diary, what sort of time was it for you? [$n = 26$])

been deterred by tense conversations she had seen on Facebook in the past. Likewise, Christian (entry 5) felt that other users were quick to get abusive if they disagreed with your posts, referring to a particularly unkind comment thread in reference to the then Chancellor of the Exchequer, George Osborne. For listeners, public political communication poses reputational risk. They are acutely aware of the real and the imagined audience—"the mental conceptualization of the people with whom we are communicating" (Litt 2012: 331)—mindful of the damage that could be caused by a wayward comment.

Some of this trepidation can be explained by the typology offered, as listeners associate political discussion on social media with the characteristics of civic instigators. Those who do take part tend to do so vociferously, as Andrea (pre-diary interview) notes, "it is very ranty and it can be a bit cringey." This is something Christian (entry 3) observed during a debate over the conduct of cyclists in London:

> I did not comment on this thread, as I never do, but I read each new comment with intrigue. What bothers me about Facebook arguments is that everyone thinks they are right about whatever point they are making. I just want to say, it is possible to have an argument where you can see both sides!

Beyond this perception of polarisation, others also highlighted the tone of political discourse on social media. Joshua (entry 12) was on the receiving end of some malicious insults from other outraged users when he commented on a Facebook page, initially set up for local gossip, to intervene in a discussion on immigration that he deemed to be racist. In his diary, Joshua noted that the unpleasant experience had deterred him from engaging in online political debate in the future. As such, the adversarial nature of political conversation, coupled with uncertainty over the reach and potential implications of a public or semi-public post, give rise to forms of social anxiety when using Facebook and Twitter.

Oliver, the most politically active participant on Facebook during the study, demonstrates how forms of public expression can fuel this unease. In his second diary entry, he noted his suspicions that some of his networked contacts on Facebook had unsubscribed from his posts as a result of his politically charged "rants." This led him to question his approach, as he felt that his "facetious, alarmist, and sometimes vulgar sentiments" may lead to fewer people engaging with him (Oliver, entry 4). This conflict between Oliver's (entry 6) desire to voice his opinions and his apprehension over the social implications of his communication left him in a difficult predicament:

> It annoys me that Facebook is used for short trivial interaction by my network. But what can I do? Either accept that and pander to it or continue to challenge that form of engagement. But if I challenge people I risk further isolating myself from others in my network.

While Oliver ultimately continued to express his views on Facebook, regardless of the reactions that he may face, these inhibitions are key to understanding why politically interested listeners are reluctant to use these platforms to regularly air their views.

This does not mean that listeners never post political material on Facebook and Twitter. As Table 6.2 shows, 15 participants shared political content at some point during the study. However, for many diarists, these posts were low in volume when compared to their contributions on other topics. Seemingly, a public or semi-public form of political expression represents a qualitatively different experience. I argue that the reputational logic that is central to the slacktivist critique, in which users act on the basis of a desired image that they wish to portray to their network, works in reverse; users are impeded by a fear of social repercussions and avoid certain forms of expression online by way of managing their identity across public and semi-public spaces. As Zoey (pre-diary interview) observes, self-expression on social networking sites requires self-confidence or at least confidence in one's beliefs. In this way, listeners often only feel comfortable posting when they possess a comprehensive understanding of an issue.

Intuitively, these topics tend to be closely tied to an individual's private interests and personal circumstances. This personalisation can come in a number of forms. Zoey, who works for a charity in the Midlands, focused on her professional interests, raising awareness of issues relating to mental health care. Deborah, a banking professional from Yorkshire, shared three politically oriented posts that were based on her identification with the Ukrainian diaspora. Liz used Twitter to share two tweets about human rights violations in Syria, an issue that she was evidently passionate about given the content of her weekly entries (entry 2; 4; 6; 9; 11). Therefore, while the lack of posts on their public profiles during the study may seem to suggest that these participants are apathetic or disengaged, the diary entries show evidence of attentive and articulate citizens who are activated into online forms of public participation on the basis of their personal interests.

This cognitive load challenges the premise that digital forms of engagement are effortless and instinctive, undertaken without any real consideration of their meaning or democratic value. By contextualising social media use with reflective diaries over a period of three months, it is possible to identify and understand the triggers for these moments of self-expression and digital micro-activism. For listeners, conscious of their audience and how they might perceive their character, a click or a status update can be a high-threshold behaviour. Publicly voicing one's political opinions can require a great deal of consideration, time, and effort. For instance, Will (entry 12) took part in a question and answer session on Twitter with Edward Snowden, the former contractor for the US government who leaked classified information from the National Security Agency (NSA). While this may seem like a relatively innocuous contribution, this 125-character tweet was carefully deliberated over as Will spent "the best part of an hour" deciding how best to articulate his contribution. As such, the low-effort nature of such actions masquerade what can be complex cognitive processes.

A Multi-Step Flow of Communication

These findings point to a more pressing concern regarding connection and communication on social media; do those who shout the loudest dominate conversations on these services? If civic instigators post the most frequently and listeners rely on social media for informational shortcuts, does this mean that there is a "spiral of silence" on Facebook and Twitter in which civic instigators shape how other users perceive public issues?

The spiral of silence, first proposed by Elisabeth Noelle-Neumann (1974), occurs when a citizen does not share their own opinion due to an underlying fear that they are in the minority, as they do not wish to risk social isolation. Findings from a study by the Pew Research Center suggest that social media platforms may exacerbate the spiral of silence, as they "do not provide new forums for those who might otherwise remain silent to express their opinions and debate issues" (Hampton et al. 2014). However, drawing inferences on general user behaviour based on this study is problematic as it focused on the leaks from Edward Snowden. As such, the issue itself may act as an intervening variable as it involves government surveillance of the very tools in question.

Evidently, this theory has relevance to the findings of this study as the majority of participants were listeners and thus wary of public forms of communication, while only a small minority were willing to regularly share political content. Furthermore, posts from civic instigators tend to have highly distinctive interpretations. For example, Matt would often share links from BBC News Online and the Mail Online by way of asserting the relevance of socialism in contemporary politics (entry 1; 8; 9; 10). The reflective diaries show that others pay attention to contentious posts like these (e.g. Annabeth, entry 2; Christian, entry 5; Joshua, entry 10). However, despite their interest and the controversial themes, other users were often unwilling to engage in discussion and correct perceived inaccuracies. Of the 135 political posts on Facebook in this study, 24 posts had no likes or comments in response. Furthermore, 82 posts had a low number of interactions, where the cumulative total of likes and comments was less than nine. The five politically oriented posts that had a very high level of interactions (defined as those posts with over 30 likes and/or comments) had either a personal orientation, such as when Oliver (entry 8) put forward a proposal to his local council, or were related to an event that triggered collective attention, as illustrated by the 13 likes and 19 comments when Joe (entry 2) shared Jeremy Paxman's interview with Russell Brand (see Chapter 5). This comment thread consisted of a visceral debate about the merits of voting between two civic instigators, rather than a debate that engaged others (Joe, entry 2). Given the frequency of posts from civic instigators, the strength of their political ideals, and the reluctance of listeners to offer a response, the opinions of those who are the most vocal often go unchallenged. As such, these findings seem to raise questions about the implications of political polarisation on social media.

However, the use of Facebook and Twitter as an informational shortcut did not result in listeners simply adopting the opinions offered by civic instigators. Rather, the diaries demonstrate a multi-step flow of communication that occurs after the point of consumption on a social networking site. These often unseen processes work in contrast to how they were originally conceived by Katz and Lazarsfeld (1955), in which opinion leaders, shaped by mass media, influence the wider population. In this study, those active users who are comparable to opinion leaders, the civic instigators, are challenged in private spaces. Listeners take to private modes of communication to contextualise, discuss, and sometimes challenge the information they receive on social networking sites. For example, Christian, a graphic designer from London, discussed the ongoing crisis in Syria at work following a post that he had seen on his Facebook News Feed. In the conversation that followed, Christian (entry 2) reflected on the possibility of military intervention given the defeat of the British government's motion to support US-led air strikes against President Bashar al-Assad's regime:

> This week I had a very long conversation with a girl at work about the issues surrounding why Britain should not get involved with the conflict in Syria. The conversation started because we both saw statements on Facebook, and this prompted her to tell me that her fiancé was in the Royal Artillery and had seen two tours of Iraq and one of Afghanistan. I asked her what she thought about the prospect of him going to Syria, and she told me that in his barracks, his squad was prepped and told to go into work with the imminent threat of being shipped out to Syria. Obviously, she was shocked and extremely worried in fighting another pointless war. I asked her why she thought it was pointless, she responded with "I accept they are killing innocent people, but can we really justify the cost of war in our current situation." I asked what the current situation

> was, and we spoke about the cuts to the NHS and policing, and the cost of the war in Iraq, both in monetary value and the cost to innocent lives. The whole conversation was prompted through social media, it sparked a greater discussion about politics and war.

Although neither Christian nor his colleague had taken to social media to express their opinion on this issue, the initial posts that they had been exposed to were key triggers for their political reflection. When we consider participation as a process, these exchanges are integral to the accumulation of civic knowledge and the formation of political identity.

There was evidence of a multi-step flow of communication across the entire sample, as participants often turned to those with whom they had a strong tie relationship to discuss politics. These conversations took place in private, either online or face-to-face. Amy spoke with her partner at home about a range of political issues that she was exposed to online, from data protection law (entry 1) to the ethics of strike action by workers on the London Underground (entry 11). Similarly, Leo (entry 7) used the cross-platform mobile messaging application WhatsApp to challenge a Facebook post that criticised the influence of the EU on policymaking in Britain. Using WhatsApp to discuss and contest content posted on social media with others, either one-to-one or in private groups, was relatively common (Abbey, entry 12; Danny, entry 5; 6; Will, entry 6). Other diarists noted that they also use the private messaging functionality on Facebook in this way, challenging the perception of Facebook as a public facing mode of communication (Charlie; Christian, pre-diary interview). In these spaces, diarists were more willing to discuss sensitive issues, such as Joshua (entry 5), who had a conversation with close friends on WhatsApp about LGBTQ rights following homophobic comments from the X Factor winner, James Arthur. Consequently, the threat of political polarisation on social media cannot simply be inferred from the content that is visible. Such judgements ignore the rich forms of private and semi-public communication that take place, as listeners challenge and contest information they receive on Facebook and Twitter.

In summary, the typology of citizen roles in social media environments illustrates the complex attitudinal characteristics that underpin political behaviour online. By focusing on public political acts online in isolation, the slacktivist critique disregards the agency of users and the different cognitive loads that are associated with public forms of self-expression. Furthermore, the critique offers a one-dimensional analysis of Facebook and Twitter as it disregards the multi-step flow of communication as it moves between public, semi-public, and private spaces. Even in these private exchanges, the lines between producer and consumer become blurred, posing new questions about the nature of mediated citizenship.

While the typology identified in this study illuminates some of the complex attitudinal motivations that underpin behaviour on social media, this is further complicated by distinctions that exist between the two social networking sites in focus, Facebook and Twitter.

A Service-Specific Logic

> I see Facebook as more like friends, and pictures, whereas Twitter is more current and relating to political things.
>
> (Claudia, pre-diary interview)

> I think most of the things that I see on Facebook are fairly superficial and I don't delve deeply into Facebook at all. It all seems to be froth and tittle and tattle… Twitter is different.
>
> (Sam, pre-diary interview)

As the quotes from Claudia and Sam suggest, there is evidence of a service-specific logic in this study; Facebook is deemed to be a social space while Twitter is an overtly politicised and news-oriented service. This logic was evident in the way that diarists used each platform to access political information (see Chapter 5), but also in how each site was used for self-expression.

By exploring the diaries and public posts of the 16 participants who used both services, it is evident that this sub-sample predominantly used Twitter, rather than Facebook, for posting political content. Facebook was often associated with specific concerns relating to reputation management. As Liz (pre-diary interview) observes, "I think it's interesting to look at politics on Facebook, but I wouldn't do it myself. It's very public." The use of the term "public" in this quote is significant given the default settings on both social networking sites. All posts on Twitter are publically accessible, whereas Facebook is a closed service, as updates are only accessible to those contacts that you approve. As such, Liz is not apprehensive of the public in a literal sense, an abstract term referring to all people, but a distinctive set of groups that trigger similar fears of other forms of openness. It is the make-up of the audience on Facebook that makes sharing sensitive posts seem more daunting. The public that Liz refers to on Facebook often includes an eclectic mix of close friends, work colleagues, and family members. Users can often feel overwhelmed as these diverse sets of social circles overlap, in what Marwick and boyd (2011) describe as a "context collapse."

The disparities between the audience on Facebook and Twitter can be demonstrated by Zoey (pre-diary interview), the only diarist to have her Facebook and Twitter account linked. This sometimes had unintended consequences, as Zoey (pre-diary interview) felt much more at ease expressing herself on Twitter:

> I've got my two accounts linked so if I put something on Twitter it automatically puts it onto Facebook. It is a bit of a nightmare because sometimes I'll put something on Twitter without thinking and then my Mum, who is friends with me on Facebook, will ask, 'What's the matter? What have you put that for?'

Even Oliver (entry 2), a civic instigator who frequently used the service to air his views, recognised the presence of a certain etiquette on Facebook; "Facebook is seen as a social tool, purely for entertainment and fun. There is a kind of 'don't talk politics at the dinner table' mentality embedded within its use." Other diarists supported this viewpoint. Claudia (pre-diary interview) and Leo (pre-diary interview) feel that clear distinctions exist over the kind of serious discussion that a user can engage in on Facebook, deeming personal achievements and significant events appropriate but politics as a topic to avoid. As such, the composition of the audience on Facebook shapes user behaviour.

On Twitter, many diarists felt more comfortable with sharing political posts. Joe, a contributor, provides the most fitting example. During the diary period, there was a significant discrepancy between the volume of political posts that he made on Twitter (90) in comparison with Facebook (18). Joe explained this deviation in his diary (entry 5), noting that Twitter was a more fitting platform because of his audience; he believed those who follow him tend to take political material seriously, whereas he feared that his Facebook network may respond with mockery. Marco, another contributor, took a similar approach, as the majority of his political contributions were shared on Twitter (27) rather than Facebook (2). Like Joe, Marco (pre-diary interview) visualised a different audience when moving between the two social networking sites, noting that those who follow him on Twitter tend to do so because of shared interests.

Even amongst those who did not have an account on the service, the majority of diarists perceived Twitter to be a space better suited to political discussion. I argue that this interpretation is a result of the real and imagined audience on each service. On Facebook, users struggle to balance their various identities: friend, family member, colleague, acquaintance, hook-up, and so on. Formulating a voice that speaks to each of these identities is difficult. On Twitter, the audience tends to be more defined, based around specific interests that the user joined the service to pursue. For instance, Amy (pre-diary interview) joined the service to follow her professional interests, using the platform to keep abreast of developments in the charity sector. Similarly, Christian (pre-diary interview) uses the site to network with fellow designers, while Leo (pre-diary interview) joined Twitter to become better informed on local news. In each of these cases, the diarist has a clear perception of what their expressions represent. Therefore, this service-specific logic can also impact the content and form of political expression.

Connecting the Typology to Political Action

The typology of citizen roles in social media environments describes how civic instigators, contributors, and listeners possess distinct attitudes towards political expression on Facebook and Twitter. These characteristics also result in different behavioural traits. Figure 6.3 shows the forms of participation that diarists were involved in over the three-month period, as disclosed in the survey completed at the end of the project.[3] While over half of participants signed a petition and donated money to a civic or political group, there was little evidence of widespread participation in more substantive forms of political action (e.g. taking part in a demonstration). However, this finding does not necessarily support the substitution thesis, in which low-effort online forms of engagement are replacing "tried and tested" offline methods. Further analysis is required to understand which diarists are participating, and why.

The substitution thesis can be explored through a comparison of the levels of digital micro-activism and instrumentalist forms of political action. In this study, those who were most active on social media, by posting political material and engaging in low-threshold forms of

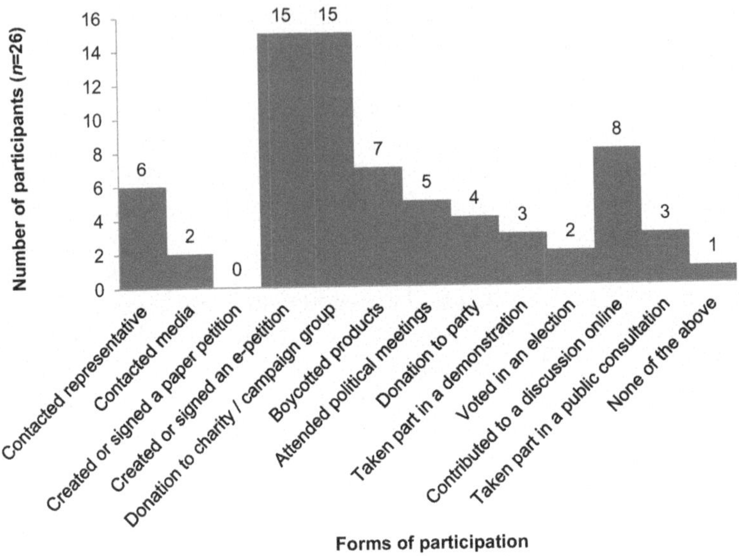

Fig. 6.3 Political action undertaken by participants during the diary period (*Source* During the time spent completing your diary, did you do any of the following to influence political representatives, public decisions, laws, or policies? [$n = 26$])

online activism, also took part in forms of substantive political action. As Table 6.3 shows, there was a correlation between citizen role and the depth of one's engagement. The civic instigators, Matt and Oliver, were two of the most active participants in the study, investing their time in a wide range of activities from political meetings to demonstrations. Contributors, such as Joe and Madeline, also engaged in high-threshold behaviours. Listeners, however, were less active, only triggered into action under specific circumstances. As such, those who most closely resembled the characteristics specified in the slacktivist critique were the most politically active citizens in this study.

For listeners, signing an e-petition was the most common form of engagement. However, this study did not find evidence of citizens engaging in digital micro-activism by way of managing their image online, which the slacktivist critique deems to be the key motivation for such behaviour. Despite 15 diarists signing an e-petition during the diary

Table 6.3 Level of participation based on the typology of citizen roles in social media environments

Citizen role	*Pseudonym*	*Forms of participation*
Civic instigator	Matt	• Donation to charity/campaign group • Boycotted products • Attended political meetings • Contributed to a discussion online
	Oliver	• Contacted representative • Created or signed an e-petition • Donation to charity/campaign group • Boycotted products • Attended political meetings • Donation to a party • Taken part in a demonstration • Contributed to a discussion online • Taken part in a public consultation
Contributor	Joe	• Contacted representative • Created or signed an e-petition • Voted in an election • Contributed to a discussion online
	Madeline	• Created or signed an e-petition • Donation to charity/campaign group • Taken part in a demonstration
Listener (Active)	Annabeth	• Donation to charity/campaign group
	Zoey	• Created or signed an e-petition
Listener (Passive)	Amy	• Donation to charity/campaign group
	Leo	• None of the above

Note The forms of participation listed in this table are based on those provided in the *Audit of Political Engagement* (Hansard Society 2018)

period, only three participants promoted a petition on their public profile during this time. Deborah (entry 4) signed a petition that her daughter posted on the service but did not share this with her own networked contacts. Similarly, Simon (entry 2; 7) reflected on a number of petitions that he had signed on Avaaz, none of which he shared on Facebook or Twitter. As such, this casts doubt on the claim that citizens engage in digital micro-activism for social benefits, rather than genuinely held personal beliefs.

The three participants who did share an e-petition on Facebook were Oliver, Madeline, and Mallory. Each of these diarists participated in campaigns that were based on their own personal interests. Oliver, who shared four petitions in total, seemed to follow the distinctive attitudinal patterns that were evident in his reflective diaries and public posts. During the study, he encouraged his friends on Facebook to: sign a petition lobbying the Secretary of State for Health, Jeremy Hunt, to abolish a legal clause that allowed the government to close hospital services without consultation; stop the ban on demonstrations at the University of Sussex; and encourage online retailer Amazon to increase pay for its workers. With each of these petitions, Oliver expressed his own views by way of encouraging others to sign. This approach differed to Madeline and Mallory, who simply shared the petition without any personal reflections. An example of this can be seen directly, as both Oliver and Madeline shared the same petition. This campaign, led by 38 Degrees, was designed to stop the Transparency of Lobbying, Non-Party Campaigning and Trade Union Administration Bill becoming law. Oliver, a civic instigator, offered his own rationale for signing the petition, arguing that the legislation would restrict political campaigning in the run-up to the 2015 general election. In comparison, Madeline, a contributor, offered no such indication of her motivations; her support was inferred from the fact that she shared the petition. This further illustrates the differences between the citizen roles.

This reluctance to regularly post personally expressive material is problematic for campaign groups and political parties. Described as informational shortcuts in Chapter 4, the leadership of political groups like 38 Degrees depend on users sharing evidence of their political behaviour and how it relates to their own private interests by way of encouraging others to participate. By providing easy access to political information for wider publics, the costs associated with involvement are reduced. While this does not necessarily lead to further action, under certain conditions it can. In this way, digital micro-activism can act as a gateway to new issues and enhanced political interest. Abbey (pre-diary interview) epitomises this process of activation through her interest and involvement in women's rights issues, which was evident through her weekly entries (entry 1; 3; 5; 7; 11) and in two tweets she posted in order to raise awareness of threats to women around the globe:

> The first time I saw *No More Page 3* [http://nomorepage3.org/] was when someone posted a link to the petition on Facebook saying, 'sign this petition, this is what it's about.' And the more I started to think about

> it, the more it was like, well, I have never been comfortable with Page 3 and, to find that I am not a weirdo in finding it a bit strange, was quite enlightening really. It just seems to be very basic. For some reason, it really appeals to me... The things that my previous colleagues used to say about women, and the way that they would treat Page 3, was embarrassing. So, I am glad that this is coming out. I love it because it's slowly leading me down the road to feminist enlightenment.

This quote illustrates the conditions under which access and exposure on social media transform into more substantive forms of engagement for listeners. Firstly, this chance sighting of an e-petition on Facebook resonated with Abbey's own pre-existing sentiments and personal experiences. This is typical for listeners, who share characteristics with the standby citizen model (Amnå and Ekman 2014); social media acts as a site of activation for these seemingly passive citizens. Secondly, Abbey's involvement was strengthened by the knowledge of a wider community of other like-minded citizens. Here, social media provides a space for connection. The presence of these communities helps foster further action.

Conclusion: Experiential Learning, Standby Citizens, and the Redundancy of the Slacktivist Critique

The rationale for this study was to observe and analyse how citizens use social networking sites for political participation in an everyday context. By drawing on data collected from Facebook and Twitter, and then contextualising these actions with rich ethnographic data in the form of diaries and interviews, this study offers a unique insight into the attitudes that guide political behaviour online. In doing so, it is clear that the slacktivist critique does not explain the individual-level attitudes that guide online self-expression and digital micro-activism. I propose a typology of citizen roles in social media environments to identify the different ways in which users engage with political material on social media in a day-to-day setting.

A small number of diarists reflect what I describe as civic instigators, active producers of expressive political content on social networking sites. However, despite the frequency of their posts, I argue that these citizens are not slacktivists. By tracking political attitudes over the course of three months using a multi-method approach, I found evidence to suggest that these digitally active citizens learn through self-expression and digital micro-activism. According to Kolb (1984: 38), an educational theorist, "learning is the process whereby knowledge is created through the transformation of experience." Civic instigators hone their personal identity through these low-threshold online interactions as part of an "experiential learning cycle," as shown in Fig. 6.4. These diarists reflect on their behaviour on social media, interpret and make sense of discursive exchanges when they occur, and then use this as a basis for future political engagement. Therefore, self-expression and digital micro-activism do not represent vacuous and ephemeral banalities but are connected to the development of a citizen's political identity.

Facebook and Twitter become sites of learning for these politically interested citizens. This reflects what Flanagan (2013: 18) describes as "mini-polities," as through their experiences in these spaces, civic instigators "formulate ideas about their membership, rights, and obligations as citizens in the broader polity." Oliver's diary exemplifies this experiential learning cycle. He often used Facebook to express his criticism of institutional politics in Britain. A theme running through his diary was the emergence of a politically active Russell Brand. At first, Oliver (entry 1)

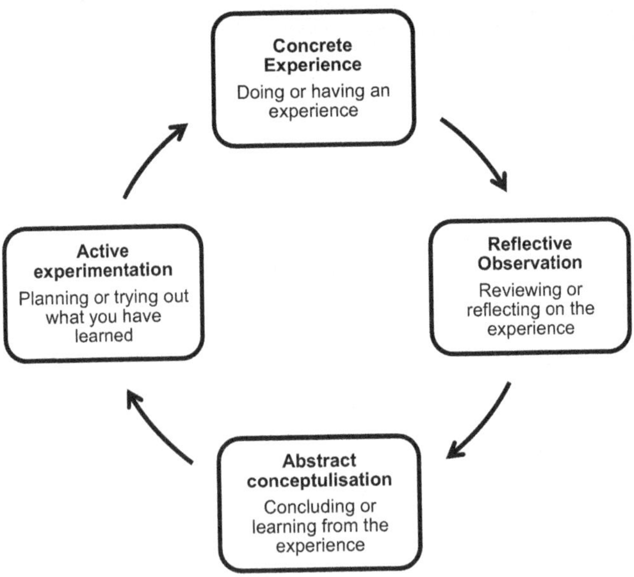

Fig. 6.4 Kolb's (1984) experiential learning cycle

was encouraged by the political vision offered in Brand's interview as the ideas resonated with his own personal frustrations; "this video was cathartic, assuring me that I am not alone in my ideas and aspirations." However, after sharing a subsequent interview with the comedian-turned-political activist on his Facebook profile (entry 2), the reaction from other users made Oliver question Brand's authenticity; "it soon dawned on me that the focus on Brand's very general message of political deviancy came at the expense of its substance." Ultimately, Oliver (entry 4) deemed Brand to be a "commodity of rebellion" that was undermining more serious political activism. Oliver discussed his own behaviours in reaction to this, reflecting on how he could tap into the interest shown by his friends in Brand. He did this by encouraging others to take part in an occupation of a university building. Therefore, this experiential learning creates the conditions for future mobilisation.

Furthermore, civic instigators and contributors, those who most closely resemble slacktivists, were the most engaged in substantive forms of political action. This correlation challenges the substitution thesis, the claim that digital micro-activism displaces tried and tested forms of participation. These findings support large-N studies that illustrate the correlation between expressive forms of digital activism and goal-oriented, public political action (Bode et al. 2014; Christensen 2011, 2012; Kristofferson et al. 2014; Vaccari et al. 2015).

It is clear that the majority of those completing the diaries were not representative of the committed activists that Gladwell (2010) and Morozov (2011) identify. While there was evidence of political learning and discussion in private spaces, examples of instrumental action were few and far between. However, as outlined in Chapter 3, such expectations are unrealistic and ultimately unhelpful. As Dalton (2007: 1) argues, rather than focusing on how good citizenship has been defined in the past, we must ask "what does it mean to be a 'good citizen' in today's society?" I argue that those citizens that I characterise as listeners are beneficial to a democracy. Listeners represent citizens who use these services to learn about news and political matters, either purposefully or as a by-product of their day-to-day use, but rarely engage in any form of public political expression. They can further be distinguished as either active listeners, those who frequently post content on non-political topics but consciously avoid anything that they deem to be political, or passive listeners, those who avoid public forms of expression entirely. For these diarists, politics still represents a taboo topic within public spaces (Eliasoph 1998). Although they value the informational shortcuts provided by social networking sites, the lines between content consumption and production were resolutely drawn; public political actions still require a public face.

Therefore, their lack of online self-expression is not indicative of disinterest but represents a distinctive attitudinal logic, one that challenges the very premise of slacktivism; political expression online is not necessarily easy. For listeners, what may seem like a simple click of a button, such as sharing a petition, is part of a complex decision-making process. This is because of the reputational risks on social networking sites, as the perception of one's audience, both real and imagined, shapes the willingness to engage. This cognitive load varies as citizens move between platforms (see Kim et al. 2018; Litt and Hargittai 2016). As a result, the slacktivist critique is correct in suggesting that image management online does play a significant role in shaping behaviour, but it constrains citizen action rather than promoting it. Those involved in this study were conscious that their posts would be deemed to be indicative of their character. As such, the slacktivist critique may even exacerbate participatory inequalities, as the more credibility and usage the term gains, the more deeply rooted these inhibitions may become.

Seemingly, when listeners do participate in self-expression and digital micro-activism these acts are not triggered by inauthentic reputational management, or the ease of the act itself, but by something much more meaningful. They overcome this cognitive load on those issues that resonate with their deeply held personal beliefs and private experiences. As such, listeners, both active and passive, reflect the characteristics of Amnå and Ekman's (2014: 262) standby citizen, those citizens who "appear passive" but "in reality are prepared for political action, should circumstances warrant."

Using the methodological orthodoxy of social media research, which emphasises publicly observable interactions, these listeners would not be accounted for when we consider online participation. However, just because they lack the same behavioural data trail as their contemporaries does not mean they are disinterested. They simply use Facebook and Twitter in a different way to civic instigators and contributors. As Joshua (entry 9) notes, "I always have it on, but I'm never using it." By using a diary methodology that traces the flow of information within and between different forms of media, this chapter illustrates how listeners form part of a multi-step flow of communication across public, semi-public, and private spaces (Katz and Lazarsfeld 1955). They are purposive in the selection of political materials that they consume, and actively express themselves on political issues in everyday life with strong tie connections in private or semi-public spaces. This often involves family members or close friends and increasingly takes place within private messaging apps, such as WhatsApp. In these private exchanges, the lines between producer and consumer become blurred even further, posing new questions about the nature of mediated citizenship. The conditions of this cross-fertilisation between access to information on public and semi-public social networking sites and discussion in private spaces further strengthens calls for research across different media.

Notes

1. Private interactions on Facebook did form part of the diaries, as a number of participants reflected on conversations with trusted contacts on Facebook Messenger. However, such disclosure was not constant across the sample, as this depended on how each diarist used the platform and whether they were willing to describe their private communications.
2. See the Research Appendix for further details on the sampling frame used. Two diarists, Arnold and Ron, did not use any form of social media. They were included as a point of comparison for the digitally active citizens that made up the rest of the sample.
3. Outside of this overview of political behaviour, these results also illustrate methodological issues. For instance, diarists sometimes omitted public political actions from their weekly entries, as they focused on their use of media for information consumption or did not perceive these acts to be political. Sam noted in his exit survey that he had taken part in a public consultation on healthcare reform but felt that this was in keeping with his professional interests rather than any political aspirations. There was also evidence of a discrepancy in how the participants interpreted the questions in the exit survey. Only eight diarists confirmed that they had contributed to a discussion online, despite the data collected from their public profiles suggesting otherwise.

References

Amnå, E., & Ekman, J. (2014). Standby Citizens: Diverse Faces of Political Passivity. *European Political Science Review, 6*(2), 261–281.

Bennett, W. L. (2008). Changing Citizenship in the Digital Age. In W. L. Bennett (Ed.), *Civic Life Online: Learning How Digital Media Can Engage Youth* (pp. 1–24). Cambridge: MIT Press.

Bennett, W. L. (2012). The Personalization of Politics: Political Identity, Social Media, and Changing Patterns of Participation. *The ANNALS of the American Academy of Political and Social Science, 644*(20), 20–39.

Bennett, W. L., Wells, C., & Freelon, D. (2011). Communicating Civic Engagement: Contrasting Models of Citizenship in the Youth Web Sphere. *Journal of Communication, 61*(5), 835–856.

Bode, L., & Vraga, E. K. (2017). Studying Politics Across Media. *Political Communication, 35*(1), 1–7.

Bode, L., Vraga, E. K., Borah, P., & Shah, D. V. (2014). A New Space for Political Behavior: Political Social Networking and Its Democratic Consequences. *Journal of Computer-Mediated Communication, 19*(3), 414–429.

Chadwick, A. (2012). Recent Shifts in the Relationship Between the Internet and Democratic Engagement in Britain and the United States: Granularity, Informational Exuberance, and Political Learning. In E. Anduiza, M. Jensen, & L. Jorba (Eds.), *Digital Media and Political Engagement Worldwide: A Comparative Study* (pp. 39–55). Cambridge: Cambridge University Press.

Christensen, H. S. (2011). Political Activities on the Internet: Slacktivism or Political Participation by Other Means? *First Monday, 16*(2). Retrieved September 23, 2011, from http://firstmonday.org/htbin/cgiwrap/bin/ojs/index.php/fm/article/viewArticle/3336/2767.

Christensen, H. S. (2012). Simply Slacktivism? Internet Participation in Finland. *eJournal of eDemocracy & Open Government, 4*(1), 1–23.

Coleman, G. (2012). Phreaks, Hackers, and Trolls: The Politics of Transgression and Spectacle. In M. Mandiberg (Ed.), *The Social Media Reader* (pp. 99–119). London: New York University Press.

Couldry, N., Livingstone, S., & Markham, T. (2010). *Media Consumption and Public Engagement: Beyond the Presumption of Attention.* Basingstoke: Palgrave Macmillan.

Crawford, K. (2011). Listening, Not Lurking: The Neglected Form of Participation. In H. Grief, L. Hjorth, & A. Lasén (Eds.), *Cultures of Participation* (pp. 63–77). Berlin: Peter Lang.

Dalton, R. J. (2007). *The Good Citizen: How a Younger Generation Is Reshaping American Politics.* Washington, DC: CQ Press.

Eliasoph, N. (1998). *Avoiding Politics: How Americans Produce Apathy in Everyday Life.* Cambridge: Cambridge University Press.

Flanagan, C. A. (2013). *Teenage Citizens: The Political Theories of the Young.* Cambridge, MA: Harvard University Press.

Gantz, W., & Trenholm, S. (1979). Why People Pass on News: Motivations for Diffusion. *Journalism & Mass Communication, 56*(2), 365–370.

Gladwell, M. (2010, October 4). Small Change: Why the Revolution Will Not Be Tweeted. *The New Yorker.* Retrieved November 3, 2010, from https://www.newyorker.com/magazine/2010/10/04/small-change-malcolm-gladwell.

Hampton, K. N., Rainie, L., Lu, W., Dwyer, M., Shin, I., & Purcell, K. (2014, September 2). Social Media and the 'Spiral of Silence'. *Pew Research Internet and American Life Project.* Retrieved September 2, 2014, from http://www.pewinternet.org/files/2014/08/PI_Social-networks-and-debate_082614.pdf.

Hansard Society. (2018). *Audit of Political Engagement 15: The 2018 Report*. London: Hansard Society.

Katz, E., & Lazarsfeld, P. F. (1955). *Personal Influence: The Part Played by People in the Flow of Mass Communications*. New York: The Free Press.

Kim, J., Lewis, S. C., & Watson, B. R. (2018). The Imagined Audience for and Perceived Quality of News Comments: Exploring the Perceptions of Commenters on News Sites and on Facebook. *Social Media + Society, 4*(1). Retrieved from https://doi.org/10.1177/2056305118765741.

Kolb, D. A. (1984). *Experiential Learning: Experience as the Source of Learning and Development*. Englewood Cliffs, NJ: Prentice Hall.

Kristofferson, K., White, K., & Peloza, J. (2014). The Nature of Slacktivism: How the Social Observability of an Initial Act of Token Support Affects Subsequent Prosocial Action. *Journal of Consumer Research, 40*(6), 1149–1166.

Lacey, K. (2013). *Listening Publics: The Politics and Experience of Listening in the Media Age*. Cambridge: Polity.

Litt, E. (2012). Knock, Knock. Who's There? The Imagined Audience. *Journal of Broadcasting & Electronic Media, 56*(3), 330–345.

Litt, E., & Hargittai, E. (2016). The Imagined Audience on Social Network Sites. *Social Media + Society, 2*(1). Retrieved from https://doi.org/10.1177/2056305116633482.

Marwick, A. E., & boyd, d. (2011). I Tweet Honestly, I Tweet Passionately: Twitter Users, Context Collapse, and the Imagined Audience. *New Media & Society, 13*(1), 114–133.

Morozov, E. (2011). *The Net Delusion: How Not to Liberate the World*. London: Penguin.

Newman, N., Fletcher, R., Kalogeropoulos, A., Levy, D. A. L., & Nielsen, R. K. (2017). *Reuters Institute Digital News Report 2017*. Oxford: University of Oxford and Reuters Institute for the Study of Journalism.

Newman, N., Levy, D. A. L., & Nielsen, R. K. (2015). *Reuters Institute Digital News Report 2015*. Oxford: University of Oxford and Reuters Institute for the Study of Journalism.

Noelle Neumann, E. (1974). The Spiral of Silence a Theory of Public Opinion. *Journal of Communication, 24*(2), 43–51.

Nonnecke, B., & Preece, J. (2003). Silent Participants: Getting to Know Lurkers Better. In C. Lueg & D. Fisher (Eds.), *From Usenet to Cowebs: Interacting with Social Information Spaces* (pp. 110–132). Amsterdam: Springer.

Papacharissi, Z. (2010). *A Private Sphere: Democracy in a Digital Age*. Cambridge: Polity.

Phillips, W. (2015). *This Is Why We Can't Have Nice Things: Mapping the Relationship Between Online Trolling and Mainstream Culture*. Cambridge: MIT Press.

Sturgeon, W. (2013, January 9). BINGO! What Makes a Daily Express Front Page? *The Media Blog*. Retrieved May 8, 2018, from http://themediablog.typepad.com/the-media-blog/2013/01/what-makes-a-daily-express-front-page.html.

Vaccari, C., Valeriani, A., Barberá, P., Bonneau, R., Jost, J. T., Nagler, J., & Tucker, J. (2015). Political Expression and Action on Social Media: Exploring the Relationship Between Lower- and Higher-Threshold Political Activities Among Twitter Users in Italy. *Journal of Computer-Mediated Communication, 20*(2), 221–239.

CHAPTER 7

Conclusion: The Candle Burns Bright

Set in the ongoing debates around slacktivism, a pejorative term that refers to inauthentic, low-threshold forms of political engagement online, this book examines the effect of routine social media use on political participation in Britain. By generating thick, descriptive data on individual-level political attitudes and behaviours, this study provides an account of how the seemingly mundane, everyday use of Facebook and Twitter can be beneficial to democracy.

I argue that the slacktivist critique has an overly narrow focus, isolating those routine actions which users undertake day-to-day from other forms of communication and modes of engagement. An alternative theoretical approach—the continuum of participation—is proposed to understand what happens before collective, or connective, action. A series of research questions were formulated based on this: What political information do citizens consume on Facebook and Twitter? Do these social networking sites provide a space for discursive engagement and, if so, what is the nature of this discussion? And, crucially, do these low-effort interactions evolve into further participatory acts? If they do, what are the attitudinal motivations driving this involvement? An experimental, mixed-methods research design was used to explore these questions in two different settings: firstly, in an activist context, through an ethnography of the political movement 38 Degrees; secondly, within day-to-day life, by combining evidence of participant behaviour online with reflective diaries.

J. Dennis, *Beyond Slacktivism*,
Interest Groups, Advocacy and Democracy Series,
https://doi.org/10.1007/978-3-030-00844-4_7

The main findings of this study suggest that Facebook and Twitter create new opportunities for cognitive engagement, discursive participation, and political mobilisation. 38 Degrees uses social media to support engagement repertoires that blend online and offline tactics. This organisational management of digital micro-activism provides participatory shortcuts for wider audiences, enabling their grass-roots members to shape campaign strategy. However, in contrast to both proponents and critics of online participation, there is no evidence of a widespread self-expressive logic. Instead, this study identifies a typology of citizen roles in social media environments. "Civic instigators," those who most closely resemble slacktivists, engage in digital micro-activism by way of refining their political identity. Meanwhile, "listeners" use social media to consume political information but refrain from public forms of expression. Instead, they take to private spaces for political discussion. When listeners do act, it is not effortless, but carefully considered. As such, I argue that these symbolic acts should not be dismissed as slacktivism but understood as forms of active citizenship.

This chapter begins by firstly outlining the main findings. Secondly, I compare the results from this micro-level study to those from macro-level projects, contextualising the book's contributions within broader national and international trends. Thirdly, in the context of the Cambridge Analytica scandal, I sketch out a research agenda for future critical research that explores the everyday experiences of digital politics at the individual level. Finally, the most significant contributions of this book are discussed in relation to the utopian-dystopian divide at the heart of this field. I reflect on how these disputes stem from fundamental differences in how participation is conceptualised.

The Continuum of Participation Revisited: Outlining the Main Findings

This book challenges slacktivism as a judgement on contemporary political action. By drawing on the continuum of participation model (see Chapter 3), in which engagement is treated a process rather than an outcome, I illustrate a number of limitations of the concept as a representation of the routine, everyday use social networking sites for political activity. Instead, I argue that Facebook and Twitter offer an important space for democratic engagement within day-to-day life.

Firstly, there was evidence that Facebook and Twitter users are exposed to political information as a by-product of the everyday use of these platforms. In an activist context, 38 Degrees members depend on the group's social media accounts for political information on topics that they deem to be "alternative," ignored by professional media. There were also examples of accidental exposure to news and current affairs within the diaries, but this was often framed around a user's pre-existing political identity. Through selective exposure on Twitter and algorithmic prioritisation on Facebook, diarists receive personally tailored information. However, this personalisation does not mean that these citizens bypass important political issues, as a comparison of the content of the diaries with the lead stories of four British newspapers showed that moments of collective exposure still occur. Rather than social media being used as an alternative to other sources of news, the diaries show how Facebook and Twitter are used to complement long-standing sources of information, a hybridisation of media habits.

Secondly, participants in this research did have political conversations that were based on their use of Facebook and Twitter, but not in the way that I expected based on the deductive framework in Chapter 3; they were not ready and willing to express themselves in public spaces online. There was little evidence to support the existence of a widespread self-expressive logic on social media amongst both 38 Degrees members and the diarists. Instead, the reputational threat of the real and imagined audience drew heavily on the minds of those taking part in this study, often impeding political expression. However, this does not mean that these users simply passively consume the information that they are exposed to online, as suggested by the slacktivist critique, but rather that they take to private spaces to discuss and contest this material. This discussion can either take place online, with WhatsApp playing a prominent role for some, or face-to-face. Although these forms of discursive engagement are not public and easy for researchers to collect, they are still examples of active citizenship and require further exploration.

Thirdly, participants used Facebook and Twitter for private expression on public political agendas, but in ways that were surprising and more nuanced than expected. In the absence of a widespread self-expressive logic, the typology of citizen types in social media environments illustrates the complex attitudinal characteristics at the individual level. Civic instigators and contributors—those most reflective of slacktivists—hone their political identity through frequent public political interactions. Meanwhile, listeners act infrequently on the basis of deeply held private motivations. In an activist context, the ethnography of 38 Degrees demonstrated how staff strategically use the low-threshold, expressive functions on Facebook and Twitter in a variety of ways across the continuum of participation: social media is used as a discursive space, so that members can influence issue selection and campaign strategy; members are encouraged to share material to raise awareness amongst wider publics; and, Facebook and particularly Twitter can be an effective space for forms of online activism. These logics are often intertwined in a single campaign.

Fourthly, the argument that low-threshold political acts on Facebook and Twitter simply replace equivalent low effort, offline forms of engagement obfuscates more complex participatory processes. For some diarists, the antecedents of political behaviour online were not low-threshold; digital micro-activism is not easy.[1] Perhaps surprisingly, social boundaries proved to be a key factor in this book. The slacktivist critique assumes that all those who engage in forms of micro-activism do so from the same state; that these actions are universally low-threshold for all participants. As the research on 38 Degrees and the media diaries show, this is not the case. Even within a relatively homogenous sampling frame, there was still a widespread divergence in the participants' willingness to engage in public forms of self-expression and micro-activism. The real and imagined audience on Facebook and Twitter poses a unique obstacle for some citizens as they navigate the various transfigurations of public, semi-public, and private spaces.

At the organisational level, the leadership at 38 Degrees seek to avoid such difficulties by using Facebook and Twitter at strategically significant points in a way that lowers the costs associated with participation. These democratic shortcuts are designed to make it easier for those citizens who are on the periphery of the "Westminster Bubble"[2] to get involved. Moving beyond the attitudinal comparison, such behavioural contrasts between new and old forms of engagement misrepresent the effectiveness of low-threshold actions. In what Karpf (2016) describes as "analytic activism," the leadership of 38 Degrees use social media data to listen and respond to the priorities of its members. This represents a significant development in organisational politics.

Fifthly, engagement in this study was based on a reflexive, individually defined notion of political identity. This was in stark contrast to the hypothesis that acts of slacktivism on social media are inauthentic, undertaken by users on the back of cascades to cultivate a managed identity online. While the slacktivist critique is correct to suggest that Facebook and Twitter can act as a site of activation in which interest for an issue is ignited, this is formed by more than just incidental exposure. As the reflections from Abbey in Chapter 6 illustrate, this activation requires a confluence of pre-existing interests and private experiences. For those diarists I describe as listeners, public expression and action is based on those issues that they are most passionate about. Given the audience dilemma, these actions are only undertaken when they are compelled to do so, most commonly on topics that relate to them personally. Conversely, civic instigators and contributors engage in low-threshold public actions online as part of a sense-making process, as they continue to formulate and adapt their own personal political identity. In a similar fashion, members of 38 Degrees mobilise around campaigns that resonate on an individual level. The identity framing by which members take collective action is inherently private. It is through exposure to emotionally salient information that the leadership brings together its ideologically disparate and geographically dispersed membership. Therefore, emotive forms of self-expression, which are derided by the slacktivist critique as inauthentic, act as an identity frame. These personal action frames provide momentum for further participation (Bennett and Segerberg 2013).

Collectively, these findings offer a sense of the individual-level experiences of those citizens who have been derided as slacktivists. By combining evidence of participant behaviour online with rich, qualitative reflections from social media users, this book seeks to offer an understanding of the quotidian experiences and personalised context that underpins some of the remarkable forms of digitally networked action that have taken place over the last decade.

Contextualising Digital Micro-Activism Nationally and Globally

The annual *Digital News Report* (http://www.digitalnewsreport.org/), provided by the Reuters Institute for the Study of Journalism, tracks digital news consumption internationally. This large-scale, representative survey offers a unique data set to contextualise the findings from this book both nationally and globally. The results demonstrate how the contributions of this study offer a starting point for further research on general behavioural trends.

When we consider the use of social media for news consumption, the evidence from the Digital News Report shows that an increasing number of citizens in the UK are using Facebook and Twitter as a source of news. As Fig. 7.1 illustrates, there has been a significant rise in the number of respondents who access news content on social networking sites in a typical week. However, in the light of fears over the impact of filter bubbles on political learning, it is important that one does not confuse use with dependency. It is not the case that social media is becoming the main source of news for all British citizens, as just nine per cent of those surveyed in the Digital News Report use it as their primary source (Newman et al. 2017). Even the most prolific users of social media in this study still combine these social platforms with newspapers, broadcast media, and direct access to professional news websites, as shown in Chapter 5. These micro-level characteristics, indicative of uses and gratifications theory, exemplify the need for further research to understand

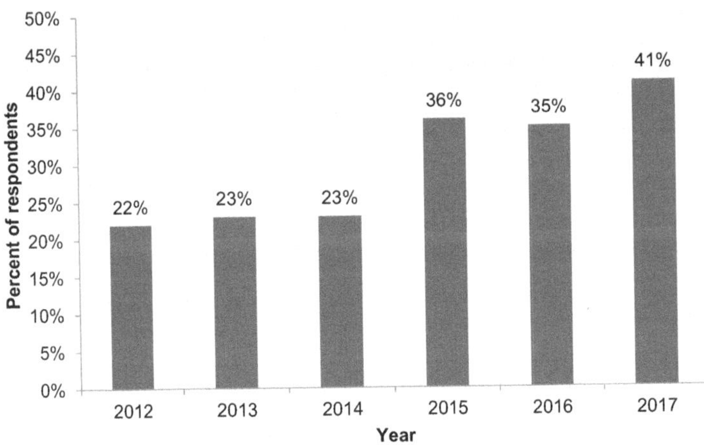

Fig. 7.1 Social media as a source of news in the UK, 2012–2017. *Note* Results are based on the following survey question: *Which, if any, of the following have you used in the last week as a source of news? Please select all that apply.* N = 1778 (2012); 2078 (2013); 2082 (2014); 2149 (2015); 2024 (2016); 2112 (2017) (*Sources* Data adapted from Newman [2012: 27], Newman and Levy [2013: 10; 2014: 14], Newman et al. [2015: 52–53; 2016, 2017])

the complex ways in which these different spaces become entwined, and whether or not these conditions are beneficial for further democratic engagement.

While access to news on social media is increasing, forms of self-expression and public discussion are relatively stagnant in the UK. The Digital News Report project also includes a range of indicators that measure whether respondents share news content online and if they interact with others. Figure 7.2 shows no evidence to support the claim that interaction and engagement with news content on social media has become more commonplace. Instead, respondents are much more likely to discuss news face-to-face. These findings, interpreted alongside the typology of citizen roles in social media environments introduced in Chapter 6, exemplify how behaviours related to news consumption

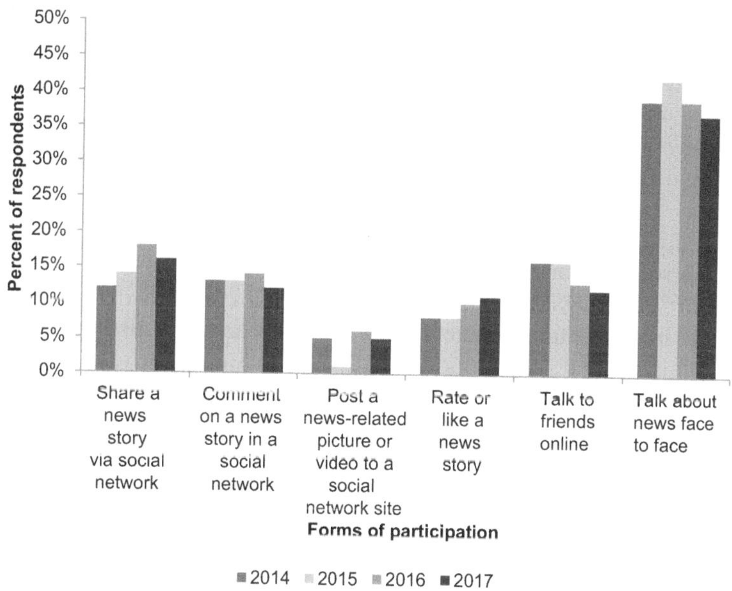

Fig. 7.2 Engagement with news coverage on social media in the UK, 2014–2017. *Note* Results are based on the following survey question: *During an average week, in which, if any, of the following ways do you share or participate in news coverage?* $N = 2082$ (2014); 2149 (2015); 2024 (2016); 2112 (2017) (*Sources* Data adapted from Newman and Levy [2013: 66; 2014: 73], Newman et al. [2015: 84; 2016, 2017])

and political expression on social media are not symbiotic. This challenges the premise that social networking sites cultivate self-expression and political discussion by virtue of their design. Further research should focus on the increasing levels of news consumption on social media, analysing the type and form of private interactions that occur post-consumption.

Although this typology may have salience in the UK, it is important to stress that the adoption of social networking sites for public expression could be dependent on cultural context. By drawing on comparative data from the Digital News Report, Table 7.1 shows the percentage of respondents who have engaged in forms of participation with news content on social media for six countries: the UK, Germany, Italy, Spain, the USA, and France. While respondents from the UK and Germany tend to be more reserved on social media, in other cultural contexts there is support for the hypothesis that online expression is growing. In France, for example, the willingness of citizens to publicly share and comment on news content has increased alongside the growth of news consumption on social media. By comparison, the results from Italy, Spain, and the USA show a significantly higher proportion of citizens sharing and commenting on news material.

These findings can be compared to the typology of citizen roles in social media environments. On a macro-level, citizens in Italy, Spain and the USA seem to share some of the behavioural traits of civic instigators and contributors, taking to public spaces to discuss and debate current events. Those in the UK seem to share the characteristics of listeners, consuming news through social media but taking to private spaces for discussion. This indicates that distinctive cultural contexts could affect online forms of political engagement. Further comparative research is therefore required to explore the relationship between political socialisation and the willingness to engage in public forms of digital expression.

Beyond the Engagement Gaze: Developing a Research Agenda

While this book challenges the attitudinal and behavioural assumptions of the slacktivist critique, it is not my intention to present a utopian account of the role of social media in political life. This is an important point given what Chadwick (2018) describes as "the engagement gaze,"

Table 7.1 Percentage distribution of participation on social media by country, 2014–2017

		As % of respondents (n)					
Forms of participation		*UK*	*Germany*	*Italy*	*Spain*	*USA*	*France*
Share a news story via a SNS	2014	12	13	35	30	22	11
	2015	14	13	30	34	21	18
	2016	18	12	31	34	25	20
	2017	16	10	31	32	29	21
Comment on a news story via a SNS	2014	13	11	23	25	21	11
	2015	13	11	25	32	21	15
	2016	14	10	27	28	22	18
	2017	12	8	23	24	24	16
Post a news-related picture or video to a SNS	2014	5	6	11	11	10	6
	2015	1	6	10	17	10	9
	2016	6	5	12	15	11	10
	2017	5	4	10	13	12	11
Rate or like a news story	2014	8	17	31	25	15	10
	2015	8	14	16	32	16	18
	2016	10	14	17	32	19	23
	2017	11	14	15	29	21	22
Talk to friends online about a news story	2014	16	13	19	24	29	15
	2015	16	15	20	32	26	18
	2016	13	9	14	27	19	15
	2017	12	8	12	26	20	16
Talk about news face to face	2014	39	39	40	48	44	30
	2015	42	40	42	48	45	33
	2016	39	34	38	43	42	32
	2017	37	31	39	41	40	30
n	2014	2082	2063	2010	2017	2197	2017
	2015	2149	1969	2006	2026	2295	2026
	2016	2024	2035	2195	2104	2181	2162
	2017	2259	2062	2011	2006	2259	2000

Sources Data adapted from Newman and Levy (2013, 2014), Newman et al. (2015, 2016, 2017)
Note Results are based on the following survey question: *During an average week, in which, if any, of the following ways do you share or participate in news coverage?* The wording for each action was altered slightly in each report, but the meaning remained the same

in which digital participation is treated as a universal good. As the behaviour of the civic instigators in Chapter 6 shows, this is not the case, as provocative and at times abusive political expression can act as an impediment to political involvement for others. Beyond the remit of this book, incivility online can have devastating consequences, as demonstrated by the instrumental role of the Facebook News Feed in spreading rumours, hate speech, and misinformation against Muslims in Sri Lanka (Taub and Fisher 2018) and the Rohingya people in Myanmar (Hogan and Safi 2018). Although this represents just one factor in the formation of these complex crises, it is clear that social networking sites have been used to push harmful narratives that have ultimately resulted in violence against minorities. With this in mind, it is essential that future individual-level research examines the connections between information consumption, opinion formation, and political action within these dangerous contexts.

What should this critical research look like? No discussion of social media and politics would be complete without mentioning Cambridge Analytica, the now defunct British political consultancy. The firm made headlines in March 2018 after *The New York Times*, *The Observer*, and Channel 4 News revealed how the company acquired personal data on 87 million Facebook users from an academic researcher's app (see Romano 2018 for an overview). Developed in 2014 by Aleksandr Kogan, "thisismydigitallife" was a personality quiz designed to reveal a participant's character traits. Although only 270,000 users took part, the app also granted the developer access to collect data on their Facebook friends. What in hindsight may seem like an obscene violation of privacy was completely acceptable at this point, as Facebook allowed third-party developers to access friend network data until 2015. Therefore, this was not a hack or a violation of Facebook policy, and this public revelation should have instead marked a meaningful turning point for the relationship between the technology firm and its userbase.

However, the critical reflections on Facebook were quickly usurped by a much more dystopian narrative, that this data was used to manipulate and control the voting intentions of the electorate. Using psychometric targeting, in which psychological profiles were added to pre-existing demographic data, former CEO Alexander Nix claimed that the firm could persuade voters by appealing to their personality traits. Although scholars had already sought to dispel any causal link between Cambridge Analytica and the result of the 2016 US presidential election (Baldwin-Philippi 2017; Tworek 2017), this narrative had real traction within popular discourse (see Gatehouse 2017). This is problematic as it obfuscates the systemic issues facing Facebook as a platform. As Karpf (2018) argues, it is essential that we do not propagate the "myth of the digital wizard." While I do not want to dismiss the significance of this scandal and the other practices that Cambridge Analytica was involved in, including the alleged use of bribes, honey traps, and the concerning ties that exist with conservative billionaire Robert Mercer, this reaction was reminiscent of the hyperbole surrounding #Kony2012—the case that inspired this book—and, seemingly as consequential, with the time spent on Facebook by US citizens going up in the wake of the scandal (Kanter 2018). Therefore, it is essential that the fundamental concerns that first emerged from this story remain at the heart of research on social media and political engagement going forwards, including: (1) the visibility and transparency of information sharing on social media; (2) the power of large technology companies; and (3) inequality online.

Firstly, in the light of the debates surrounding the transparency of political micro-targeting and the spread of misinformation, future studies should examine the dynamics of visibility online. In the diary study, I was surprised at how the majority of the politically interested, social media savvy sample reflected the listener categorisation, consuming political information from Facebook and Twitter but refraining from public forms of expression. In line with other scholars (Crawford 2011; Karpf 2016; Tufekci 2018), I contend that listening may be the most potent political resource on social platforms, even more so than the expression of voice. This attention is structured and ultimately controlled by large technology companies. When Facebook and Twitter change the algorithms for content prioritisation on their platforms, information distribution can change dramatically. This has been illustrated by those sites that have seen their audience traffic plummet as a result of tweaks made to the News Feed on Facebook. Upworthy, the media company known for its politically progressive viral content, was victim to such changes, witnessing its unique monthly website visitors drop from a high of 87 million in December 2013 to 20 million by November 2014 (Sanders 2017). Similarly, in an experiment across five countries in 2018, Facebook removed all posts by Pages from the News Feed, adding them instead to a newly created Explore Feed. While this may seem fairly insignificant and well within the rights of the company as the service provider, it negates the fact that many media organisations rely on Facebook traffic for their audience. Filip Struhárik (2017), a Slovakian journalist who was affected by the changes, reported a dramatic reduction in the number of interactions (likes, shares, and comments) for mainstream news media outlets.

Although the experiment is now over, this move represents the direction of travel for Facebook. In 2018 the company updated the News

Feed algorithm to prioritise posts from friends over Pages, a change described as showing users more "updates that spark conversation" (Mosseri 2018). However, as the results of the diary study show, even politically interested citizens are often unwilling to share or debate news online. These listeners often rely on Pages that they follow for updates on current affairs and, seeing as data already shows a steady decline in Facebook-referred traffic for news organisations (Owen 2018), new questions must be asked about how the news consumption experience on Facebook is changing and how this impacts political citizenship. Matt Karolian (2018), Director of Audience Engagement at *The Boston Globe*, has already advocated for publishers to consider alternative platforms and services to reach their audience, highlighting the growth in dedicated bots for news dissemination through private messaging applications and mobile-focused solutions, such as Instagram and Snapchat. These semi-public and private forms of communication mirror those adopted by the listeners in this study, many of whom are already dependent on WhatsApp for political talk. As the uses of these platforms evolve and change, it is vital that individual-level research is conducted that describes and explains these emerging media habits.

Secondly, although the shocking undercover footage of Alexander Nix offering to use sex workers to entrap rival politicians meant that Cambridge Analytica was firmly in the public spotlight, Facebook was at the centre of this scandal, and the story has illustrated the immense power the company has within society. Nielsen (2018) describes this influence as "platform power," identifying how: (1) technology companies like Facebook, Google, and Twitter increasingly set the technical standards for news dissemination online; (2) these platforms have ultimate control over this distribution, through shaping the algorithms that deliver content to end-users and by updating the rules and community standards that determine what material is acceptable; and (3) that these decisions are made in secret, with little transparency. As this book illustrates, some citizens are dependent on social platforms for their political agency. This dependency, coupled with the apparent vulnerability of these platforms for abuse, demonstrates why it is imperative that researchers treat these companies as valid objects of study. For instance, Kreiss and McGregor (2018) illustrate how staff at Facebook and Twitter played an active role in shaping campaign communications during the 2016 US presidential election. The involvement of these organisations went beyond merely selling a product, in this case, digital advertising. Instead, staff worked closely with political campaigns on the adverts they produced by way of securing their commitment and adoption of their platform (Kreiss and McGregor 2018: 167). As Kreiss and McGregor (2018: 172) argue, "What is clear is that political communication scholars need to consider technology, and especially social media, firms as more active agents in political processes than previously appreciated in the literature."

Finally, while this book offers an empirically grounded, optimistic account of how the routine use of Facebook and Twitter can benefit democratic citizenship, these findings are an illustration of participatory habits amongst a specific population, those that resemble the characteristics of slacktivists. Those alienated or apathetic citizens who are deemed most susceptible to misinformation and political micro-targeting were not part of this research. Here, I refer to what Ford and Goodwin (2014) describe as the "left-behind," older, white, socially conservative voters in more economically marginal areas whose support was integral to the referendum result in the UK. Similarly, in the context of eight years of austerity and growing levels of poverty (Goodman 2018), there is an urgent need to explore the conditions of digital citizenship amongst disaffected communities. Schradie (2015) offers a powerful critique of cyber-optimism, highlighting how the assumed political benefits derived from social media overlook the structural inequalities that are embedded within them, stating that "poor and working-class people are denied full civic and political citizenship using the internet" (Schradie 2015: 76). Therefore, there is a need for rich, ethnographic research that explores the race, class, and gender dynamics of political social media use.

Ultimately, this book offers an account of how citizens mix social media into everyday political practices at the individual level. It illustrates the day-to-day conditions under which Facebook and Twitter become civically relevant and enhance democratic engagement. It is unquestionably optimistic in its contribution, but only so far as to challenge a critique that has undermined and questioned what I contend are invaluable and significant political acts. Beyond this rebuttal, I do not wish to make generalisable claims about the enduring and transformational utility of these tools. Instead, by exploring the process of political engagement across different media, I believe future research can help illuminate the precise conditions of the aforementioned challenges.

The Power of Participation

The extent to which one buys into this neo-optimism depends on a key question that runs throughout this book, one that is controversial and likely to divide scholars; how *should* we define participation? Your response to this question will frame the value that you assign to this research.

Some scholars argue that participation must be public and seek to change the goal-orientated behaviour of others (see Carpentier 2011 for an overview). It is this action-focused definition of participation that sustains the slacktivist critique. If you approach the concept from this perspective, then the findings of this research may seem to have little value. However, by adopting this logic one equates participation with cause and effect, disregarding the democratic benefits that are accrued prior to instrumentalist forms of political engagement. Such an interpretation ignores the pre-conditions that are necessary for substantive forms of activism. For example, Dahlgren (2011: 8) argues that "participation has a clear material and actionist dimension, and cannot be reduced to how we think or feel". I disagree. We cannot truly understand political action unless we attempt to unpick the experiences, interactions, and emotions that result in mobilisation.

This limitation can be demonstrated if we consider the concept of power. Different actors seek to exercise power or influence those who possess it in order to affect change. Carpentier (2011: 69) argues that it is the absence of conflict over decision-making that distinguishes participation from information consumption or political discussion. However, by adopting this narrow conceptualisation of participation, we revert back to a one-dimensional view of power, in which power is behavioural and can only be understood in terms of its effects (Dahl 1961; Hay 2007: 173). Actions do not occur spontaneously. As decades of rights-based movements have shown, activism is deeply ingrained in everyday experiences. These protest movements often target both material and symbolic goals, as political elites also wield influence over the ways in which individual-level preferences are formed (Bachrach and Baratz 1962; Lukes 2005). Indeed, the literature on media effects, which comprises some of the most important theoretical contributions to political communication as a discipline, is reliant on such a definition. As such, I argue that the processes that citizens take prior to forms of public-facing action also have value.

Therefore, the findings of this book dispute the notion that political participation is a public-only phenomenon. Each empirical chapter illustrates how politics is increasingly understood through the prism of everyday, personal experiences: 38 Degrees members mobilise around the campaigns that are personally relevant; the evidence from the diaries suggests that citizens understand news and current affairs through the lens of their own individually-driven interests, and listeners overcome the cognitive load online when mobilised by an issue that resonates with their political identity. This personalisation is representative of a distinct generational shift in citizenship within Western democracies (see Bennett 2008, 2012; Dalton 2008; Inglehart 1990). These findings suggest that we cannot separate our private, everyday experiences from our public actions. As such, participation should be conceptualised as a process, whereby listening, everyday political conversations, and private forms of expression are all indicators of the health of a democracy. While these private political interactions do not always result in instrumental forms of action, these behaviours *are* empirically significant. I argue that they should not be analysed separately.

Future research should avoid using easily accessible, publicly available data as a reflection of the routine, day-to-day use of social media. Public modes of expression form just one function of the many different ways that citizens use these tools in everyday life. Private and semi-public forms of digitally mediated self-expression can still be beneficial for cultivating active citizenship. Whether it was Claire, a member of 38 Degrees, whose interest in a number of issues was triggered by casually browsing the movement's posts on Facebook (Interview 8, June 2013), or Deborah, who was motivated to sign a petition based on a link shared by her daughter (entry 4), social media can act as a site of activation in which interest for an issue is ignited or strengthened. This activation is an important dynamic when we consider the characteristics of contemporary citizenship, such as Schudson's (1999) concept of the monitorial citizen and Amnå and Ekman's (2014) notion of the standby citizen. The digitally active citizens in this study use Facebook and Twitter in a similar way, as they monitor the information space, waiting for an issue that they identify with. To this end, listening and private forms of communication are significant for understanding digital citizenship.

In this way, these findings support Papacharissi's (2010: 167) hypothesis that the convergence of the private-personal and the public political facilitates new forms of collective action between like-minded individuals. Fuchs (2014: 186) is critical of this approach, arguing:

> Papacharissi reduces collective action to individual action and the public sphere to the private sphere. She ignores the materiality of protest action. Her approach is individualistic, reductionist and philosophically idealistic.

However, Fuchs' criticisms are unfounded as he and Papacharissi are theorising about intrinsically different phenomena.

Papacharissi (2010: 89) explains how the norms of democratic citizenship are evolving in the light of the development of online digital media. Such work is based on the idea that political identity in advanced industrial democracies is no longer collective in a traditional sense, but privatised, a result of years of social fragmentation (Inglehart 1990). In this way, social media acts as a facilitator, enabling autonomous citizens to craft political identity and connect with others. In contrast, Fuchs (2014: 186) stresses the value of real space activism, arguing that such interpretations overlook the importance of "co-presence and physicality." He contends that a cohesive political movement relies on the social bonds that are built face-to-face, rather than online, and that offline forms of protest are more effective than digitally mediated action.

This argument is symptomatic of the slacktivist critique. Both claims are examples of "either/or" propositions, ones that ignore the relationships that are formed between the Internet and offline activism. Although Fuchs (2014: 186) does acknowledge that social media can be beneficial as an organisational tool, by rejecting Papacharissi's hypothesis he tacitly equates participation to public political action. In doing so, he negates the value of digital technologies, as they are not deemed capable of cultivating the strong tie connections required for high-cost activism. However, such activism accounts for a tiny proportion of the many ways in which citizens can participate in public life and disregards the process by which citizens become engaged. The local mobilisation efforts to minimise the impact of the UK's 2012 Health and Social Care Act, discussed in Chapter 4, are an example of this. In the first instance a weak tie network between like-minded individuals was necessary, formed through the leadership's use of e-petitions and Facebook groups. This then provided the infrastructure for local collective action, as over 150 groups formed, meeting face-to-face to lobby their CCG. The strong tie bonds that formed were therefore dependent on the weak tie networks. Crucially, the success of this campaign was not the result of *just* face-to-face interactions or *just* digital communication, but it was part of a process that required both; private and semi-public connections can foster public action.

The majority of those participants involved in this research are interested in politics and well-informed on those issues that they deemed to be important, yet they are uncomfortable in expressing these opinions in public spaces. If we move beyond the reification of public-only participation when researching social media, we can see how the everyday use of platforms like Facebook, Twitter, and private messaging applications like WhatsApp, benefits political citizenship. The slacktivist critique ignores these lifestyle-based forms of political talk and self-expression. This is problematic, as these experiences shape the dynamics of collective action. As Eliasoph (1998: 8) argues, "the ability to discuss politics allows citizens to generate power together." This is not to say that this relationship between private connection and public action did not exist before social media, but platforms such as Facebook and Twitter can certainly make the process easier for citizens to act collectively on their personal preferences.

Ironically, the emphasis on effort within the slacktivist critique is emblematic of the very technological determinism that cyber-pessimists seek to counter. Emphasising the individual-level costs associated with a technological function, such as clicking a button, disregards the cognitive processes that result in such an act. While it may be the case that some of these actions are done with very little forethought or planning, to assume that all are done on this basis is inaccurate. For some, these actions can be deliberated over at great length. Likewise, it seems quite perverse to suggest that just because these actions require less effort than other forms of activism did in the past, these citizens are somehow acting inauthentically. If these actions help to reduce costs at the individual level and enable a broader, more diverse range of citizens to participate in substantive action repertoires, should they not be valued? These tools are evidently not designed to "save the world," and to judge them in such terms is disingenuous. No form of communication will bring about systemic political change, but, in both activist contexts and day-to-day life, social media can be of benefit to citizens.

As the title of the introduction to this book suggests, it is only when we adjust our focus away from deterministic, impossibly grand claims about the impact of social media that we begin to see the symbolic possibilities for democratic enrichment in the milieu of everyday life: the candle burns bright.

Notes

1. Doubt must also be raised over whether sending a postcard or placing a sticker on a car bumper also represent easy, low-threshold acts, as similar social anxieties may be present.
2. The Westminster Bubble is a characterisation of those working in Parliament as being isolated from life outside it. The politicians, civil servants, and journalists working in and around Westminster are considered as a community removed from the experiences and concerns of the general public (see Grant and Warhurst 2015).

References

Amnå, E., & Ekman, J. (2014). Standby Citizens: Diverse Faces of Political Passivity. *European Political Science Review, 6*(2), 261–281.

Bachrach, P., & Baratz, M. (1962). Two Faces of Power. *The American Political Science Review, 56*(4), 947–952.

Baldwin-Philippi, J. (2017). The Myths of Data-Driven Campaigning. *Political Communication, 34*(4), 627–633.

Bennett, W. L. (2008). Changing Citizenship in the Digital Age. In W. L. Bennett (Ed.), *Civic Life Online: Learning How Digital Media Can Engage Youth* (pp. 1–24). Cambridge: MIT Press.

Bennett, W. L. (2012). The Personalization of Politics: Political Identity, Social Media, and Changing Patterns of Participation. *The ANNALS of the American Academy of Political and Social Science, 644*(20), 20–39.

Bennett, W. L., & Segerberg, A. (2013). *The Logic of Connective Action: Digital Media and the Personalization of Contentious Politics.* Cambridge: Cambridge University Press.

Carpentier, N. (2011). *Media and Participation: A Site of Ideological-Democratic Struggle.* Bristol: Intellect.

Chadwick, A. (2013). *The Hybrid Media System: Politics and Power.* Oxford: Oxford University Press.

Chadwick, A. (2018). *Thinking About the Role of Social Media in the Formation of Public Opinion.* Paper presented at the International Communication Association Annual Conference, Prague, Czech Republic.

Crawford, K. (2011). Listening, Not Lurking: The Neglected Form of Participation. In H. Grief, L. Hjorth, & A. Lasén (Eds.), *Cultures of Participation* (pp. 63–77). Berlin: Peter Lang.

Dahl, R. A. (1961). *Who Governs? Democracy and Power in an American City.* London: Yale University Press.

Dahlgren, P. (2011). Parameters of Online Participation: Conceptualizing Civic Contingencies. *Communication Management Quarterly, 21*(4), 87–110.

Dalton, R. J. (2008). *Citizens Politics: Public Opinion and Political Parties in Advanced Industrial Democracies* (5th ed.). Washington, DC: CQ Press.

Eliasoph, N. (1998). *Avoiding Politics: How Americans Produce Apathy in Everyday Life*. Cambridge: Cambridge University Press.

Ford, R., & Goodwin, M. (2014). *Revolt on the Right: Explaining the Radical Right in Britain*. London: Routledge.

Fuchs, C. (2014). *Social Media: A Critical Introduction*. London: Sage.

Gatehouse, G. (2017, June 27). Did Cambridge Analytica Play a Role in the EU Referendum? *BBC News*. Retrieved May 27, 2018, from http://www.bbc.co.uk/news/av/uk-40423629/did-cambridge-analytica-play-a-role-in-the-eu-referendum.

Goodman, P. S. (2018, May 28). In Britain, Austerity Is Changing Everything. *The New York Times*. Retrieved May 28, 2018, from https://www.nytimes.com/2018/05/28/world/europe/uk-austerity-poverty.html.

Grant, W., & Warhurst, C. (2014/2015, February 1). Could the 'Westminster Bubble' Be Detrimental to British Politics? Retrieved August 8, 2015, from http://www2.warwick.ac.uk/knowledge/socialscience/westminsterbubble/.

Hay, C. (2007). *Why We Hate Politics*. Cambridge: Polity Press.

Hogan, L., & Safi, M. (2018, April 3). Revealed: Facebook Hate Speech Exploded in Myanmar During Rohingya Crisis. *The Guardian*. Retrieved May 27, 2018, from https://www.theguardian.com/world/2018/apr/03/revealed-facebook-hate-speech-exploded-in-myanmar-during-rohingya-crisis.

Inglehart, R. (1990). *Culture Shift in Advanced Industrial Society*. Princeton, NJ: Princeton University Press.

Kanter, J. (2018, May 20). The Backlash That Never Happened: New Data Shows People Actually Increased Their Facebook Usage After the Cambridge Analytica Scandal. *Business Insider*. Retrieved May 27, 2018, from http://www.businessinsider.com/people-increased-facebook-usage-after-cambridge-analytica-scandal-2018-5.

Karolian, M. [mkarolian]. (2018, January 12). The Summary Slide on My @BostonGlobe 2017 Strategy Deck Doesn't Include Anything Re: Facebook Pages. Pages Are Ineffective as They Don't Cultivate Community and Relationships. We've Known This for Years. *Tweet*. Retrieved May 27, 2018, from https://twitter.com/mkarolian/status/951626154154299393.

Karpf, D. (2016). *Analytic Activism: Digital Listening and the New Political Strategy*. Oxford: Oxford University Press.

Karpf, D. (2018, April 24). A World Without Wizards: On Facebook and Cambridge Analytica. *Civic Hall*. Retrieved May 27, 2018, from https://civichall.org/civicist/world-without-wizards-facebook-cambridge-analytica/.

Kreiss, D., & McGregor, S. C. (2018). Technology Firms Shape Political Communication: The Work of Microsoft, Facebook, Twitter, and Google with Campaigns During the 2016 U.S. Presidential Cycle. *Political Communication, 35*(2), 155–177.

Lukes, S. (2005). *Power: A Radical View*. Basingstoke: Palgrave Macmillan.

Mosseri, A. (2018, January 11). Bringing People Closer Together. *Facebook Newsroom*. Retrieved May 27, 2018, from https://newsroom.fb.com/news/2018/01/news-feed-fyi-bringing-people-closer-together/.

Newman, N. (2012). *Reuters Institute Digital News Report 2012: Tracking the Future of News*. Oxford: Reuters Institute for the Study of Journalism, University of Oxford.

Newman, N., & Levy, D. A. L. (2013). *Reuters Institute Digital News Report 2013*. Oxford: Reuters Institute for the Study of Journalism, University of Oxford.

Newman, N., & Levy, D. A. L. (2014). *Reuters Institute Digital News Report 2014*. Oxford: Reuters Institute for the Study of Journalism, University of Oxford.

Newman, N., Levy, D. A. L., & Nielsen, R. K. (2015). *Reuters Institute Digital News Report 2015*. Oxford: Reuters Institute for the Study of Journalism, University of Oxford.

Newman, N., Fletcher, R., Levy, D. A. L., & Nielsen, R. K. (2016). *Reuters Institute Digital News Report 2016*. Oxford: Reuters Institute for the Study of Journalism, University of Oxford.

Newman, N., Fletcher, R., Kalogeropoulos, A., Levy, D. A. L., & Nielsen, R. K. (2017). *Reuters Institute Digital News Report 2017*. Oxford: Reuters Institute for the Study of Journalism, University of Oxford.

Nielsen, R. K. (2018, March 29). *The Power of Platforms*. Retrieved May 27, 2018, from https://www.slideshare.net/RasmusKleisNielsen/the-power-of-platforms-inaugural-lecture-by-rasmus-kleis-nielsen-u-of-oxford.

Owen, L. H. (2018, January 11). Facebook Drastically Changes News Feed to Make It "Good for People" (and Bad for Most Publishers). *NiemanLab*. Retrieved May 27, 2018, from http://www.niemanlab.org/2018/01/facebook-drastically-changes-news-feed-to-make-it-good-for-people-and-bad-for-most-publishers/.

Papacharissi, Z. (2010). *A Private Sphere: Democracy in a Digital Age*. Cambridge: Polity Press.

Romano, A. (2018, March 20). The Facebook Data Breach Wasn't a Hack. It Was a Wake-Up Call. *Vox*. Retrieved May 27, 2018, from https://www.vox.com/2018/3/20/17138756/facebook-data-breach-cambridge-analytica-explained.

Sanders, S. (2017, June 20). Upworthy Was One of The Hottest Sites Ever. You Won't Believe What Happened Next. *NPR*. Retrieved June 1, 2018, from https://www.npr.org/sections/alltechconsidered/2017/06/20/533529538/upworthy-was-one-of-the-hottest-sites-ever-you-wont-believe-what-happened-next.

Schradie, J. (2015). Silicon Valley Ideology and Class Inequality: A Virtual Poll Tax on Digital Politics. In D. Freelon & S. Coleman (Eds.), *Handbook of Digital Politics* (pp. 67–84). Cheltenham: Edward Elgar.

Schudson, M. (1999). *The Good Citizen: A History of American Public Life*. Cambridge, MA: Harvard University Press.

Struhárik, F. (2017, December 17). Facebook Has Hurt Mainstream Media More Than Fake News Sites. Retrieved May 27, 2018, from https://medium.com/estadodelasredessociales2017/facebook-has-hurt-mainstream-media-more-than-fake-news-sites-113277bada8.

Taub, A., & Fisher, M. (2018, April 21). Where Countries Are Tinderboxes and Facebook Is a Match. *The New York Times*. Retrieved May 27, 2018, from https://www.nytimes.com/2018/04/21/world/asia/facebook-sri-lanka-riots.html.

Tufekci, Z. (2018, January 16). It's the (Democracy-Poisoning) Golden Age of Free Speech. *Wired*. Retrieved May 27, 2018, from https://www.wired.com/story/free-speech-issue-tech-turmoil-new-censorship/.

Tworek, H. (2017, May 15). Cambridge Analytica, Trump, and the New Old Fear of Manipulating the Masses. *NiemanLab*. Retrieved May 27, 2018, from http://www.niemanlab.org/2017/05/cambridge-analytica-trump-and-the-new-old-fear-of-manipulating-the-masses/.

Research Appendix

The mixed-method research design used in this study is, at its core, a workaround; a creative fix designed to explore the relatively uncharted terrain of digital engagement at the individual level. As many of the methods used have not gone through the years of refinement like their more traditional counterparts, this research appendix is an important way of ensuring transparency amongst the scholarly community (Karpf 2012b). Reflecting on the shortcomings of the experimental methodology is important, as I envisage that this information can be critiqued, improved upon, and adapted for use in future studies.

Supporting Information for Chapter 4

List of Interviews

Anonymity was offered as part of the agreement allowing internal access to 38 Degrees. The gender of interviewees should not be implied from their pseudonyms (Tables A.1 and A.2).

J. Dennis, *Beyond Slacktivism*, Interest Groups, Advocacy and Democracy Series, https://doi.org/10.1007/978-3-030-00844-4

Table A.1 Interviews with staff at 38 Degrees

No.	*Pseudonym*	*Role*	*Date*
1	Jessica	Member Services Manager	May, 2013
2	Anna	Campaigns By You Manager	May, 2013
3	Jonathan	Campaigns Manager	May, 2013
4	Amy	Campaigns Director	May, 2013
5	Adam	Technology Manager	May, 2013
6	Paul	Campaigner	May, 2013
7	David Babbs	Executive Director	June, 2013

Note Given his role within 38 Degrees, David agreed to be interviewed without anonymity

Table A.2 Interviews with members of 38 Degrees

No.	*Pseudonym*	*Age*	*City*	*Profession*	*Date*
8	Claire	25	Leicester	Archive centre operative	June, 2013
9	Mike	24	London	Engineering	June, 2013
10	Daniela	21	London	Student	June, 2013
11	Siobhan	20	London	Student	June, 2013
12	Nina	22	London	Unemployed	June, 2013
13	Geraldine	68	Liverpool	Retired	June, 2013
14	Helen	49	Essex	Civil servant	July, 2013
15	George	63	Birmingham	Retired	August, 2013
16	Mary	63	Hertfordshire	Retired	October, 2013
17	Ian	60	Brighton	Teacher	October, 2013
18	Jack	56	London	Civil servant	October, 2013
19	Liam	38	London	Charity sector	October, 2013
20	Joanna	57	Essex	Volunteer	October, 2013
21	Joan	73	London	Artist	October, 2013
22	Danni	24	London	Advertising	November, 2013

Supporting Information for Chapters 5 and 6

Sampling Frame and Demographic Information

This convenience sample was designed to identify participants with media habits that were reflective of the slacktivist critique. The sample is heavily skewed towards citizens who use digital media. Of the 29 diarists, 24 had a Facebook account and 20 used Twitter. Just two participants, Arnold and Ron, did not use either service. Furthermore, 15 diarists stated that they use online providers as their main source of news,

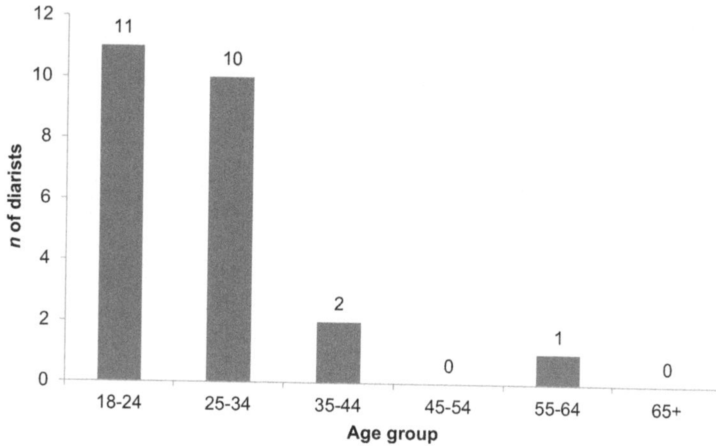

Fig. A.1 Number of diarists with a Facebook account by age group

with four participants using social networking sites for this purpose. This does not mirror general trends, as television is still the most widely used medium for news consumption in Britain (Ofcom 2014: 2).

No quotas for age, gender, or socio-economic groupings were used during recruitment. As a result, there was a slight over-representation of young people with either a Facebook account, as shown in Fig. A.1, or a Twitter account, illustrated in Fig. A.2.

However, as Fig. A.3 shows, this reflects a similar trend across the wider British public, with younger Internet users more likely to have set up an account on a social networking site (Ofcom 2013a: 25). While this offers a more accurate representation of the target population, this study has an over-representation of younger age groups.

The sample also had a gender and socio-economic status bias. There was a slight over-representation of males with 16 male and 13 female participants. Secondly, as Table A.3 shows, there was a significant over-representation of citizens who were either in the process of undertaking or had already completed an undergraduate degree when compared to UK census data. Likewise, the occupational status of those involved was not representative of the wider population, with all but one diarist in work and many with incomes higher than the national average (£26,500). As Sloam (2012) argues, this has implications for the findings of this research as new repertoires of political engagement tend to

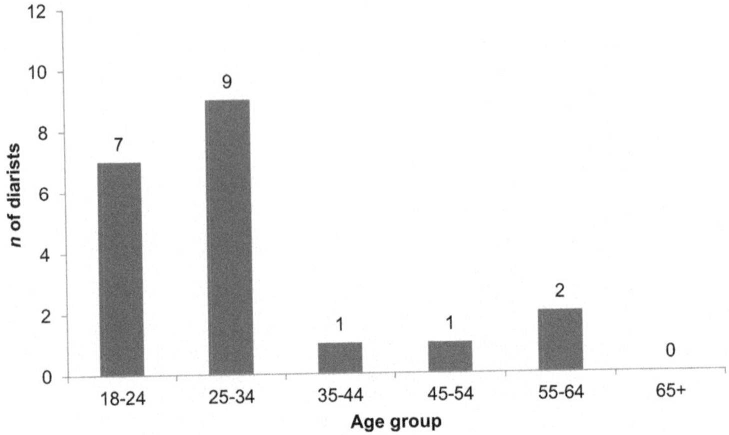

Fig. A.2 Number of diarists with a Twitter account by age group

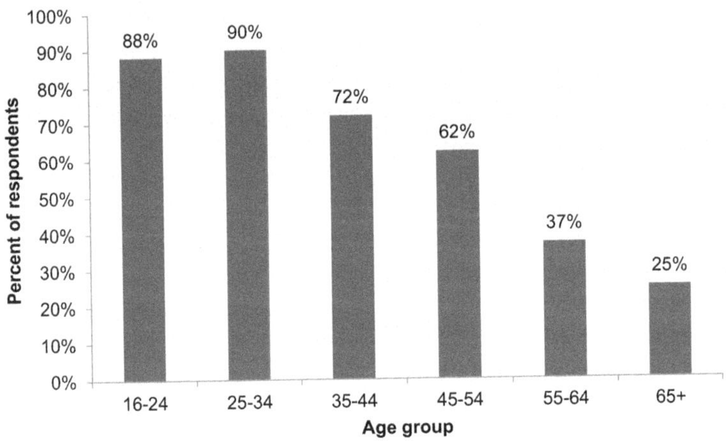

Fig. A.3 Internet users in Britain who have set up a profile on a social networking site by age group (*Source* Ofcom [2013a: 25]. *Note* Results are based on the following survey question: *Which, if any, of these things have you ever done online: Set up your own social networking site page or profile on a site or app such as Facebook, Twitter, LinkedIn, Instagram, Tumblr or Pinterest.* N=1346)

Table A.3 Details of the diarists

Pseudonym	*Age group*	*Gender*	*Region*	*Profession*	*Highest completed level of education*	*Facebook user*	*Twitter user*	*Diary medium*
Leo	25–34	M	London	Financial sector	University or college degree (e.g. BA; BSc)	Yes	Yes	Email
Claudia	25–34	F	London	Charity and voluntary sector	University or college degree	Yes	Yes	Word document
Madeline	25–34	F	South East	Higher education	Higher university or college degree (e.g. MA; MSc; PhD; PGCE)	Yes	Yes	Shared Evernote notebook
Angela	55–64	F	East Midlands	Clerical work	Lower secondary school qualification (e.g. O levels; GCSEs)	No	Yes	Email
Sam	55–64	M	East Midlands	Healthcare sector	University or college degree	No	Yes	Shared Evernote notebook
Will	25–34	M	East of England	Financial sector	University or college degree	Yes	Yes	Email
Deborah	55–64	F	Yorkshire and the Humber	Retail sector	Lower secondary school qualification	Yes	No	Email
Joshua	18–24	M	East Midlands	Recruitment	University or college degree	Yes	Yes	Email
Charlie	25–34	M	London	Charity and voluntary sector	University or college degree	Yes	Yes	Shared Google Drive document
Annabeth	18–24	F	Yorkshire and the Humber	Student	Upper secondary school qualification (e.g. A levels; Highers)	Yes	Yes	Email
Louise	18–24	F	South East	Student	Upper secondary school qualification	Yes	No	Shared Evernote notebook

Table A.3 (continued)

Pseudonym	*Age group*	*Gender*	*Region*	*Profession*	*Highest completed level of education*	*Facebook user*	*Twitter user*	*Diary medium*
Danny	25–34	M	East of England	Civil servant	University or college degree	Yes	Yes	Word document
Oliver	25–34	M	South East	Higher education	University or college degree	Yes	No	Word document
Joe	18–24	M	South East	Student	Upper secondary school qualification	Yes	Yes	Email
Abbey	25–34	F	East Midlands	Clerical work	University or college qualification below a degree (e.g. Higher National Diploma; Higher National Certificate; City and Guilds Advanced Certificate; Nursing Diploma)	Yes	Yes	Facebook message
Liz	18–24	F	South East	Student	Upper secondary school qualification	Yes	Yes	Word document
Thomas	18–24	M	South East	Student	Upper secondary school qualification	Yes	Yes	Email
Zoey	35–44	F	East Midlands	Charity and voluntary sector	Upper secondary school qualification	Yes	Yes	Email
Andrea	18–24	F	South East	Student	Upper secondary school qualification	Yes	No	Word document
Marco	18–24	M	South East	Student	Upper secondary school qualification	Yes	Yes	Shared Evernote notebook

(continued)

Table A.3 (continued)

Pseudonym	*Age group*	*Gender*	*Region*	*Profession*	*Highest completed level of education*	*Facebook user*	*Twitter user*	*Diary medium*
Matt	18–24	M	South East	Student	Upper secondary school qualification	Yes	No	Word document
Mallory	18–24	F	South East	Student	Upper secondary school qualification	Yes	Yes	Word document
Arnold	55–64	M	East Midlands	Construction	Lower secondary school qualification	No	No	Handwritten
Simon	18–24	M	South East	Student	Upper secondary school qualification	Yes	No	Word document
Cathy	45–54	F	East Midlands	Charity and voluntary sector	Upper secondary school qualification	No	Yes	Email
Amy	25–34	F	East of England	Charity and voluntary sector	University or college degree	Yes	Yes	Email
Ron	*65+*	*M*	*Yorkshire and the Humber*	*Retired*	*Lower secondary school qualification*	*No*	*No*	*Word document*
Alan	*35–44*	*M*	*East Midlands*	*Unemployed*	*Lower secondary school qualification*	*Yes*	*No*	*Word document*
Christian	*25–34*	*M*	*London*	*Digital and creative services*	*University or college degree*	*Yes*	*Yes*	*Email*

Note Louise did not consent to the researcher using her Facebook data during the project. Thomas deleted his Twitter account during the diary period. Ron, Alan, and Christian withdrew from the project before completion be structured in favour of citizens with higher levels of education and higher levels of household income.

The convenience sample was also designed to recruit citizens with some interest in politics. As with media habits, political interest was an important variable in order to identify participants who may represent the slacktivist critique. As such, this means that the findings of this study are limited to those citizens with some level of interest in politics. Political interest was calculated through a measure of political activity. Participants were asked what political actions they had completed over the previous 12 months. This question, and the responses offered, was based on those included in the *Audit of Political Engagement* (Hansard Society 2014: 90). By comparing the results, there are two measures in which the sample had significantly lower levels of political activity, singing a paper petition and taking part in a public consultation. Otherwise, the participants in this research are generally representative of the target population, i.e. politically active individuals in Britain.

Details on the Dataset

The data set for this study consists of the diaries, content from Facebook and Twitter where applicable, pre-diary interviews, and post-diary survey data. Diarists were asked to complete weekly, free-form diary updates over a period of three months. A diary template was provided on request. This was designed to be plain, to minimise researcher influence. Diarists were not given direction over the length or structure of the diary, but encouraged to develop a style that worked for them. This was done purposefully to motivate reflection on what participants deem to be political (Couldry et al. 2010: 48).

Participants were recruited through advertisements across two pre-existing networks available to the researcher: students at Royal Holloway, University of London, and volunteers at the South Derbyshire Centre for Voluntary Services. Participants were paid a fee of £10 for their involvement and entered into a prize draw for a tablet computer.

The attrition rate was relatively low. Of the 30 diarists that were originally recruited for the study, four participants withdrew before completion. Alan, Christian, and Ron gave consent for their partially completed diaries to be included in the research, contributing five, six, and seven entries, respectively. As such, none of these diarists took part in the exit survey. Furthermore, due to a range of factors including family crises, vacations, and the logistics of participant recruitment, diaries were not always completed concurrently. This did not jeopardise comparability between the diaries and the newspaper sources, as mentions of political issues were weighted to account for the number of active diarists.

Participants were given the option to record their diaries through a number of different mediums to minimise the inconvenience caused and to avoid participant withdrawal. Diarists used the following methods to submit their entries: email (12 participants); Microsoft Word, using a template provided by the researcher (10); Evernote, using a shared notebook (4); Google Drive (1); Facebook, through a series of messages (1); and 1 participant completed their diary by hand.

The diary entries submitted varied dramatically, both in terms of their depth but also substance. Joshua would send a few lines, highlighting the topics that caught his attention over the last week, while Joe would go into great depth. Precisely what formed the main topic of reflection differed from diarist to diarist. Some, such as Deborah, Leo, and Thomas, used the diary to discuss specific items in the news each week. Others, like Charlie, Christian, and Claudia, reflected on their use of social media, even addressing slacktivism directly at times. These different styles are important, as they illustrate that the diaries were already highly interpretive before any analysis was undertaken.

All diarists with a Facebook and Twitter profile were asked to provide evidence of their public interactions. All but one diarist, Louise, agreed to this. In order to collect this data, I added all of their diarists as a friend on Facebook and then sorted them into a private list. This enabled me to access all posts made without algorithmic restrictions. I collected all posts made by the diarists during their involvement in the project. This did not include comments or likes on the content of other Facebook users or private interactions.

All diarists gave permission for their posts on Twitter to be used in the research. However, one diarist was excluded from the analysis. Although Thomas originally provided consent, he left the service before the data collection took place. The data collected from Twitter included all public interactions made by diarists during the diary period, including public responses to other accounts (@mentions).

Limitations

A number of research limitations should be noted. Firstly, just as users alter their behaviour online depending on their audience, there was a level of performance in each diary (Couldry et al. 2010: 53). I attempted to identify any inconsistencies by drawing on multiple data sources. Secondly, it is not possible to claim that the entries provided an entirely accurate representation of normal, day-to-day experiences. Arnold, Joe, and Joshua all noted that they were more attentive to political news during the diary period than they otherwise would be.

The exit survey raised a number of practical limitations. Firstly, some participants reported that they had difficulty recalling detailed reflections due to the weekly format. As such, issues and events that occurred closer to the date in which the diarist prepared the entry were more likely to included, irrespective of their comparative importance to earlier topics. Secondly, a number of participants highlighted the demands of the research on their time. Both Angela and Sam informed the researcher relatively early on in the project that they found writing the entries to be cumbersome, so, to avoid them withdrawing from the project, guidance was offered as to make their entries briefer.

News Comparison: Research Notes

A timeline was used as to compare the relative prominence of news stories in the British press with those issues raised in the diaries. To do this, I adopted the same approach as used by Couldry et al. (2010: 212) in *Media Consumption and Public Engagement*:

> For the diaries, each mention of a news story was recorded and dated, and references to news items across the sample were added up and calculated week-to-week. In some cases the specific date of diary entries was not clear, and had to be inferred by previous and subsequent entries as well as the content of the entry. These totals were then weighted so as to control for the number of diarists writing in any given week.

A weighted value was calculated to account for the fluctuation in the number of active diarists each week. To do this, the maximum number of diarists active during a single week was identified; there were 27 diarists active during the week ending 16 November 2013. During those weeks in which there were fewer than 27 diarists active, the weighted value was calculated using this formula:

$$\text{Weighted value} = \text{Observed counts} \times \frac{27}{\text{No. of active diarists}}$$

There were three weeks during the project where the formula may have oversimplified the prominence of certain stories, as the total number of diarists was fewer than 10.

The press timeline is based on data collected over the course of the diary period from the front pages of four British newspapers: the *Sun*, the *Daily Mail*, *The Times*, and the *Guardian*. These four sources were selected in order to compare the prominence of stories in this study with those in *Media Consumption and Public Engagement*. This study collated the front pages of these publications using Paperboy (http://www.thepaperboy.com/uk/), a free-to-access digital archive of image files of newspapers from around the globe.

In order to compare the press timeline with the diarist timeline, the volume of mentions of news items in the newspapers had to be weighted. As in the design used by Couldry et al. (2010: 213), a news reference point was selected; this was the news item that received the most mentions by diarists in a single week. This occurred during the week ending 7 December 2013, in which 21 diarists discussed the passing of Nelson Mandela. The number of references made by diarists to this event was then divided by the number of mentions on the same issue in the four selected newspapers; 7 mentions. As such, a ratio of 3 was used to weight mentions of news items.

The timelines are structured on a weekly basis, with each week starting on a Saturday. While this may seem unorthodox, this is because participants often sent their weekly entries on a Saturday. The timelines span four months and, as such, do not cover the entire diary period. This decision was made to avoid those weeks in which only a handful of diarists were active.

All three timelines include only the two codes that had the largest weighted volume for each week. Codes emerged inductively from an initial analysis of the diaries and were then systematically applied to both the diaries and the newspaper front pages. As Table A.4 shows, the news items were categorised through precise references, but also amalgamated into broader topics when appropriate.

Table A.4 Key to the news comparison timelines

Abbreviation	*News item*
Bad weather	Storms, flooding and heavy snowfall in Britain
Leveson	"The Leveson Inquiry," a judicial public inquiry into the culture, practices, and ethics of the British press following the phone hacking scandal
Snowden	Edward Snowden, an American computer professional who leaked classified information from the National Security Agency (NSA)
Health	Specific items relating to healthcare in the UK, including debates surrounding the legal status of drugs, NHS reforms etc.
Philippines Typhoon	Typhoon Haiyan, a tropical cyclone that devastated Southeast Asia
Co-Op	Allegations of drug abuse and financial impropriety against the former Co-operative Bank chairman, Paul Flowers
Slavery	Cases of slavery in the UK and USA
Immigration and EU	Immigration and items relating to European Union, in particular the lifting of migration restrictions for Bulgarian and Romanian citizens
Nigella Lawson	A series of stories relating to the celebrity chef Nigella Lawson, including allegations of drug abuse, the trial of two of her personal assistants, and her divorce from Charles Saatchi
Helicopter crash	A police helicopter crash at a pub in Glasgow
Mandela	Death of Nelson Mandela, who served as President of South Africa from 1994 to 1999
Child abuse scandals	Child abuse allegations, including both mentions of cases relating to "Operation Yewtree," an investigation into the historical sexual abuse of children, and the trial of the musician, Ian Watkins
Economy	Items relating to the state of the British economy
David Cameron	Specific items relating to the Prime Minister, David Cameron
Michael Schumacher	A skiing accident involving the Formula 1 driver, Michael Schumacher
Welfare reforms	Items on reforms of the welfare system in the UK, including the Under Occupancy Penalty, popularly branded the Bedroom Tax, child tax credits etc.
Mark Duggan	Inquest into the death of Mark Duggan
Rennard scandal	Allegations of sexual abuse aimed at the Liberal Democrat peer, Lord Chris Rennard
Liberal Democrats	Specific items relating to the Liberal Democrats
Labour Party	Specific items relating to the Labour Party, including the party's relationship with the union, Unite
Brand and Paxman	BBC *Newsnight* interview with celebrity-activist Russell Brand, by journalist Jeremy Paxman
Energy prices	Items on the cost of energy in the UK

(continued)

Table A.4 (continued)

Abbreviation	*News item*
Paul Walker	Death of Paul Walker, actor
MPs' pay rise	Stories on a suggested 11% pay rise for MPs
Apollo theatre	Collapse of the Apollo Theatre in London
One Direction	Liam Payne, a member of One Direction, apologises for a dangerous photo
Volgograd	Terrorist attack at the Winter Olympics in Russia
"Benefits Street"	Channel 4 documentary series exploring the life of people on benefits
Women's rights	Items on the rights of women, including equal pay
Afghanistan	Exit strategy for UK armed forces in Afghanistan
Environment	Items relating to the environment
Ukraine	Protests and conflict in Ukraine
Social media	Items on social media, including Twitter abuse and "Neknominate," an online drinking game in which the participant must film themselves drinking a beverage and upload the footage online before nominating others

Coding Framework

All data collected from Facebook and Twitter was coded on NVivo using this framework.

Facebook:

A. **Type of post** (*discrete coding*)

1. Status update: text only
2. Status update: image
3. Status update: video
4. Sharing content: text only or link
5. Sharing content: image
6. Sharing content: video
7. Changing profile picture
8. Changing cover photo
9. Creating/sharing an event
10. Re-sharing content from a Friend, Page or application: text only or link
11. Re-sharing content from a Friend, Page or application: image
12. Re-sharing content from a Friend, Page or application: video
13. Adding photograph(s) to album/uploading an album
14. Location tag

B. **Content of post** (*non-discrete coding*)

1. Personal: friends and family; health; careers and work; etc.
2. Humour
3. Music and radio
4. Film
5. TV
6. Technology and video games
7. Other visual arts
8. Books and literature
9. Sports and exercise
10. Celebrity and gossip
11. Travel
12. Food and drink
13. Retail and commerce
14. Fashion
15. Religion, faith, and spirituality
16. Science and space
17. Environment and energy
18. Animals and pets
19. Vehicles
20. Crime and legal
21. Social media (e.g. reflecting on the service itself or on the behaviour of users on the service)
22. Charity, community, and social causes
23. Current events and news
24. Politics and political events
25. Other
26. Health (non-personal)
27. Weather
28. Education

C. **Level of interaction on post** (*discrete coding; cumulative total*)

1. None: No likes, comments, or shares
2. Low: Between 1 and 9 likes, comments, and shares
3. Medium: Between 10 and 19 likes, comments, and shares
4. High: Between 20 and 29 likes, comments, and shares
5. Very high: Above 30 likes, comments, and shares

D. **Politics: Type of post** (*non-discrete coding*)

1. Sharing information from a broadcast or print media source (recognised media outlets)
2. Sharing information from an alternative source, including new media outlets (e.g. BuzzFeed, Upworthy, Vice) an advocacy group; a citizen activist
3. Sharing information from a networked contact (e.g. a Friend on Facebook)
4. Expression of opinion contained within a status update
5. Expression of opinion: link to user-generated content (e.g. blog post; vlog)
6. Sharing evidence of/promoting an action: e-petition
7. Sharing evidence of/promoting an action: donating to a civic or political cause
8. Sharing evidence of/promoting an action: consumer activism (e.g. boycotting and buycotting)
9. Sharing evidence of/promoting an action: contacting political representatives
10. Sharing evidence of/promoting an action: contacting the broadcast or print media
11. Sharing evidence of/promoting an action: volunteering
12. Sharing evidence of/promoting an action: activity related to group membership
13. Sharing evidence of/promoting an action: forms of public demonstration
14. Sharing evidence of/promoting an action: forms of illegal protest activity
15. Sharing evidence of/promoting an action: voting
16. Organising, or contributing to the organisation of, a political action
17. Other
18. Sharing information from a political party or political representative
19. Sharing evidence of/promoting an action: contribution to a public meeting, consultation, or debate

Twitter:

A. **Type of tweet** (*discrete coding*)

1. Tweet—no link, no user mentions, and not a Retweet (RT)
2. Tweet—interaction (@mention) with another user(s)

3. Retweet of another user (done natively or in the traditional style)
4. Modified tweet (MT) from another user
5. Tweet—@reply

B. **Content being shared** (*discrete coding*)

1. No links
2. Embedded content (e.g. images; YouTube videos)
3. Link to external content (e.g. blogs; e-petition; news)

C. **Content of post** (*non-discrete; links are included in the coding if they are still accessible*)

1. Personal: friends and family; health; careers and work; etc.
2. Humour
3. Music and radio
4. Film
5. TV
6. Technology and video games
7. Other visual arts
8. Books and literature
9. Sports and exercise
10. Celebrity and gossip
11. Travel
12. Food and drink
13. Retail and commerce
14. Fashion
15. Religion, faith, and spirituality
16. Science and space
17. Environment and energy
18. Animals and pets
19. Vehicles
20. Crime and legal
21. Social media (e.g. reflecting on the service itself or on the behaviour of users on the service)
22. Charity, community, and social causes
23. Current events and news
24. Politics and political events
25. Other

26. Health (non-personal)
27. Weather
28. Education

D. **Politics: Type of post** (*non-discrete coding*)

1. Sharing information from a broadcast or print media source (recognised media outlets)
2. Sharing information from an alternative source, including new media outlets (e.g. BuzzFeed, Upworthy, Vice); an advocacy group; a citizen activist
3. Sharing information from a networked contact (e.g. another user on Twitter)
4. Expression of opinion contained within a tweet
5. Expression of opinion: link to user-generated content (e.g. blog post; vlog)
6. Sharing evidence of/promoting an action: e-petition
7. Sharing evidence of/promoting an action: donating to a civic or political cause
8. Sharing evidence of/promoting an action: consumer activism (e.g. boycotting and buycotting)
9. Sharing evidence of/promoting an action: contacting political representatives
10. Sharing evidence of/promoting an action: contacting the broadcast or print media
11. Sharing evidence of/promoting an action: volunteering
12. Sharing evidence of/promoting an action: activity related to group membership
13. Sharing evidence of/promoting an action: forms of public demonstration
14. Sharing evidence of/promoting an action: forms of illegal protest activity
15. Sharing evidence of/promoting an action: voting
16. Organising, or contributing to the organisation of, a political action
17. Other
18. Sharing information from a political party or political representative
19. Sharing evidence of/promoting an action: contribution to a public meeting, consultation, or debate

Post-diary Survey Questions

This survey was shared with participants in June 2014. This provided a period of reflection so that diarists could consider their involvement in the project. The survey was designed using Google Sheets, and all data was stored on Google Drive.

1. How did you find completing the diary? Did you enjoy it? Did it cause you any problems?
2. Thinking back to the period of time when you were completing your diary—what sort of time was it for you?
   a. Very busy
   b. Busy
   c. Normal
   d. A quiet period
   e. A very quiet period
3. While you were filling in the diary, did you notice anything that surprised you regarding your media habits?
4. In your diary, did you find yourself commenting on topics you wouldn't have expected to comment on?
5. During the diary period, where did you get your news from? Please indicate all that apply.
   a. TV
   b. Radio
   c. Newspaper
   d. Online news websites (e.g. BBC; The Huffington Post)
   e. Blogs
   f. Social media (e.g. Facebook; Twitter; Reddit; YouTube)
   g. Magazines
   h. Word of mouth
   i. Other—please specify
6. During the diary period, where did you get the majority of your news from? Please select one option only.
   a. TV
   b. Radio
   c. Newspaper
   d. Online news websites (e.g. BBC; The Huffington Post)
   e. Blogs
   f. Social media (e.g. shared on Facebook and Twitter)
   g. Magazines

h. Word of mouth
i. Other—please specify

7. During the diary, did you undertake any political actions, such as contacting an MP or signing a petition?
   a. Yes
   b. No
   c. I don't know
8. Has doing the diary changed your media use at all?
   a. Yes
   b. No
   c. I don't know
9. Has doing the diary changed your view about:
   a. The role that media play in your life?
   b. What public issues are important?
10. In the last 12 months, have you done any of the following to influence political representatives, public decisions, laws, or policies? Please tick all of those that apply:
    a. Contacted a local councillor or MP/MSP/Welsh Assembly Member
    b. Contacted the media
    c. Created or signed a paper petition
    d. Created or signed an e-petition
    e. Donated money or paid a membership fee to a charity or campaigning organisation
    f. Boycotted certain products for political, ethical, or environmental reasons
    g. Attended political meetings
    h. Donated money or paid a membership fee to a political party
    i. Taken part in a demonstration, picket, or march
    j. Voted in an election
    k. Contributed to a discussion or campaign online or on social media
    l. Taken part in a public consultation
    m. None of the above
11. If yes, please tick all those that occurred while you were completing your diary:
    a. Contacted a local councillor or MP/MSP/Welsh Assembly Member

b. Contacted the media
c. Created or signed a paper petition
d. Created or signed an e-petition
e. Donated money or paid a membership fee to a charity or campaigning organisation
f. Boycotted certain products for political, ethical, or environmental reasons
g. Attended political meetings
h. Donated money or paid a membership fee to a political party
i. Taken part in a demonstration, picket, or march
j. Voted in an election
k. Contributed to a discussion or campaign online or on social media
l. Taken part in a public consultation
m. N/A

Bibliography

38 Degrees. (2013a, January 31). Success! *Facebook Update*. Retrieved May 20, 2018, from https://www.facebook.com/peoplepowerchange/photos/a.457255765787.382103.200006375787/10152483133555788/?type=3.

38 Degrees. (2013b, April 17). Are Npower the New Starbucks? *Facebook Update*. Retrieved September 15, 2015, from https://www.facebook.com/peoplepowerchange/posts/10152754455415788.

38 Degrees. (2013c, April 30). Npower's Tax Dodging Explained. *Facebook Update*. Retrieved March 24, 2014, from https://www.facebook.com/photo.php?fbid=10152789416335788&set=a.457255765787.382103.200006375787.

38 Degrees. (2013d, May 28). The Conservatives Seem to Be Considering Plans to Limit the Number of Times We'd Be Allowed to Visit a GP… *Facebook Update*. Retrieved July 10, 2014, from https://www.facebook.com/peoplepowerchange/posts/10152866604640788.

38 Degrees. (2013e, May 29). Already 145,000 of Us Have Signed the Petition to Jeremy Hunt Telling Him Not to Limit How Many Times We Can Visit Our GP!… *Facebook Update*. Retrieved July 10, 2014, from https://www.facebook.com/peoplepowerchange/posts/10152869643835788.

38 Degrees. (2013f, May 30). Fantastic News! Our People-Powered Petition of 182,000 People Has Obviously Had the Right Effect! *Facebook Update*. Retrieved July 12, 2014, from https://www.facebook.com/peoplepowerchange/photos/a.457255765787.382103.200006375787/10152872307590788.

J. Dennis, *Beyond Slacktivism*, Interest Groups, Advocacy and Democracy Series, https://doi.org/10.1007/978-3-030-00844-4

38 Degrees. (2014a, January 7). *New Year Survey*. Retrieved January 7, 2014, from https://secure.38degrees.org.uk/new%C2%ADyear%C2%ADsurvey.

38 Degrees. (2014b, July 7). *Choose Your Priority Issues*. Retrieved July 9, 2014, from https://secure.38degrees.org.uk/page/s/priorities-your-most-important-issues.

Allocca, K. (2011, February 1). Why Videos Go Viral. *TED*. Retrieved May 1, 2012, from http://www.ted.com/talks/kevin_allocca_why_videos_go_viral.html.

Almond, G., & Verba, S. (1963). *The Civic Culture: Political Attitudes and Democracy in Five Nations*. Princeton, NJ: Princeton University Press.

Amazing Pics [AmazingPicz]. (2014, February 20). Retweet If You Say No to Animal Testing. #Animalrights. *Tweet*. Retrieved April 24, 2018, from https://twitter.com/amazingpicx/status/436359414820270080.

Amnå, E., & Ekman, J. (2014). Standby Citizens: Diverse Faces of Political Passivity. *European Political Science Review, 6*(2), 261–281.

Amry, H. [LibyaLiberty]. (2012, September 17). I'm Having Such a Good Hair Day: No One Even Knows. #Muslimrage. *Tweet*. Retrieved April 24, 2018, from https://twitter.com/LibyaLiberty/status/247737358320037888.

Anderson, C. (2004, January 10). The Long Tail. *Wired*. Retrieved May 14, 2018, from https://www.wired.com/2004/10/tail.

Andrejevic, M. (2009). Critical Media Studies 2.0: An Interactive Upgrade. *Interactions: Studies in Communication & Culture, 1*(1), 35–51.

Anstead, N., & Chadwick, A. (2018). A Primary Definer Online: The Construction and Propagation of a Think Tank's Authority on Social Media. *Media, Culture & Society, 40*(2), 246–266.

Anstead, N., & O'Loughlin, B. (2011). The Emerging Viewertariat and BBC Question Time: Television Debate and Real-Time Commenting Online. *International Journal of Press/Politics, 16*(4), 440–462.

Anstead, N., & O'Loughlin, B. (2015). Social Media Analysis and Public Opinion: The 2010 UK General Election. *Journal of Computer-Mediated Communication, 20*(2), 204–220.

Apostolova, V., Uberoi, E., & Johnston, N. (2017). *Political Disengagement in the UK: Who Is Disengaged?* (Briefing Paper Number CBP7501). Retrieved from http://researchbriefings.parliament.uk/ResearchBriefing/Summary/CBP-7501.

Arnstein, S. R. (1969). A Ladder of Citizen Participation. *Journal of the American Institute of Planners, 35*(4), 216–224.

Aslan, B., Dennis, J., & O'Loughlin, B. (2015). Balding Goes Trolling? Amplification, Engagement and Controversy at the 2012 Olympics. *Participations: Journal of Audience & Reception Studies, 12*(1), 577–607.

Audickas, L., Dempsey, N., & Keen, R. (2018). *Membership of UK Political Parties* (Briefing Paper Number SN05125). Retrieved from https://researchbriefings.parliament.uk/ResearchBriefing/Summary/SN05125.

Babbs, D. (2013, May 14). Npower: 48 Hrs to Vote. *38 Degrees*. Retrieved May 22, 2013, from http://blog.38degrees.org.uk/2013/05/14/npower-48-hrs-to-vote/.

Bachrach, P., & Baratz, M. (1962). Two Faces of Power. *The American Political Science Review, 56*(4), 947–952.

Baek, Y. M., Wojcieszak, M., & Delli Carpini, M. X. (2012). Online Versus Face-to-Face Deliberation: Who? Why? What? With What Effects? *New Media & Society, 14*(3), 363–383.

Bakardjieva, M. (2009). Subactivism: Lifeworld and Politics in the Age of the Internet. *The Information Society: An International Journal, 25*(2), 91–104.

Bakshy, E., Messing, S., & Adamic, L. (2015). Exposure to Ideologically Diverse News and Opinion on Facebook. *Science, 348*, 1130–1132.

Baldwin-Philippi, J. (2017). The Myths of Data-Driven Campaigning. *Political Communication, 34*(4), 627–633.

Barberá, P., Jost, J. T., Nagler, J., Tucker, J. A., & Bonneau, R. (2015). Tweeting from Left to Right: Is Online Political Communication More Than an Echo Chamber? *Psychological Science: A Journal of the Association for Psychological Science, 26*(10), 1531–1542.

Bastien, F. (2009). Beyond Sex and Saxophones: Interviewing Practices and Political Substance on Televised Talk Shows. *The Canadian Political Science Review, 3*(2), 70–88.

Bauerlin, M. (2009). *The Dumbest Generation: How the Digital Age Stupefies Young Americans and Jeopardizes Our Future or Don't Trust Anyone Under 30*. New York: Tarcher.

Bauman, Z. (2001). *The Individualized Society*. Cambridge: Polity.

Baym, G. (2005). The Daily Show: Discursive Integration and the Reinvention of Political Journalism. *Political Communication, 22*(3), 259–276.

Baym, N. K. (2010). *Personal Connections in the Digital Age*. Cambridge: Polity.

Beam, M. A., Hutchens, M. J., & Hmiclowski, J. D. (2018). Facebook News and (De)Polarization: Reinforcing Spirals in the 2016 US Election. *Information, Communication & Society, 21*(7), 940–958.

Beattie, J. (2013, May 27). Secret Tory Plan to Limit Your Number of GP Appointments. *Daily Mirror*. Retrieved May 31, 2013, from http://www.mirror.co.uk/news/uk-news/secret-tory-plan-cap-gp-1914881.

Bell, E. (2016, July 3). The Truth About Brexit Didn't Stand a Chance in the Online Bubble. *The Guardian*. Retrieved May 13, 2018, from https://www.theguardian.com/media/2016/jul/03/facebook-bubble-brexit-filter.

Bellamy, R. (2008). Evaluating Union Citizenship: Belonging, Rights and Participation with the E.U. *Citizenship Studies, 12*(6), 597–611.

Bennett, W. L. (1990). Toward a Theory of Press-State Relations in the United States. *Journal of Communication, 40*(2), 103–125.

Bennett, W. L. (2008). Changing Citizenship in the Digital Age. In W. L. Bennett (Ed.), *Civic Life Online: Learning How Digital Media Can Engage Youth* (pp. 1–24). Cambridge: MIT Press.

Bennett, W. L. (2012). The Personalization of Politics: Political Identity, Social Media, and Changing Patterns of Participation. *The ANNALS of the American Academy of Political and Social Science, 644*(20), 20–39.

Bennett, W. L., & Livingston, S. (2018). The Disinformation Order: Disruptive Communication and the Decline of Democratic Institutions. *European Journal of Communication, 33*(2), 122–139.

Bennett, W. L., & Pfetsch, B. (2018). Rethinking Political Communication in a Time of Disrupted Public Spheres. *Journal of Communication, 68*(2), 243–253.

Bennett, W. L., & Segerberg, A. (2013). *The Logic of Connective Action: Digital Media and the Personalization of Contentious Politics.* Cambridge: Cambridge University Press.

Bennett, W. L., Wells, C., & Freelon, D. (2011). Communicating Civic Engagement: Contrasting Models of Citizenship in the Youth Web Sphere. *Journal of Communication, 61*(5), 835–856.

Bimber, B., Flanagin, A. J., & Stohl, C. (2012). *Collective Action in Organizations: Interaction and Engagement in an Era of Technological Change.* Cambridge: Cambridge University Press.

Bochel, C. (2013). Petitions Systems: Contributing to Representative Democracy? *Parliamentary Affairs, 66*(4), 798–815.

Bode, L. (2017). Gateway Political Behaviors: The Frequency and Consequences of Low-Cost Political Engagement on Social Media. *Social Media + Society, 3*(4). Retrieved from https://doi.org/10.1177/2056305117743349.

Bode, L., & Vraga, E. K. (2017). Studying Politics Across Media. *Political Communication, 35*(1), 1–7.

Bode, L., Vraga, E. K., Borah, P., & Shah, D. V. (2014). A New Space for Political Behavior: Political Social Networking and Its Democratic Consequences. *Journal of Computer-Mediated Communication, 19*(3), 414–429.

Boulianne, S. (2009). Does Internet Use Affect Engagement? A Meta-Analysis of Research. *Political Communication, 26*(2), 193–211.

Boulianne, S. (2015). Social Media Use and Participation: A Meta-Analysis of Current Research. *Information, Communication & Society, 18*(5), 524–538.

boyd, D., & Crawford, K. (2012). Critical Questions for Big Data: Provocations for a Cultural, Technological, and Scholarly Platform. *Information Communication and Society, 15*(5), 662–679.

boyd, D., & Ellison, N. B. (2007). Social Network Sites: Definition, History, and Scholarship. *Journal of Computer-Mediated Communication, 13*(1), 210–230.

Brand, R. (2014). *Revolution*. London: Random House.

Brundidge, J. (2010). Toward a Theory of Citizen Interface with Political Discussion and News in the Contemporary Public Sphere. *International Journal of Communication, 4*, 1056–1078.

Brundidge, J., & Rice, R. E. (2009). Political Engagement Online: Do the Information Rich Get Richer and the Like-Minded Get More Similar? In A. Chadwick & P. N. Howard (Eds.), *Routledge Handbook of Internet Politics* (pp. 144–157). Abingdon: Routledge.

Bucy, E. P., & Gregson, K. S. (2001). Media Participation: A Legitimizing Mechanism of Mass Democracy. *New Media and Society, 3*(3), 357–380.

Cammaerts, B., & Van Audenhove, L. (2005). Online Political Debate, Unbounded Citizenship, and the Problematic Nature of a Transnational Public Sphere. *Political Communication, 22*(2), 179–196.

Campbell, A., Gurin, G., & Miller, W. E. (1954). *The Voter Decides*. Evanston, IL: Row, Peterson and Co.

Carpentier, N. (2011). *Media and Participation: A Site of Ideological-Democratic Struggle*. Bristol: Intellect.

Carswell, D. (2012). *The End of Politics and the Birth of iDemocracy*. Hull: Biteback Publishing.

Carvin, S. (2012, March 7). *Invisible Children—Pretty Dang Visible*. Retrieved May 12, 2012, from http://duckofminerva.blogspot.com/2012/03/invisible-children-pretty-dang-visible.html.

Castells, M. (2000). *The Rise of the Network Society*. Oxford: Blackwell.

Castells, M. (2001). *The Internet Galaxy: Reflections on the Internet, Business, and Society*. Oxford: Oxford University Press.

Castells, M. (2009). *Communication Power*. Oxford: Oxford University Press.

Chadwick, A. (2006). *Internet Politics: States, Citizens and New Communication Technologies*. Oxford: Oxford University Press.

Chadwick, A. (2007). Digital Network Repertoires and Organizational Hybridity. *Political Communication, 24*(3), 283–301.

Chadwick, A. (2011). The Political Information Cycle in a Hybrid News System: The British Prime Minister and the Bullygate Affair. *The International Journal of Press/Politics, 16*(1), 3–29.

Chadwick, A. (2012). Recent Shifts in the Relationship Between the Internet and Democratic Engagement in Britain and the United States: Granularity, Informational Exuberance, and Political Learning. In E. Anduiza, M. Jensen, & L. Jorba (Eds.), *Digital Media and Political Engagement Worldwide: A Comparative Study* (pp. 39–55). Cambridge: Cambridge University Press.

Chadwick, A. (2013). *The Hybrid Media System: Politics and Power*. Oxford: Oxford University Press.

Chadwick, A. (2018). *Thinking About the Role of Social Media in the Formation of Public Opinion*. Paper presented at the International Communication Association Annual Conference, Prague, Czech Republic.

Chadwick, A., & Dennis, J. (2017). Social Media, Professional Media and Mobilisation in Contemporary Britain: Explaining the Strengths and Weaknesses of the Citizens' Movement 38 Degrees. *Political Studies, 65*(1), 42–60.

Chadwick, A., Dennis, J., & Smith, A. P. (2016). Politics in the Age of Hybrid Media: Power, Systems, and Media Logics. In A. Bruns, E. Skogerbø, C. Christensen, A. O. Larsson, & G. Enli (Eds.), *Routledge Companion to Social Media and Politics* (pp. 7–22). London: Routledge.

Chadwick, A., O'Loughlin, B., & Vaccari, C. (2017). Why People Dual Screen Political Debates and Why It Matters for Democratic Engagement. *Journal of Broadcasting & Electronic Media, 61*(2), 220–239.

Chadwick, A., Vaccari, C., & O'Loughlin, B. (2018). Do Tabloids Poison the Well of Social Media? Explaining Democratically Dysfunctional News Sharing. *New Media & Society, 2*(3). Retrieved from https://doi.org/10.1177/1461444818769689.

Chiluwa, I., & Ifukor, P. (2015). 'War Against Our Children': Stance and Evaluation in #BringBackOurGirls Campaign Discourse on Twitter and Facebook. *Discourse and Society, 26*(3), 267–296.

Christensen, H. S. (2011). Political Activities on the Internet: Slacktivism or Political Participation by Other Means? *First Monday, 16*(2). Retrieved September 23, 2011, from http://firstmonday.org/htbin/cgiwrap/bin/ojs/index.php/fm/article/viewArticle/3336/2767.

Christensen, H. S. (2012). Simply Slacktivism? Internet Participation in Finland. *eJournal of eDemocracy & Open Government, 4*(1), 1–23.

Coleman, S. (2007). How Democracies Have Disengaged from Young People. In B. D. Loader (Ed.), *Young Citizens in the Digital Age: Political Engagement, Young People and New Media* (pp. 166–185). Abingdon: Routledge.

Coleman, G. (2012). Phreaks, Hackers, and Trolls: The Politics of Transgression and Spectacle. In M. Mandiberg (Ed.), *The Social Media Reader* (pp. 99–119). London: New York University Press.

Coleman, S., & Blumler, J. G. (2009). *The Internet and Democratic Citizenship: Theory, Practice and Policy*. Cambridge: Cambridge University Press.

Conservative Policy Forum. (2013, May 14). *Local Health Discussion Brief*. Retrieved July 2, 2013, from http://www.conservativepolicyforum.com/sites/www.conservativepolicyforum.com/files/local_health_discussion_brief.doc.

Constine, J. (2016, September 6). How Facebook News Feed Words. *TechCrunch*. Retrieved May 14, 2018, from https://techcrunch.com/2016/09/06/ultimate-guide-to-the-news-feed/.

Couldry, N. (2003). *Media Rituals: A Critical Approach*. Abingdon: Routledge.

Couldry, N. (2012). *Media, Society, World: Social Theory and Digital Media Practice*. Cambridge: Polity.

Couldry, N., Livingstone, S., & Markham, T. (2010). *Media Consumption and Public Engagement: Beyond the Presumption of Attention*. Basingstoke: Palgrave Macmillan.

Cracknell, R. (2014, May 1). 'First Class the Post': The Rise of Postal Voting. *House of Commons Library*. Retrieved July 21, 2015, from http://commonslibraryblog.com/2014/05/01/postal-voting-in-the-uk/.

Crawford, K. (2011). Listening, Not Lurking: The Neglected Form of Participation. In H. Grief, L. Hjorth, & A. Lasén (Eds.), *Cultures of Participation* (pp. 63–77). Berlin: Peter Lang.

Dahl, R. A. (1961). *Who Governs? Democracy and Power in an American City*. London: Yale University Press.

Dahlgren, P. (2005). The Internet, Public Spheres, and Political Communication: Dispersion and Deliberation. *Political Communication, 22*, 147–162.

Dahlgren, P. (2009). *Media and Political Engagement: Citizens, Communication and Democracy*. Cambridge: Cambridge University Press.

Dahlgren, P. (2011). Parameters of Online Participation: Conceptualizing Civic Contingencies. *Communication Management Quarterly, 21*(4), 87–110.

Daily Telegraph. (2013, May 26). Conservatives Consider Limit on GP Visits. *Daily Telegraph*. Retrieved July 9, 2014, from http://www.telegraph.co.uk/health/healthnews/10081220/Conservatives-consider-limit-on-GP-visits.html.

Dalton, R. J. (2007). *The Good Citizen: How a Younger Generation Is Reshaping American Politics*. Washington, DC: CQ Press.

Dalton, R. J. (2008). *Citizens Politics: Public Opinion and Political Parties in Advanced Industrial Democracies* (5th ed.). Washington, DC: CQ Press.

Davies, D. T. C. (2014). HC Deb 11 March 2014, Vol 577, Col 256.

Davison, P. (2012). The Language of Internet Memes. In M. Mandiberg (Ed.), *The Social Media Reader* (pp. 120–134). London: New York University Press.

Dean, J. (2005). Communicative Capitalism: Circulation and the Foreclosure of Politics. *Cultural Politics, 1*(1), 51–74.

Delli Carpini, M. X., & Williams, B. A. (2000). Let Us Infotain You: Politics in the New Media Environment. In W. L. Bennett & R. Entman (Eds.), *Mediated Politics: Communication in the Future of Democracy* (pp. 160–181). Cambridge: Cambridge University Press.

Delli Carpini, M. X., Cook, F. L., & Jacobs, L. R. (2004). Public Deliberation, Discursive Participation and Citizenship Engagement: A Review of the Empirical Literature. *Annual Review of Political Science, 7*(1), 315–344.

Dennis, J., & Sampaio-Dias, S. (2017). Not Just Swearing and Loathing on the Internet: Analysing BuzzFeed and VICE During #GE2017. In E. Thorsen, D. Jackson, & D. Lilleker (Eds.), *UK Election Analysis 2017: Media, Voters and the Campaign* (pp. 66–67). Bournemouth: The Centre for the Study of Journalism, Culture and Community, Bournemouth University.

Denver, D. (2006). *Elections and Voters in Britain* (2nd ed.). Basingstoke: Palgrave Macmillan.

Deuze, M. (2012). *Media Life*. Cambridge: Polity.

Downs, A. (1957). *An Economic Theory of Democracy*. New York: Harper.

Drumbl, M. A. (2012). Child Soldiers and Clicktivism: Justice, Myths, and Prevention. *Journal of Human Rights Practice, 4*(3), 481–485.

Dubois, E., & Blank, G. (2018). The Echo Chamber Is Overstated: The Moderating Effect of Political Interest and Diverse Media. *Information, Communication & Society, 21*(5), 729–745.

Dunleavy, P. (2005). Facing Up to Multi-Party Politics: How Partisan Dealignment and PR Voting Have Fundamentally Changed Britain's Party Systems. *Parliamentary Affairs, 58*(3), 503–532.

Eliasoph, N. (1998). *Avoiding Politics: How Americans Produce Apathy in Everyday Life*. Cambridge: Cambridge University Press.

Ellison, N. B., Steinfield, C., & Lampe, C. (2007). The Benefits of Facebook "Friends": Social Capital and College Students' Use of Online Social Network Sites. *Journal of Computer-Mediated Communication, 12*(4), 1143–1168.

Engelhardt, J. v., & Jansz, J. (2014). Challenging Humanitarian Communication: An Empirical Exploration of Kony 2012. *The International Communication Gazette, 76*(6), 464–484.

Entman, R. (2004). *Projections of Power: Framing News Public Opinion and US Foreign Policy*. Chicago, IL: Chicago University Press.

Eveland, W. P., & Hively, M. H. (2009). Political Discussion Frequency, Network Size, and "Heterogenity" of Discussion as Predictors of Political Knowledge and Participation. *Journal of Communication, 59*(2), 205–224.

Fisher, M. (2012, March 8). The Soft Bigotry of Kony 2012. *The Atlantic*. Retrieved December 31, 2012, from http://www.theatlantic.com/international/print/2012/03/the-soft-bigotry-of-kony-2012/254194/.

Flanagan, C. A. (2013). *Teenage Citizens: The Political Theories of the Young*. Cambridge, MA: Harvard University Press.

Fletcher, R., & Nielsen, R. K. (2017a). Are News Audiences Increasingly Fragmented? A Cross-National Comparative Analysis of Cross-Platform News Audience Fragmentation and Duplication. *Journal of Communication, 67*(4), 476–498.

Fletcher, R., & Nielsen, R. K. (2017b). Are People Incidentally Exposed to News on Social Media? A Comparative Analysis. *New Media & Society, 20*(7), 2450–2468. Retrieved from https://doi.org/10.1177/1461444817724170.

Fletcher, R., & Nielsen, R. K. (2018). Generalised Scepticism: How People Navigate News on Social Media. *Information, Communication & Society*. Retrieved from https://doi.org/10.1080/1369118X.2018.1450887.

Flynn, K. (2018, January 12). Current Facebook Wants to Go Back to Being Old Facebook. *Mashable*. Retrieved May 20, 2018, from https://mashable.com/2018/01/12/zuckerberg-facebook-before-news-feed-meaningful.

Ford, R., & Goodwin, M. (2014). *Revolt on the Right: Explaining the Radical Right in Britain*. London: Routledge.

Fox, S. (2014). Is It Time to Update the Definition of Political Participation? Political Participation in Britain: The Decline and Revival of Civic Culture. *Parliamentary Affairs, 67*(2), 495–505.

Fox, Z. (2012, April 24). The Decline of Kony 2012: Where Did the Online Buzz Go? *Mashable*. Retrieved December 31, 2012, from http://mashable.com/2012/04/24/kony-2012-decline/.

Freelon, D., McIlwain, C., & Clark, M. (2016). Beyond the Hashtags: #Ferguson, #BlackLivesMatter, and the Online Struggle for Offline Justice. *Center for Media and Social Impact, American University*. Retrieved April 24, 2018, from https://papers.ssrn.com/sol3/papers.cfm?abstract_id=2747066.

Fuchs, C. (2014). *Social Media: A Critical Introduction*. London: Sage.

Fung, A. (2006). Varieties of Participation in Complex Governance. *Public Administration Review, 66*, 66–75.

Gallagher, R. J., Reagan, A. J., Danforth, C. M., & Dodds, P. S. (2018). Divergent Discourse Between Protests and Counter-Protests: #BlackLivesMatter and #AllLivesMatter. *PLOS One, 13*(4). Retrieved from https://doi.org/10.1371/journal.pone.0195644.

Gallucci, N. (2018, March 27). America's Youth Could Put Slacktivism Behind Us Once and for All. *Mashable*. Retrieved April 24, 2018, from https://mashable.com/2018/03/27/trump-era-end-of-slacktivism.

Gantz, W., & Trenholm, S. (1979). Why People Pass on News: Motivations for Diffusion. *Journalism & Mass Communication, 56*(2), 365–370.

Garcia, A. (2013, March 26). The Best Going Red for Equality Equal Signs from Social Media Today. *The Gaily Grind*. Retrieved August 5, 2013, from http://www.thegailygrind.com/2013/03/26/the-best-going-red-for-equality-equal-signs-from-social-media-today.

Gatehouse, G. (2017, June 27). Did Cambridge Analytica Play a Role in the EU Referendum? *BBC News*. Retrieved May 27, 2018, from http://www.bbc.co.uk/news/av/uk-40423629/did-cambridge-analytica-play-a-role-in-the-eu-referendum.

Geertz, C. (1975). Thick Description: Toward an Interpretive Theory of Culture. In C. Geertz (Ed.), *The Interpretation of Cultures: Selected Essays* (pp. 3–32). New York: Basic Books.

Gerbaudo, P. (2012). *Tweets and the Streets: Social Media and Contemporary Action*. London: Pluto Press.

Gerodimos, R., & Ward, J. (2007). Rethinking Online Youth Civic Engagement: Reflections on Web Content Analysis. In B. D. Loader (Ed.), *Young Citizens in the Digital Age: Political Engagement, Young People and New Media* (pp. 114–126). Abingdon: Routledge.

Giddens, A. (1991). *Modernity and Self-Identity: Self and Society in the Late Modern Age*. Cambridge: Polity.

Gil de Zúñiga, H., Molyneux, L., & Zheng, P. (2014). Social Media, Political Expression, and Political Participation: Panel Analysis of Lagged and Concurrent Relationships. *Journal of Communication, 64*(4), 612–634.

Gladwell, M. (2010, October 4). Small Change: Why the Revolution Will Not Be Tweeted. *The New Yorker.* Retrieved November 3, 2010, from https://www.newyorker.com/magazine/2010/10/04/small-change-malcolm-gladwell.

Goffman, E. (1990). *The Presentation of Self in Everyday Life*. London: Penguin.

Goffman, E., Lemert, C. C., & Branaman, A. (1997). *The Goffman Reader.* Cambridge, MA: Blackwell.

Goodin, R. E., Rice, J. M., Parpo, A., & Eriksson, L. (2008). *Discretionary Time: A New Measure of Freedom*. Cambridge: Cambridge University Press.

Goodman, P. S. (2018, May 28). In Britain, Austerity is Changing Everything. *The New York Times*. Retrieved May 28, 2018, from https://www.nytimes.com/2018/05/28/world/europe/uk-austerity-poverty.html.

Graber, D. A. (2004). Mediated Politics and Citizenship in the Twenty-First Century. *Annual Review of Psychology, 55,* 545–571.

Graham, T., Jackson, D., & Wright, S. (2015). From Everyday Conversation to Political Action: Talking Austerity in Online 'Third Spaces'. *European Journal of Communication, 30*(6), 648–665.

Graham, T., & Wright, S. (2014). Discursive Equality and Everyday Talk Online: The Impact of "Superparticipants". *Journal of Computer-Mediated Communication, 19*(3), 625–642.

Granovetter, M. S. (1973). The Strength of Weak Ties. *American Journal of Sociology, 78*(6), 1360–1380.

Grant, W., & Warhurst, C. (2014, February 1). *Could the 'Westminster Bubble' Be Detrimental to British Politics?* Retrieved August 8, 2015, from http://www2.warwick.ac.uk/knowledge/socialscience/westminsterbubble/.

Gregory, S. (2012). Kony 2012 Through a Prism of Video Advocacy Practices and Trends. *Journal of Human Rights Practice, 4*(3), 463–468.

Hall, N. (2017). Innovations in Activism in the Digital Era. In Hertie School of Governance (Ed.), *The Governance Report 2017* (pp. 143–156). Oxford: Oxford University Press.

Halupka, M. (2014). Clicktivism: A Systematic Heuristic. *Policy and Internet, 6*(2), 115–132.

Halupka, M. (2018). The Legitimisation of Clicktivism. *Australian Journal of Political Science, 53*(1), 130–141.

Hampton, K. N., Rainie, L., Lu, W., Dwyer, M., Shin, I., & Purcell, K. (2014, September 2). Social Media and the 'Spiral of Silence'. *Pew Research Internet and American Life Project*. Retrieved September 2, 2014, from http://www.pewinternet.org/files/2014/08/PI_Social-networks-and-debate_082614.pdf.

Hansard Society. (2014). *Audit of Political Engagement 11: The 2014 Report*. London: Hansard Society.

Hansard Society. (2018). *Audit of Political Engagement 15: The 2018 Report*. London: Hansard Society.

Hardy, B., & Scheufele, D. A. (2006). Examining Differential Gains from Internet Use: Comparing the Moderating Role of Talk and Online Interactions. *Journal of Communication, 55*(1), 71–84.

Hargittai, E., Neuman, W. R., & Curry, O. (2012). Taming the Information Tide: Perceptions of Information Overload in the American Home. *The Information Society: An International Journal, 28*(3), 161–173.

Hay, C. (2002). *Political Analysis: A Critical Introduction*. Basingstoke: Palgrave Macmillan.

Hay, C. (2007). *Why We Hate Politics*. Cambridge: Polity.

Hensby, A., Sibthorpe, J., & Driver, S. (2011). Resisting the 'Protest Business': Bureaucracy, Postbureaucracy and Active Membership in Social Movement Organizations. *Organization, 19*(6), 809–823.

Hogan, L., & Safi, M. (2018, April 3). Revealed: Facebook Hate Speech Exploded in Myanmar During Rohingya Crisis. *The Guardian*. Retrieved May 27, 2018, from https://www.theguardian.com/world/2018/apr/03/revealed-facebook-hate-speech-exploded-in-myanmar-during-rohingya-crisis.

Hooghe, M., & Dejaeghere, Y. (2007). Does the 'Monitorial Citizen' Exist? An Empirical Investigation into the Occurrence of Postmodern Forms of Citizenship in the Nordic Countries. *Scandinavian Political Studies, 30*(2), 249–271.

Hotz, A. (2012, September 17). Newsweek 'Muslim Rage' Cover Invokes a Rage of Its Own. *The Guardian*. Retrieved August 12, 2013, from http://www.theguardian.com/media/us-news-blog/2012/sep/17/muslim-rage-newsweek-magazine-twitter.

Howard, P. N. (2011). *Castells and the Media*. Cambridge: Polity.

Howard, P. N., Woolley, S., & Calo, R. (2018). Algorithms, Bots, and Political Communication in the US 2016 Election: The Challenge of Automated Political Communication for Election Law and Administration. *Journal of Informational Technology & Politics, 15*(2), 81–93.

Hunt, J. [Jeremy_Hunt]. (2013, May 30). In Case Being Misled by 'Neutral' 38 Degrees E-Petition, It Is Not and Was Never Going to Be Conservative Policy to Limit GP Appointments. *Tweet*. Retrieved July 10, 2014, from https://twitter.com/Jeremy_Hunt/status/340046406926598144.

Inglehart, R. (1990). *Culture Shift in Advanced Industrial Society*. Princeton, NJ: Princeton University Press.

Iyengar, S., Hahn, K. S., Krosnick, J. A., & Walker, J. (2008). Selective Exposure to Campaign Communication: The Role of Anticipated Agreement and Issue Public Membership. *The Journal of Politics, 70*(1), 186–200.

James, S. B. (2014, January 22). Tory MP Brands 38 Degrees Campaign as 'Stupid'. *Third Sector*. Retrieved from http://www.thirdsector.co.uk/Policy_and_Politics/article/1228234/tory-mp-brands-38-degrees-campaign-stupid/.

Jarvis, J. (2009). *What Would Google Do?* New York: Collins Business.

Jarvis, J. (2011). *Public Parts: How Sharing in the Digital Age Improves the Way We Work and Live*. London: Simon & Schuster.

Jasper, J. M. (1997). *The Art of Moral Protest: Culture, Biography, and Creativity in Social Movements*. London: University of Chicago Press.

Jenkins, H. (2006). *Convergence Culture: Where Old and New Media Collide*. New York: New York University.

Jenkins, H., & Carpentier, N. (2013). Theorizing Participatory Intensities: A Conversation About Participation and Politics. *Convergence: The International Journal of Research into New Media, 19*(3), 265–286.

Jones, J. P. (2005). *Entertaining Politics: New Political Television and Civic Culture*. Oxford: Rowman & Littlefield.

Jordan, G., & Maloney, W. (2007). *Democracy and Interest Groups: Enhancing Participation?* Basingstoke: Palgrave Macmillan.

Jurgenson, N. (2011, September 13). *Digital Dualism and the Fallacy of Web Objectivity*. Retrieved February 25, 2013, from http://thesocietypages.org/cyborgology/2011/09/13/digital-dualism-and-the-fallacy-of-web-objectivity.

Jurgenson, N. (2012, October 24). Speaking in Memes. *The New Inquiry*. Retrieved August 13, 2013, from http://thenewinquiry.com/essays/speaking-in-memes.

Kačinskas, R. [rkacinskas]. (2018). *Twitter Account*. Retrieved May 20, 2018, from https://twitter.com/rkacinskas.

Kahne, J., Middaugh, E., Lee, N. J., & Feezell, J. (2012). Youth Online Activity and Exposure to Diverse Perspectives. *New Media & Society, 14*(3), 492–512.

Kant, T. (2016). *Making It Personal: Web Users and Algorithmic Personalisation* (Doctoral thesis, University of Sussex).

Kanter, J. (2018, May 20). The Backlash That Never Happened: New Data Shows People Actually Increased Their Facebook Usage After the Cambridge Analytica Scandal. *Business Insider*. Retrieved May 27, 2018, from http://www.businessinsider.com/people-increased-facebook-usage-after-cambridge-analytica-scandal-2018-5.

Kaplan, A. M., & Haenlein, M. (2010). Users of the World, Unite! The Challenges and Opportunities of Social Media. *Business Horizons, 53*(1), 59–68.

Karolian, M. [mkarolian]. (2018, January 12). The Summary Slide on My @ Bostonglobe 2017 Strategy Deck Doesn't Include Anything Re: Facebook Pages. Pages Are Ineffective as They Don't Cultivate Community and Relationships. We've Known This for Years. *Tweet*. Retrieved May 27, 2018, from https://twitter.com/mkarolian/status/951626154154299393.

Karpf, D. (2010). Online Political Mobilization from the Advocacy Group's Perspective: Looking Beyond Clicktivism. *Policy and Internet, 2*(4), 7–41.

Karpf, D. (2012a). *The MoveOn Effect: The Unexpected Transformation of American Political Advocacy*. Oxford: Oxford University Press.

Karpf, D. (2012b). Social Science Research Methods in Internet Time. *Information, Communication and Society, 15*(5), 639–661.

Karpf, D. (2016). *Analytic Activism: Digital Listening and the New Political Strategy*. Oxford: Oxford University Press.

Karpf, D. (2018, April 24). A World Without Wizards: On Facebook and Cambridge Analytica. *Civic Hall*. Retrieved May 27, 2018, from https://civichall.org/civicist/world-without-wizards-facebook-cambridge-analytica/.

Katz, E., & Lazarsfeld, P. F. (1955). *Personal Influence: The Part Played by People in the Flow of Mass Communications*. New York: The Free Press.

Keen, A. (2008). *The Cult of the Amateur: How Blogs, Myspace, YouTube, and the Rest of Today's User-Generated Media Are Destroying Our Economy, Our Culture, and Our Values*. New York: Random House.

Kemp, S. (2017, January 24). Digital in 2017: Global Overview. *We Are Social*. Retrieved January 30, 2017, from https://wearesocial.com/special-reports/digital-in-2017-global-overview.

Kersten, M. (2012, March 7). Taking 'Kony 2012' Down a Notch. *Justice in Conflict*. Retrieved March 7, 2012, from http://justiceinconflict.org/2012/03/07/taking-kony-2012-down-a-notch/.

Kettell, S. (2006). *Dirty Politics? New Labour, British Democracy and the Invasion of Iraq*. London: Zed Books.

Khazan, O. (2013, April 30). Unicef Tells Slacktivists: Give Money, Not Facebook Likes. *The Atlantic*. Retrieved August 2, 2013, from http://www.theatlantic.com/international/archive/2013/04/unicef-tells-slacktivists-give-money-not-facebook-likes/275429.

Kim, J., Lewis, S. C., & Watson, B. R. (2018). The Imagined Audience for and Perceived Quality of News Comments: Exploring the Perceptions of Commenters on News Sites and on Facebook. *Social Media + Society, 4*(1). Retrieved from https://doi.org/10.1177/2056305118765741.

Kirkpatrick, D. D. (2012, September 17). Newsweek's 'Muslim Rage' Cover Mocked Online. *The New York Times*. Retrieved August 12, 2013, from http://thelede.blogs.nytimes.com/2012/09/17/newsweeks-muslim-rage-cover-mocked-online/.

Knibbs, K. (2013, March 26). The Birth of Marriage Equality Meme. *Digital Trends*. Retrieved August 5, 2013, from http://www.digitaltrends.com/social-media/red-equal-signs-take-over-facebook-the-birth-of-a-marriage-equality-meme.

Kolb, D. A. (1984). *Experiential Learning: Experience as the Source of Learning and Development*. Englewood Cliffs, NJ: Prentice Hall.

Kreiss, D. (2010). *Taking Our Country Back? Political Consultants and the Crafting of Networked Politics from Howard Dean to Barack Obama* (Doctoral dissertation, Stanford University).

Kreiss, D. (2012). *Taking Our Country Back: The Crafting of Networked Politics from Howard Dean to Barack Obama*. Oxford: Oxford University Press.

Kreiss, D., & McGregor, S. C. (2018). Technology Firms Shape Political Communication: The Work of Microsoft, Facebook, Twitter, and Google with Campaigns During the 2016 U.S. Presidential Cycle. *Political Communication, 35*(2), 155–177.

Kristofferson, K., White, K., & Peloza, J. (2014). The Nature of Slacktivism: How the Social Observability of an Initial Act of Token Support Affects Subsequent Prosocial Action. *Journal of Consumer Research, 40*(6), 1149–1166.

Kümpel, A. S., Karnowski, V., & Keyling, T. (2015). News Sharing in Social Media: A Review of Current Research on News Sharing Users, Content, and Networks. *Social Media + Society, 1*(2). Retrieved from https://doi.org/10.1177/2056305115610141.

Küng, L. (2015). *Innovators in Digital News*. London: I.B. Tauris.

Lacey, K. (2013). *Listening Publics: The Politics and Experience of Listening in the Media Age*. Cambridge: Polity.

LaFrance, A. (2017, October 18). The Power of Personalization. *NiemanLab*. Retrieved May 14, 2018, from http://niemanreports.org/articles/the-power-of-personalization.

Lessig, L. (2008). *Remix: Making Art and Commerce Thrive in the Hybrid Economy*. New York: Penguin Press.

Liddle, R. (2013, March 10). Placards? They're so Last Year. Make Way for the Mighty Mouse. *The Sunday Times*. Retrieved March 10, 2013, from http://www.thesundaytimes.co.uk/sto/Magazine/Features/article1225047.ece?shareToken=1eb4425e171e4a1ecda5d2c956c0540d.

Litt, E. (2012). Knock, Knock. Who's There? The Imagined Audience. *Journal of Broadcasting & Electronic Media, 56*(3), 330–345.

Litt, E., & Hargittai, E. (2016). The Imagined Audience on Social Network Sites. *Social Media + Society, 2*(1). Retrieved from https://doi.org/10.1177/2056305116633482.

Livingstone, S. (2011). Digital Learning and Participation Among Youth: Critical Reflections on Future Research Priorities. *International Journal of Learning and Media, 2*(2–3), 1–13.

Lotan, G. (2012, March 14). [Data Viz] Kony2012: See How Invisible Networks Helped a Campaign Capture the World's Attention. *SocialFlow*. Retrieved December 31, 2012, from http://blog.socialflow.com/post/7120244932/data-viz-kony2012-see-how-invisible-networks-helped-a-campaign-capture-the-worlds-attention.

Lukes, S. (2005). *Power: A Radical View*. Basingstoke: Palgrave Macmillan.

Madianou, M. (2013). Humanitarian Campaigns in Social Media: Network Architectures and Polymedia Events. *Journalism Studies, 14*(2), 249–266.

Main, S. (2013, November 21). 18 Reasons Cats Think Humans Are Terrible at Being Cats. *BuzzFeed*. Retrieved September 11, 2014, from http://www.buzzfeed.com/samimain/ways-cats-think-humans-are-terrible-at-being-cats.

Mallikarjuna, K. (2013, September 24). 11 Delightful Poems Found in Pornhub Comments. *BuzzFeed*. Retrieved September 11, 2014, from http://www.buzzfeed.com/kmallikarjuna/11-delightful-poems-found-in-pornhub-comments.

Margetts, H., John, P., Hale, S., & Yasseri, T. (2015). *Political Turbulence: How Social Media Shape Collective Action*. Princeton, NJ: Princeton University Press.

Marwick, A. E., & boyd, d. (2011). I Tweet Honestly, I Tweet Passionately: Twitter Users, Context Collapse, and the Imagined Audience. *New Media & Society, 13*(1), 114–133.

McCann, J. (2013, May 26). Fury as Tories Look to Limit the Number of Times You Can See Your GP Each Year. *The Daily Mail*. Retrieved July 9, 2014, from http://www.dailymail.co.uk/news/article-2331068/Fury-Tories-look-limit-number-times-GP-year.html.

McGowan, M. [The Artist Taxi Driver]. (2018). *Facebook Account*. Retrieved May 20, 2018, from https://www.facebook.com/mark.mcgowan.969.

McKelvey, F., & Piebiak, J. (2016). Porting the Political Campaign: The NationBuilder Platform and the Global Flows of Political Technology. *New Media & Society, 20*(3), 901–918.

McLeod, J. M., Scheufele, D. A., & Moy, P. (1999). Community, Communication, and Participation: The Role of Mass Media and Interpersonal Discussion in Local Political Participation. *Political Communication, 16*(3), 315–336.

Meraz, S., & Papacharissi, Z. (2013). Networked Gatekeeping and Networked Framing on #Egypt. *The International Journal of Press/Politics, 18*(2), 138–166.

Merrick, J. (2013, May 26). Cap on Number of GP Visits Being Considered by Tories. *The Independent*. Retrieved May 31, 2013, from http://www.independent.co.uk/life-style/health-and-families/health-news/cap-on-number-of-gp-visits-being-considered-by-tories-8632396.html.

Mirkinson, J. (2012, September 17). Newsweek's 'Muslim Rage' Cover Draws Angry Protest. *The Huffington Post*. Retrieved August 12, 2013, from http://www.huffingtonpost.com/2012/09/17/newsweek-muslim-rage-cover_n_1890124.html.

Mitchell, A., Simmons, K., Matsa, K. E., Silver, L., Shearer, E., Johnson, C., et al. (2018, May 14). Many Western Europeans Get News via Social Media, but in Some Countries, Substantial Minorities Do Not Pay Attention to the Source. *Pew Research Center*. Retrieved May 14, 2018, from http://www.journalism.org/2018/05/14/many-western-europeans-get-news-via-social-media-but-in-some-countries-substantial-minorities-do-not-pay-attention-to-the-source.

Möller, J., Trilling, D., Helberger, N., & van Es, B. (2018). Do Not Blame It on the Algorithm: An Empirical Assessment of Multiple Recommender Systems and Their Impact on Content Diversity. *Information, Communication & Society, 21*(7), 959–977.

Morozov, E. (2009, May 19). The Brave New World of Slacktivism. *Foreign Policy*. Retrieved April 18, 2011, from http://neteffect.foreignpolicy.com/posts/2009/05/19/the_brave_new_world_of_slacktivism.

Morozov, E. (2011). *The Net Delusion: How Not to Liberate the World*. London: Penguin.

Morozov, E. (2013). *To Save Everything, Click Here: The Folly of Technological Determinism*. London: Allen Lane.

Mossberger, K., Tolbert, C. J., & Stansbury, M. (2003). *Virtual Inequality: Beyond the Digital Divide*. Washington, DC: Georgetown University Press.

Mosseri, A. (2018, January 11). Bringing People Closer Together. *Facebook Newsroom*. Retrieved May 27, 2018, from https://newsroom.fb.com/news/2018/01/news-feed-fyi-bringing-people-closer-together/.

Nasr, R. (2012, September 18). Newsweek Muslim Rage Cover: Someone at Newsweek Needs to Get Fired for This. *PolicyMic*. Retrieved August 12, 2013, from http://www.policymic.com/articles/14908/newsweek-muslim-rage-cover-someone-at-newsweek-needs-to-get-fired-for-this.

Negroponte, N. (1995). *Being Digital*. London: Hodder & Stoughton.

Neuman, W. R., Bimber, B., & Hindman, M. (2011). The Internet and Four Dimensions of Citizenship. In R. Y. Shapiro & L. R. Jacobs (Eds.), *The Oxford Handbook of American Public Opinion and the Media* (pp. 22–42). Oxford: Oxford University Press.

Neuman, W. R., Just, M. R., & Crigler, A. N. (1992). *Common Knowledge: News and the Construction of Political Meaning*. Chicago, IL: University of Chicago Press.

Newman, N. (2012). *Reuters Institute Digital News Report 2012: Tracking the Future of News*. Oxford: Reuters Institute for the Study of Journalism, University of Oxford.

Newman, N., Fletcher, R., Kalogeropoulos, A., Levy, D. A. L., & Nielsen, R. K. (2017). *Reuters Institute Digital News Report 2017*. Oxford: Reuters Institute for the Study of Journalism, University of Oxford.

Newman, N., Fletcher, R., Levy, D. A. L., & Nielsen, R. K. (2016). *Reuters Institute Digital News Report 2016*. Oxford: Reuters Institute for the Study of Journalism, University of Oxford.

Newman, N., & Levy, D. A. L. (2013). *Reuters Institute Digital News Report 2013*. Oxford: Reuters Institute for the Study of Journalism, University of Oxford.

Newman, N., & Levy, D. A. L. (2014). *Reuters Institute Digital News Report 2014*. Oxford: Reuters Institute for the Study of Journalism, University of Oxford.

Newman, N., Levy, D. A. L., & Nielsen, R. K. (2015). *Reuters Institute Digital News Report 2015*. Oxford: Reuters Institute for the Study of Journalism, University of Oxford.

Nielsen, R. K. (2018, March 29). *The Power of Platforms*. Retrieved May 27, 2018, from https://www.slideshare.net/RasmusKleisNielsen/the-power-of-platforms-inaugural-lecture-by-rasmus-kleis-nielsen-u-of-oxford.

Nielsen, R. K., & Graves, L. (2017). *"News You Don't Believe": Audience Perspectives on Fake News*. Oxford: Reuters Institute for the Study of Journalism.

Noelle-Neumann, E. (1974). The Spiral of Silence a Theory of Public Opinion. *Journal of Communication, 24*(2), 43–51.

Nonnecke, B., & Preece, J. (2003). Silent Participants: Getting to Know Lurkers Better. In C. Lueg & D. Fisher (Eds.), *From Usenet to Cowebs: Interacting with Social Information Spaces* (pp. 110–132). Amsterdam, The Netherlands: Springer.

Norris, P. (2000). *A Virtuous Circle: Political Communication in Postindustrial Societies*. Cambridge: Cambridge University Press.

Norris, P. (2011). *Democratic Deficit: Critical Citizens Revisited*. Cambridge: Cambridge University Press.

O'Loughlin, B. (2011). Information Overload, Paradigm Underload? The Internet and Political Disruption. *Global Policy, 2*(3), 349–351.

O'Loughlin, B., Vaccari, C., Dennis, J., & Aslan Ozgul, B. (2017). Twitter and Global Political Crises: Cycles of Insecurity in #PrayforParis and #PrayforSyria. *Middle East Journal of Culture and Communication, 10*(2–3), 175–203.

Obama, M. [FLOTUS44]. (2014, May 7). Our Prayers Are with the Missing Nigerian Girls and Their Families. It's Time to #BringBackOurGirls. -mo. *Tweet*. Retrieved April 24, 2018, from https://twitter.com/flotus44/status/464148654354628608.

Obar, J. A., Zube, P., & Lampe, C. (2012). Advocacy 2.0: An Analysis of How Advocacy Groups in the United States Perceive and Use Social Media as Tools for Facilitating Civic Engagement and Collective Action. *Journal for Information Policy, 2,* 1–25.

Olson, C. C. (2016). #BringBackOurGirls: Digital Communities Supporting Real-World Change and Influencing Mainstream Media Agendas. *Feminist Media Studies, 16*(5), 772–787.

Olson, M. (1971). *The Logic of Collective Action: Public Goods and the Theory of Groups.* Cambridge, MA: Harvard University Press.

Owen, L. H. (2018, January 11). Facebook Drastically Changes News Feed to Make It "Good for People" (and Bad for Most Publishers). *NiemanLab.* Retrieved May 27, 2018, from http://www.niemanlab.org/2018/01/facebook-drastically-changes-news-feed-to-make-it-good-for-people-and-bad-for-most-publishers/.

Oyston, G. (2012, March 8). *We Got Trouble.* Retrieved March 8, 2012, from http://visiblechildren.tumblr.com/post/18890947431/we-got-trouble.

Papacharissi, Z. (2010). *A Private Sphere: Democracy in a Digital Age.* Cambridge: Polity.

Papacharissi, Z. (2012). Without You, I'm Nothing: Performances of the Self on Twitter. *International Journal of Communication, 6,* 1989–2006.

Papacharissi, Z. (2014). *Affective Publics: Sentiment, Technology, and Politics.* Oxford: Oxford University Press.

Pariser, E. (2011). *The Filter Bubble: What the Internet Is Hiding from You.* New York: Penguin Press.

Pattie, C., Seyd, P., & Whiteley, P. (2004). *Citizenship in Britain: Values, Participation and Democracy.* Cambridge: Cambridge University Press.

Phillips, W. (2015). *This Is Why We Can't Have Nice Things: Mapping the Relationship Between Online Trolling and Mainstream Culture.* Cambridge: MIT Press.

Powers, E. (2017). My News Feed Is Filtered? Awareness of News Personalization Among College Students. *Digital Journalism, 5*(10), 1315–1335.

Prior, M. (2005). News vs. Entertainment: How Increasing Media Choice Widens Gaps in Political Knowledge and Turnout. *American Journal of Political Science, 49*(3), 577–592.

Prior, M. (2007). *Post-broadcast Democracy: How Media Choice Increases Inequality in Political Involvement and Polarizes Elections.* Cambridge: Cambridge University Press.

Procter, R., Vis, F., & Voss, A. (2013). Reading the Riots on Twitter: Methodological Innovation for the Analysis of Big Data. *International Journal of Social Research Methodology, 16*(3), 197–214.

Putnam, R. D. (2000). *Bowling Alone: The Collapse and Revival of American Community*. London: Simon & Schuster.

Putnam, R. D., Feldstein, L., & Cohen, D. (2004). *Better Together: Restoring the American Community*. London: Simon & Schuster.

Rainie, L., & Smith, A. (2012). *Social Networking Sites and Politics*. Washington, DC: Pew Research Centre.

Rainie, L., & Wellman, B. (2012). *Networked: The New Social Operating System*. Cambridge: MIT Press.

Rickett, O. (2013, November 22). Want to Change the World? It Won't Happen Via Your Mouse Button. *The Guardian*. Retrieved March 20, 2014, from http://www.theguardian.com/commentisfree/2013/nov/22/change-the-world-charity-facebook-e-petition.

Rihanna. [rihanna]. (2012, March 6). Please Go to http://Www.Invisiblechildren.Com Even If Its 10 Minutes... Trust Me, You Need to Know About This! #1love. *Tweet*. Retrieved December 31, 2012, from http://twitter.com/rihanna/status/177302109937614848.

Romano, A. (2018, March 20). The Facebook Data Breach Wasn't a Hack. It Was a Wake-Up Call. *Vox*. Retrieved May 27, 2018, from https://www.vox.com/2018/3/20/17138756/facebook-data-breach-cambridge-analytica-explained.

Rotman, D., Vieweg, S., Chi, E. H., Preece, J., Shneiderman, B., Pirolli, P., et al. (2011). *From Slacktivism to Activism: Participatory Culture in the Age of Social Media*. Paper presented at the Conference of Human Factors in Computing Systems, Vancouver, Canada.

Ryan, D. (2007). Getting the Word Out: Notes on the Social Organization of Notification*. *Sociological Theory, 24*(3), 228–254.

Salmons, J. (2012, November 16). *Deep Data: Digging into Social Media with Qualitative Methods*. Retrieved January 20, 2013, from http://nsmnss.blogspot.co.uk/2012/11/deep-data-digging-into-social-media_16.html.

Sanders, S. (2017, June 20). Upworthy Was One of the Hottest Sites Ever. You Won't Believe What Happened Next. *NPR*. Retrieved June 1, 2018, from https://www.npr.org/sections/alltechconsidered/2017/06/20/533529538/upworthy-was-one-of-the-hottest-sites-ever-you-wont-believe-what-happened-next.

Sayer Vincent. (2017, January 31). *38 Degrees: Report and Financial Statements for the Year Ended 30 September 2016*. Retrieved May 20, 2018, from https://files.38degrees.org.uk/items/files/000/000/097/original/38_Degrees_final_accounts_2016_%281%29.pdf.

Scheufele, D. A. (2001). Democracy for Some? How Political Talk Both Informs and Polarizes the Electorate. In R. P. Hart & D. Shaw (Eds.), *Communication and U.S. Elections: New Agendas* (pp. 19–32). Lanham, MD: Rowman & Littlefield.

Schradie, J. (2015). Silicon Valley Ideology and Class Inequality: A Virtual Poll Tax on Digital Politics. In D. Freelon & S. Coleman (Eds.), *Handbook of Digital Politics* (pp. 67–84). Cheltenham: Edward Elgar.

Schudson, M. (1999). *The Good Citizen: A History of American Public Life*. Cambridge, MA: Harvard University Press.

Shifman, L. (2013). *Memes in Digital Culture*. Cambridge: MIT Press.

Shirky, C. (2008). *Here Comes Everybody: The Power of Organizing Without Organizations*. London: Allen Lane.

Shirky, C. (2010). *Cognitive Surplus: Creativity and Generosity in a Connected Age*. London: Allen Lane.

Shirky, C. (2011, January/February). The Political Power of Social Media: Technology, the Public Sphere and Political Change. *Foreign Affairs*. Retrieved March 15, 2011, from http://www.foreignaffairs.com/articles/67038/clay-shirky/the-political-power-of-social-media.

Shontell, A. (2012, December 11). Inside BuzzFeed: The Story of How Jonah Peretti Built the Web's Most Beloved New Media Brand. *Business Insider*. Retrieved September 11, 2014, from http://www.businessinsider.com/buzzfeed-jonah-peretti-interview-2012-12.

Shulman, S. (2009). The Case Against Mass E-Mails: Perverse Incentives and Low Quality Public Participation in U.S. Federal Rulemaking. *Policy and Internet, 1*(1), 23–53.

Skoric, M. M., & Kwan, G. (2011). Do Facebook and Video Games Promote Political Participation Among Youth? *Journal of eDemocracy, 3*(1), 70–79.

Sloam, J. (2012). Introduction: Youth Citizenship and Politics. *Parliamentary Affairs, 65*(1), 4–12.

Sloan, L. (2017). Who Tweets in the United Kingdom? Profiling the Twitter Population Using the British Social Attitudes Survey 2015. *Social Media + Society, 3*(1). Retrieved from https://doi.org/10.1177/2056305117698981.

Speaking of Research. (2014, February 27). *Fact into Fiction—Why Context Matters with Animal Images*. Retrieved May 14, 2018, from https://speakingofresearch.com/2014/02/27/fact-into-fiction-why-context-matters-with-animal-images.

Stanyer, J. (2005). The British Public and Political Attitude Expression: The Emergence of a Self-Expressive Political Culture? *Contemporary Politics, 11*(1), 19–32.

Stoker, G. (2006). *Why Politics Matter: Making Democracy Work*. Basingstoke: Palgrave Macmillan.

Struhárik, F. (2017, December 17). *Facebook Has Hurt Mainstream Media More Than Fake News Sites*. Retrieved May 27, 2018, from https://medium.com/estadodelasredessociales2017/facebook-has-hurt-mainstream-media-more-than-fake-news-sites-113277bada8.

Sturgeon, W. (2013, January 9). BINGO! What Makes a Daily Express Front Page? *The Media Blog*. Retrieved May 8, 2018, from http://themediablog.

typepad.com/the-media-blog/2013/01/what-makes-a-daily-express-front-page.html.

Sunday Times. (2018, April 29). *Exposed: Russian Twitter Bots Tried to Swing General Election for Jeremy Corbyn.* Retrieved May 14, 2018, from https://www.thetimes.co.uk/article/exposed-russian-twitter-bots-tried-to-swing-general-election-for-jeremy-corbyn-zffv8652x.

Sunstein, C. R. (2007). *Republic.Com 2.0.* Princeton, NJ: Princeton University Press.

Sunstein, C. R. (2018, January 22). Guest Post: Is Social Media Good or Bad for Democracy? *Facebook Newsroom.* Retrieved May 27, 2018, from https://newsroom.fb.com/news/2018/01/sunstein-democracy/.

Svensson, J. (2011). Theorizing Citizenships in Late Modern ICT Societies. *Triple C: Cognition, Communication, Co-operation, 9*(2), 644–656.

Swirko, C. (2011, August 10). Seized Cats Being Readied for Adopt-a-Thon on August 26–28. *The Gainesville Sun.* Retrieved May 14, 2018, from http://www.gainesville.com/news/20110810/seized-cats-being-readied-for-adopt-a-thon-on-aug-26-28.

Taub, A., & Fisher, M. (2018, April 21). Where Countries Are Tinderboxes and Facebook Is a Match. *The New York Times.* Retrieved May 27, 2018, from https://www.nytimes.com/2018/04/21/world/asia/facebook-sri-lanka-riots.html.

Tewksbury, D., & Rittenberg, J. (2012). *News on the Internet: Information and Citizenship in the 21st Century.* Oxford: Oxford University Press.

The Simpsons Against the Conservatives. (2017, June 11). Perhaps This Pamphlet Will Prove Helpful. *Facebook Update.* Retrieved April 25, 2018, from https://www.facebook.com/TheSimpsonsAgainstTheConservatives/photos/a.140507476486819.1073741827.139908539880046/168792716991628.

Theocharis, Y. (2012). Cuts, Tweets, Solidarity and Mobilisation: How the Internet Shaped the Student Occupations. *Parliamentary Affairs, 65*(1), 162–194.

Theocharis, Y., & van Deth, J. W. (2018). The Continuous Expansion of Citizen Participation: A New Taxonomy. *European Political Science Review, 10*(1), 139–163.

Toff, B., & Nielsen, R. K. (2018). "I Just Google It": Folk Theories of Distributed Discovery. *Journal of Communication.* Retrieved from https://doi.org/10.1093/joc/jqy009.

Tufekci, Z. (2012). We Were Always Human. In N. L. Whitehead & M. Wesch (Eds.), *Human No More: Digital Subjectivities, Unhuman Subjects, and the End of Anthropology* (pp. 33–47). Boulder, CO: University of Colorado.

Tufekci, Z. [zeynep]. (2014a, February 2). These Symbolic, Epistemic Acts Online–Derided as "Slacktivism"—May Well Be Among the Most Important

Effects of the Internet. *Tweet*. Retrieved February 3, 2014, from https://twitter.com/zeynep/status/430093891300524032.
Tufekci, Z. (2014b, August 14). *What Happens to #Ferguson Affects Ferguson: Net Neutrality, Algorithmic Filtering and Ferguson*. Retrieved September 14, 2015, from https://medium.com/message/ferguson-is-also-a-net-neutrality-issue-6d2f3db51eb0.
Tufekci, Z. (2018, January 16). It's the (Democracy-Poisoning) Golden Age of Free Speech. *Wired*. Retrieved May 27, 2018, from https://www.wired.com/story/free-speech-issue-tech-turmoil-new-censorship/.
Tworek, H. (2017, May 15). Cambridge Analytica, Trump, and the New Old Fear of Manipulating the Masses. *NiemanLab*. Retrieved May 27, 2018, from http://www.niemanlab.org/2017/05/cambridge-analytica-trump-and-the-new-old-fear-of-manipulating-the-masses/.
Vaccari, C. (2013). *Digital Politics in Western Democracies: A Comparative Study*. Baltimore, MD: Johns Hopkins University Press.
Vaccari, C. (2014, November 9). *Response to the Consultation Themes Set Forth by the Digital Democracy Commission*. Retrieved August 8, 2015, from http://www.parliament.uk/documents/speaker/digital-democracy/VaccariSCDDresponsefinal.pdf.
Vaccari, C. (2018, February 13). *How Prevalent Are Filter Bubbles and Echo Chambers on Social Media? Not as Much as Conventional Wisdom Has It*. Retrieved May 20, 2018, from https://cristianvaccari.com/2018/02/13/how-prevalent-are-filter-bubbles-and-echo-chambers-on-social-media-not-as-much-as-president-obama-thinks.
Vaccari, C., Chadwick, A., & O'Loughlin, B. (2015). Dual Screening the Political: Media Events, Social Media, and Citizen Engagement. *Journal of Communication, 65*(6), 1041–1061.
Vaccari, C., Valeriani, A., Barberá, P., Bonneau, R., Jost, J. T., Nagler, J., et al. (2015). Political Expression and Action on Social Media: Exploring the Relationship Between Lower- and Higher-Threshold Political Activities Among Twitter Users in Italy. *Journal of Computer-Mediated Communication, 20*(2), 221–239.
Valenzuela, S., Kim, Y., & Gil de Zúñiga, H. (2011). Social Networks That Matter: Exploring the Role of Political Discussion for Online Political Participation. *International Journal of Public Opinion Research, 24*(2), 163–184.
Valeriani, A., & Vaccari, C. (2016). Accidental Exposure to Politics on Social Media as Online Participation Equalizer in Germany, Italy, and the United Kingdom. *New Media & Society, 18*(9), 1857–1874.
van Dijck, J. (2013). 'You Have One Identity': Performing the Self on Facebook and LinkedIn. *Media, Culture & Society, 35*(2), 199–215.

Vegh, S. (2003). Classifying Forms of Online Activism: The Case of Cyberprotests Against the World Bank. In M. D. Ayers & M. McCaughey (Eds.), *Cyberactivism: Online Activism in Theory and Practice* (pp. 71–96). Abingdon: Routledge.

Verba, S., & Nie, N. H. (1972). *Participation in America: Political Democracy and Social Equality*. London: Harper & Row.

Verba, S., Nie, N. H., & Kim, J. (1978). *Participation and Political Equality: A Seven-Nation Comparison*. Cambridge: Cambridge University Press.

Verba, S., Schlozman, K., & Brady, H. (1995). *Voice and Equality: Civic Voluntarism in American Politics*. Cambridge, MA.: Harvard University Press.

Vromen, A. (2017). *Digital Citizenship and Political Engagement: The Challenge from Online Campaigning and Advocacy Organisations*. Basingstoke: Palgrave Macmillan.

Vromen, A., & Coleman, W. (2013). Online Campaigning Organizations and Storytelling Strategies: Getup! in Australia. *Policy and Internet, 5*(1), 76–100.

Wahl-Jorgensen, K. (2018). The Emotional Architecture of Social Media. In Z. Papacharissi (Ed.), *A Networked Self and Platforms, Stories, Connections*. Oxon: Routledge.

Ward, D. [DWard]. (2013, June 4). Having Considered All Arguments & Listened to Debate Today, I Will Be Voting for #vote4cleanpower and the #2030decarb Target in #Energybill. *Tweet*. Retrieved May 20, 2018, from https://twitter.com/DWard/status/341906513117474816.

Wardle, C. (2017, February 16). Fake News. It's Complicated. *First Draft*. Retrieved May 11, 2018, from https://medium.com/1st-draft/fake-news-its-complicated-d0f773766c79.

Wasserman, T. (2012, March 12). 'Kony 2012' Tops 100 Million Views, Becomes the Most Viral Video in History [Study]. *Mashable*. Retrieved December 31, 2012, from http://mashable.com/2012/03/12/kony-most-viral/.

Webb, R. (2013, October 30). Dear Russell, Choosing to Vote Is the Most British Kind of Revolution There Is. *New Statesman*. Retrieved April 20, 2014, from http://www.newstatesman.com/2013/10/russell-brand-robert-webb-choosing-vote-most-british-kind-revolution-there.

White, M. (2010, August 12). Clicktivism Is Ruining Leftist Activism. *The Guardian*. Retrieved January 31, 2012, from http://www.guardian.co.uk/commentisfree/2010/aug/12/clicktivism-ruining-leftist-activism.

White, M. (2011). *Activism vs. Slacktivism*. Paper Presented at the FairSay eCampaigning Forum 2011, University of Oxford. Retrieved from https://www.youtube.com/watch?v=sHN4JNW9Yx8.

Whiteley, P. (2012). *Political Participation in Britain: The Decline and Revival of Civic Culture*. Basingstoke: Palgrave Macmillan.

Willingham, A. J. (2018, March 26). Slacktivism Is Over. The #NeverAgain Movement Is About What's Next. *CNN*. Retrieved April 24, 2018, from https://edition.cnn.com/2018/03/25/us/march-for-our-lives-slacktivism-trnd.

Woodstock, L. (2014). The News-Democracy Narrative and the Unexpected Benefits of Limited News Consumption: The Case of News Resisters. *Journalism, 15*(7), 834–849.

Wright, S. (2012). Politics as Usual? Revolution, Normalization and a New Agenda for Online Deliberation. *New Media & Society, 14*(2), 244–261.

Yacobi, B. G. (2012). The Limits of Authenticity. *Philosophy Now, 92*(September/October), 28–30.

Yang, H., & DeHart, J. L. (2016). Social Media Use and Online Political Participation Among College Students During the US Election 2012. *Social Media + Society, 2*(1). Retrieved from https://doi.org/10.1177/2056305115623802.

Zuckerman, E. (2008, March 8). *The Cute Cat Theory Talk at Etech*. Retrieved August 23, 2013, from http://www.ethanzuckerman.com/blog/2008/03/08/the-cute-cat-theory-talk-at-etech.

Zuckerman, E. (2012a, August 3). *Unpacking Kony 2012*. Retrieved March 11, 2012, from http://www.ethanzuckerman.com/blog/2012/03/08/unpacking-kony-2012.

Zuckerman, E. (2012b, April 20). *The Tweetbomb and the Ethics of Attention*. Retrieved April 25, 2012, from http://www.ethanzuckerman.com/blog/2012/04/20/the-tweetbomb-and-the-ethics-of-attention/.

Zuckerman, E. (2014, September 1). *Self-Segregation on Social Networks and the Implications for the Ferguson, MO Story*. Retrieved September 1, 2014, from http://www.ethanzuckerman.com/blog/2014/08/27/self-segregation-on-social-networks-and-the-implications-for-the-ferguson-mo-story.

Zukin, C., Keeter, S., Andolina, M., Jenkins, K., & Delli Carpini, M. X. (2006). *A New Engagement: Political Participation, Civic Life, and the Changing American Citizen*. Oxford: Oxford University Press.

Index

A

B

J. Dennis, *Beyond Slacktivism*,
Interest Groups, Advocacy and Democracy Series,
https://doi.org/10.1007/978-3-030-00844-4

The manufacturer's authorised representative in the EU is Springer Nature Customer Service Centre GmbH, Europaplatz 3, 69115 Heidelberg, Germany. If you have any concerns regarding our products, please contact ProductSafety@springernature.com

Printed and bound by CPI Group (UK) Ltd, Croydon, CR0 4YY
22/09/2026
02221063-0003